THEBES IN EGYPT

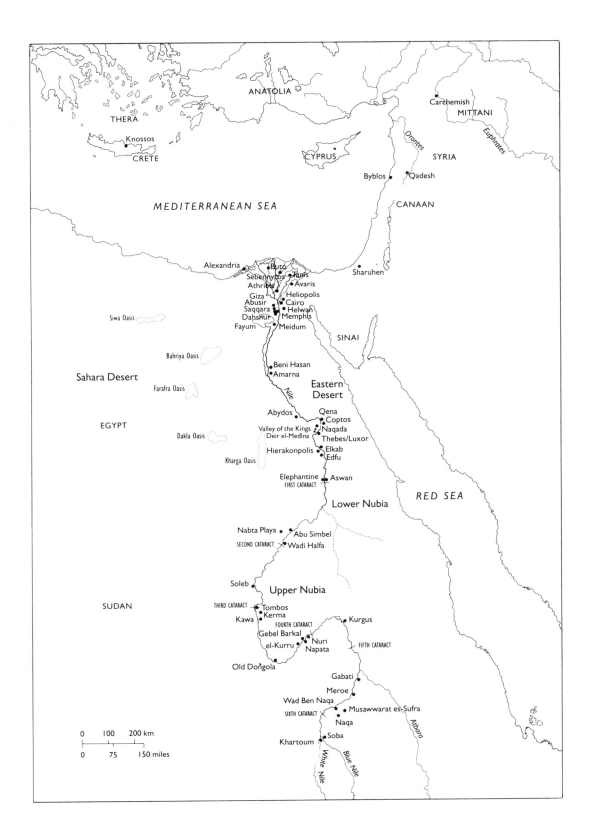

THERA

Knossos
CRETE

ANATOLIA

CYPRUS

Carchemish
MITTANI

Orontes
SYRIA

Euphrates

Byblos • Qadesh

MEDITERRANEAN SEA

CANAAN

Alexandria
Buto
Sebennytos • Tanis
Athribis • Avaris
Giza • Heliopolis
Abusir • Cairo
Saqqara • Helwan
Dahshur • Memphis
Fayum • Meidum

Sharuhen

SINAI

Siwa Oasis

Sahara Desert

Bahriya Oasis

Farafra Oasis

EGYPT

Dakla Oasis

Beni Hasan
Amarna

Nile

Eastern
Desert

Abydos
Qena
Coptos
Naqada
Valley of the Kings
Deir el-Medina
Thebes/Luxor
Hierakonpolis
Elkab
Edfu

Kharga Oasis

Elephantine
FIRST CATARACT
Aswan

RED SEA

Lower Nubia

Nabta Playa • Abu Simbel
SECOND CATARACT • Wadi Halfa

Soleb

Upper Nubia

SUDAN

THIRD CATARACT • Tombos
Kerma
Kawa
FOURTH CATARACT
Gebel Barkal
el-Kurru • Nuri
Napata

Kurgus

FIFTH CATARACT

Old Dongola

Gabati

Meroe

Wad Ben Naqa
SIXTH CATARACT
Naqa

Khartoum

Soba

Atbara

White Nile

Blue Nile

Musawwarat es-Sufra

0   100   200 km

0   75   150 miles

THEBES IN EGYPT

A GUIDE TO THE TOMBS
AND TEMPLES
OF ANCIENT LUXOR

Nigel and Helen Strudwick

CORNELL UNIVERSITY PRESS

Ithaca, New York

Authors' note

The nature of the ancient source
material used for this book means
that there is no general agreement
among scholars about dates and
(particularly) the transcription of
proper names. The authors have
adopted one convenient chronology
and their own preferences for the
spelling of names.

First published in the United States
in 1999 by Cornell University Press

First published in Great Britain in
1999 by British Museum Press

ISBN 0–8014–3693–1 (cloth)
    0–8014–8616–5 (paper)

Librarians: Library of Congress
Cataloging-in-Publication Data are
available.

Printed in Slovenia

CONTENTS

PREFACE

No visit to Egypt is complete without a trip to Luxor and a tour of the sites of ancient Thebes. Guidebooks on the site abound, as do picture books, but there is nothing currently in print which aims to help the reader to understand the site as a whole and to provide the background necessary for the fuller appreciation of the achievements of the ancient Egyptians in this area. In 1964 Charles Nims published *Thebes of the Pharaohs*, but this has been out of print for many years and, as is always to be hoped, our knowledge of the site has moved on since then.This book is intended to fill that gap. It results from many years of working in ancient Thebes and many days spent visiting the monuments, walking in the hills and talking to friends and colleagues who have lived and worked at the site.

We are immensely grateful to Emma Way and the British Museum Press for agreeing to publish a work we have wanted to write for many years. A special word of thanks must be reserved for our editor, Joanna Champness, for seeing the book through the various stages of gestation and providing help and support along the way. We would like to thank the following for helping us with illustrations for this book: Susan Allen, Jean-Claude Golvin, Marsha Hill, Anthony Leahy, Patricia Spencer and Elisabetta Valtz.

Colleagues whom we should thank include Aly Abdalla, Jan Assmann, John Baines, Edwin Brock, Lyla Brock, Debbie Darnell, Vivian Davies, Eberhard Dziobek, Heike Guksch, Janusz Karkowski, Jiro Kondo, Christine Lilyquist, Daniel Polz, Nicholas Reeves and Gyözö Vörös. We are grateful to Caroline Simpson for discussions with her about the history of the West Bank villages. We owe a particular debt to all our friends from Chicago House, and most particularly to Lanny Bell, Peter Dorman and Ray Johnson. For many years we have enjoyed the friendship of Karl and Friederike Seyfried and have profited greatly from our many long discussions about the Theban necropolis. Our thanks must also go to the Chairmen and the Permanent Committee of the Supreme Council for Antiquities in Egypt, who have the unenviable responsibility of looking after the monuments and who have given us permission to work in Luxor since 1984. We are especially indebted to our colleagues in Luxor, in particular to Mohammed el-Saghir, Mohammed Nasr, Sabri Abd el-Aziz, Mohammed el-Bialy, Ibrahim Soleiman and Ramadan Ahmed Aly. We cannot end without also thanking our loyal Egyptian workmen from Qurna and the dedicated members of our mission in Thebes.

A TOUR OF THE SITES
OF LUXOR

The modern Egyptian town of Luxor lies within one of the largest archaeological sites in the world, that of ancient Thebes. Few other such places in the world contain so many well-preserved monuments of an ancient civilization, and there is surely none which has yielded such a huge number of ancient objects in the course of scientific and non-scientific excavation. These objects range from colossal statues, through coffins and funerary figures, down to pieces of jewellery and the pottery of everyday life.

Egypt is a country famed for its ancient monuments, and was the home to one of the very first cultures which can rightly be called a civilization. The Sumerians of ancient Iraq may have discovered writing two hundred years or so before the inhabitants of the Nile valley, but once Egypt became a united country, in about 3000 BC, a culture was created which bore the same hallmarks for a period in excess of three thousand years. Of all other ancient societies, only those of China and India have lasted longer, but they have also experienced far greater periods of turbulence and instability than are known for ancient Egypt.

Luxor has been a United Nations World Heritage Site since 1979,[1] and, with such internationally famous locations as the Valley of the Kings and the temples of Karnak within its boundaries, it is rivalled in Egypt as a tourist attraction only by the pyramids of Giza. Guidebooks for visitors abound in all languages, but they inevitably concentrate on the principal monuments accessible to the tourist. The purpose of this book is to go further, and show how the tourist attractions fit into the wider history and meaning of the site. Along the way the reader will encounter important tombs, temples and individuals who do not feature in the guidebooks, but they are of the highest importance for understanding what the site of Luxor, ancient Thebes, is all about.

The site of Luxor/Thebes

The modern city of Luxor is located about 600 km south of Cairo, the capital of the Arab Republic of Egypt. The Nile valley south of Cairo is known generally as Upper Egypt, as it is further towards the source of the river Nile; conversely, the area north of Cairo, as the river nears the sea, is known as Lower Egypt. No one can study or visit Egypt without being impressed by the effect the river has on the country. Put very simply, if there were no Nile, there would have been no ancient and modern Egypt, since the flow of the Nile from central Africa, and the annual flooding which happened until a few years ago, have created between them one of the great fertile areas of the world. Luxor is just to the south of a great bend in the Nile; to the north of this bend the major fertile areas, and thus the principal settlements, lie to the west of the river, but south of this bend they are to be found on the east. Thus Luxor is located on the East Bank of the river. The city is connected to Cairo by road and rail, and has an important international airport, mainly to handle the tourist traffic, the principal local source of foreign currency and income. In ancient times there was only the river, which provided a means of transport as well as the water which gave life to the fields.

The importance of Luxor did not come about because it was built on an important trading route, or because it was easily defended, as with so many ancient and medieval settlements. Its prominence today is largely due to accidents of fortune that in two periods of relative chaos and instability (about 2010 and 1550 BC) its rulers were able to re-establish the centralized Egyptian state, and in doing so promoted their local deity to be the most important in the land. Even when these rulers moved away to new capital cities, they continued to honour the gods of Thebes, where most of the kings in the period 1550–1070 BC were buried. Hence, in ancient times the economic well-being of Thebes was largely due to these religious and funerary functions, which continue in a very different way to be the life-blood of the modern city.

The spread of the site and its names

The toponym Luxor really covers only the modern inhabited area on the east bank of the Nile, stretching from slightly to the north of the temple of Karnak to about 5 km to the south of the Temple of Luxor. On the west it is of course bounded by the river, and on the east it spreads 1–2 km into the cultivation, but it is mainly a north–south city, and one which is expanding all the time; its growth since the mid-1970s has been phenomenal. The population of Egypt as a whole has grown enormously since that time, and Luxor has witnessed a dramatic expansion in tourist facilities in those years. Recently a bridge has been opened about 8 km to the south of the city which has made motorized access to the West Bank much easier than before.

The name Luxor is a European form of the Arabic name of the city, el-Uqsor, usually interpreted as 'the palaces'. 'Palaces' of course is a general term here being applied to a range of large structures, the identity of which was unknown to those who coined the name. This neatly brings us to the point that, as far as the ancient monuments are concerned, the city of Luxor forms only one side of the equation. The Nile valley is bounded on the east

A bird's-eye view of Thebes as it might have appeared in the late New Kingdom

and west by cliffs. The west was always considered by the ancient Egyptians as the land of the dead, as the setting of the sun was a metaphor for death, and the western cliffs of the Nile valley were an ideal site for burial so long as they were not too far from the settlements in which the local population lived. At Luxor the hills of the east are some way into the desert, perhaps 10–15 km;[2] however, the western cliffs are only 3–4 km from the river, and this, combined with the spectacular aspect they present to the visitor, must have meant that they and their adjacent desert plains were an ideal location for burial.

The ancient Egyptian term for the city and adjacent area was ⌐ᵃ *Waset*, and is written with a special form of the hieroglyph meaning 'dominion'. Another term, which is found particularly from the New Kingdom on, is ⊗ᵃ *niut*, literally, 'the city'. Both terms covered both banks of the river, in fact the whole area which this book covers. The epithet 𓉺 *iun resy*, 'the southern Heliopolis', is also found in hieroglyphic texts, presumably relating the importance of the city to the other major religious centre of Egypt in the north. Better known is the name Thebes, given to the area by the Greeks. This conveniently covers the entire area as well, and is still the most commonly used toponym for the whole site. The Greeks frequently refer to it as the 'city of the hundred gates', starting at least as far back as Homer (*Iliad* IX, 381–4), and it was fabled as being full of treasure. Presumably someone saw similarities with the Greek city of Thebes and bestowed the name on Waset in Egypt. The official name of the city itself during much of the Graeco-Roman period was Diospolis Magna.

A brief tour

The following is a rapid tour round the site to orientate the reader before he or she moves to the rest of the book. It is based on the modern layout so that the current terminology can be grasped, but the stress is on the ancient monuments, starting on the East Bank.

The East Bank

The northern end of the modern city of Luxor is formed of settlements which have grown up in the vicinity of the temples of Karnak. The structures here, considered in Chapter 3, form the largest religious complex in Egypt and perhaps in the world. Its origins go back to the Old Kingdom, and the main East Bank settlement in ancient times was probably in this area; settlement remains going back at least to the Middle Kingdom have been unearthed near Karnak. The main processional way into the temple before the New Kingdom led from the west where there was a canal and basin. The development in the New Kingdom of another temple to the south in the centre of modern Luxor (Luxor Temple) meant that a new processional way was constructed in that direction. Luxor Temple was located almost immediately adjacent to the river, and was connected to Karnak by this processional way, and there was also access via a quay on the river.

Obtaining an idea of the spread of the ancient city is severely hampered by the existence of the modern town. It was originally a number of villages probably centred on the remains of Karnak, but these small settlements have grown into a modern town of perhaps two hundred thousand people. Much of the centre of modern Luxor developed after the establishment of the mosque of Abu el-Haggag partly on the site of Luxor Temple (p. 209). Areas of the ancient town have occasionally been located during building work; one of these is locally known as Abu Daoud, and is located next to the modern

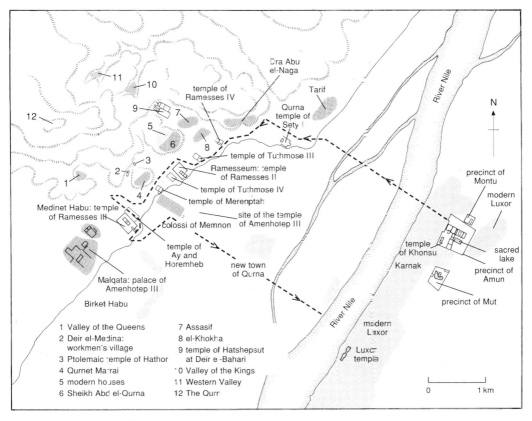

Map of Thebes, showing the route of the tour in this chapter

road to the airport, where a small temple and other buildings of the Ramesside period were found.

No sites are located immediately to the south of these East Bank settlements, but the temple of Medamud, a cult centre of the god Montu, is located 8 km to the north-east.

The West Bank

In ancient times the normal crossing point from east to west for the inhabitants of the East Bank city was presumably located near the riverbank at Karnak. There are two modern ferry crossings to the west: the ferry used by the local population and the independent traveller is located outside Luxor Temple, and its landing point on the west is almost directly opposite; the tourist ferry, however, has several embarkation points on the east, and a special landing on the west north of the other ferry. With the advent of the Luxor bridge it is unclear whether these patterns might change.

The name given today to the whole of the West Bank is Qurna, presumably derived from the name of the minor peak which overlooks the central area of the site, called the Qurn, probably meaning 'horn'. From this is derived the appellation 'Qurnawi' given to the local people. There are a series of toponyms which describe the various sub-areas of the West Bank mentioned on the tour. Some of these names have been given to them by archaeologists, and the terms have persisted, even though the local inhabitants do not know their origins. There are also other much more localized designations for some areas, and there is often disagreement among the people as to which term applies to which part of the settlement. Preference is given here to the terms normally used by archaeologists, and which appear in other publications about the site.

Having crossed the Nile, the ancient route from opposite Karnak led more or less directly west to the modern area known as et-Tarif (Tarif). This is where the main West Bank settlement was located from the Early Dynastic Period to the New Kingdom at least, and it has an associated necropolis. The area of Tarif is now the most consistently expanding settlement on the West Bank, stretching several kilometres to the north. The ancient centre was probably just to the north and east of the main visible monument in the area, the mortuary temple of Sety I, often called the Qurna temple.

From Tarif the road heads west past the Qurna temple, and at a crossroads it is possible to continue west along a gently sloping road for about 4 km to the Valley of the Kings. This was the route used for effecting the royal buri-

The West Bank of the Nile at Luxor

The hill known as the Qurn with some of the 'tombs of the Nobles' in the foreground

als and the transporting of heavy items to the valley, although the most usual ancient access on foot was over the hills. To the north, in a grove of trees, can be seen the house built in 1910 by Howard Carter, which he refers to in his letters as 'Castle Carter'. In the distance to the north-west beyond the Carter house is the highest peak on the West Bank, on top of which may just be seen the remains of an Eleventh Dynasty temple. Adjacent to this is a path which led out to the ancient desert routes across the Nile bend, and also to some nearby stone quarries, used today for the materials worked on in the numerous 'alabaster factories'. Just before the crossroads are modern shrines to Sayida Zeinab and Abu el-Qumsan; the latter was a local holy man, and his festival, shortly before the start of Ramadan, is an occasion for great local celebration.

Turning south, the road passes through the area of Dra Abu el-Naga, where are located many tombs of the Seventeenth to Twentieth Dynasties, including those of the Seventeenth Dynasty kings, and a large cemetery for the non-elite population of the New Kingdom. As the modern visitor reaches the alabaster factories which mark the beginning of the village of Dra Abu el-Naga, the road forks. Straight ahead is the road to Deir el-Bahari. The branch going to the south-east has been in existence only since the mid-1980s, when the Deir el-Bahari road, which formerly continued south, was closed and diverted to the edge of the cultivation to remove the stress being given to a number of monuments by the vibration of tour buses.

By the mosque in Dra Abu el-Naga the metalled road turns west, and there is a spectacular view of the temples of Hatshepsut and Nebhepetre Mentuhotep II at Deir el-Bahari, with the Middle Kingdom cliff tombs which overlook them. The mosque at the corner is the most important place of worship on the West Bank, and the current cleric, Sheikh Tayyib, is regarded with great respect and affection by the population of Luxor and those further afield. From the hill to the south of the road, known as 'hill 104' to archaeologists (from its height above sea level), we see the temples at Deir el-Bahari, and the remains of their causeways, as well as parts of numerous large and small tombs. The area between the temples and the cultivation is known as the Assasif, and is archaeologically perhaps the most complex area of the whole site, although fortunately it has also received some of the best excavation work too. To the right of the car park at Deir el-Bahari can be seen the white path up the side of the valley which takes the more energetic visitor by foot to the Valley of the Kings, or south to Deir el-Medina.

On the old road, to the south of Assasif, there is a small long hill extending in the Deir el-Bahari direction, which makes the Assasif something of a shallow valley. This hill is known as el-Khokha,l and bears one of the local villages, as well as a host of rock-cut tombs from the Old and New Kingdoms. The more adventurous tourist may stop and visit the half a dozen or so tombs which are open, but the majority will continue further south. After a short while the new road joins the older one, and, after mounds of mud brick which belong to the largely destroyed temple of Tuthmose III, straight ahead is the Ramesseum, the mortuary temple of Ramesses II, with its impressive statues of the king and battle scenes.

Towards the Qurn at this point, another 300 m along the road, is another hill honeycombed with tombs. This is Sheikh Abd el-Qurna, apparently named after a holy man who was supposed to have lived on the top of it and worshipped the Qurn. In this hill are many of the most famous and most visited of the Tombs of the Nobles, and in the houses around it live the descendants of those who used to rob the tombs in search of antiquities to satisfy the European lust for collecting.

The road resumes its southern orientation beside the car park for the Tombs of the Nobles, and as it rises up towards the house of the German Archaeological Institute on the west, the traveller may just catch a glimpse of part of the workmen's village of Deir el-Medina behind the hill which is now on the right. From this village starts the path that the workmen took to the Valley of the Kings, and which is taken by many unhurried visitors today. The hill to the south of the German house, home like the others to both tombs and houses, is called Qurnet Marrai. The tombs are almost all of the

View over the Assasif, with the temple of Hatshepsut at Deir el-Bahari in the background

The modern village of Dra Abu el-Naga from the hill to the west of it

View towards the hill of Sheikh Abd el-Qurna showing some of the 'Tombs of the Nobles'

The West Bank looking north from Deir el-Medina and Qurnet Marrai

One of the Colossi of Memnon at the entrance to the mortuary temple of Amenhotep III

New Kingdom, and on the top of the hill are the remains of a monastery. As the road starts to descend, on the left is the enclosure of the mortuary temple of Merenptah, partially built with stones from the similar structure of Amenhotep III; adjacent to it is the first excavation house of the Oriental Institute of Chicago, long given up. It is now the Marsam hotel.

The road continues to a junction with the road from the ferry. Here is the Inspectorate of Antiquities, where tickets for the monuments can be purchased, and where the offices of the site director and inspectors are located. Turning to the west again, and then travelling south a little, the road passes a junction for the village of Deir el-Medina, and then there is a T junction which allows a choice between turning right to the Valley of the Queens, lying at the foot of the impressive cliffs, or turning left to go to Medinet Habu. There is also, it should be noted, an unpaved road leading straight ahead – this leads, local security permitting, to the remains of the palace of Amenhotep III at Malqata, and ultimately to the small temple of Deir es-Shelwit.

Taking the road to Medinet Habu, on the right are the enclosure walls of the great temple, with the many late Roman and Coptic houses built into them. On the left are the remains of the mortuary temples of kings Ay and Horemheb. The visitor to the village of Medinet Habu cannot fail to be impressed by the massive remains of the temple of Ramesses III with the additional buildings of other periods. An alternative return is by the newer back route out of this village, which joins the main road to the ferry just to the east of the Inspectorate.

Further east on this road are seemingly shapeless lumps of limestone lying in the fields. Only on reaching the Colossi of Memnon is it apparent that in fact they and the two statues, together with a large stela glimpsed from near the Inspectorate, are all that remains of the mortuary temple of Amenhotep III, which would have been one of the largest structures in Egypt.

The road continues towards the ferry. Just before we cross the sugar-cane railway, we pass the model village of Qurna Gedida (New Qurna), built by the eminent architect Hassan Fakhry in the 1940s in an unsuccessful attempt to woo those who lived in the vicinity of the tombs away with the promise of new, well-built homes. At the crossroads by the police checkpoint the road continues straight ahead towards the ferries, or turns right to the south to cross the river by the new bridge.

A SHORT HISTORY OF THEBES

The purpose of this chapter is to set the historical background for the rest of the book. It does not pretend to be a summary of the history of Egypt; rather, it concentrates on events as they affected Thebes, and outlines other matters only in so far as they contribute to the broader picture. However, the opportunity is taken here to cover a number of small issues, isolated monuments and so on, which do not feature in the remaining chapters of this book.

Prehistory to the end of the Early Dynastic Period (*c*.90,000–2707 BC)

Indications of habitation from Egyptian prehistory are often overlooked by Egyptologists. Most are not trained to recognize the often subtle traces of early settlement, and they have not been helped in the case of Thebes by the almost continuous excavation and disturbance of the whole site over the past two hundred years.

The earliest material from the Theban region dates to the Middle and Upper Palaeolithic periods, which cover a huge span of time from 90,000 to about 10,000 BC. Most attested activity in this period is in what we now call the Sahara and on the cliffs at the edge of the Nile valley; the desert was much more habitable in those days, and the hunter-gatherer peoples of the Palaeolithic era seem rarely to have moved into the valley. Palaeolithic activity in Thebes is almost always observed from the discovery of stone tools, most of which have been located on the valley margins; where remains have been found on the edge of the cultivated area itself, such as the Upper and Middle Palaeolithic material discovered in the 1960s in the area of Tarif, it seems likely that they were brought down there by water deposition.

In the Neolithic period people began to settle in the valley, and began the climb which was to result in the dynastic culture of Egypt. Clearly there were settlements of some sort in the Theban area, shown by the discovery in Tarif of further stone tools, which range in date from before the existence of the recognized prehistoric Nile cultures, through these cultures, primarily Naqada I and II (*c*.3700–3300 BC), to the Early Dynastic Period. This neatly links in with pottery evidence, also from Tarif, which begins in Naqada I and continues to the Old Kingdom. Most dramatic of all, parts of buildings dating to Naqada I and II have been found. Also characteristic of the Early Dynastic Period are fragments of stone vessels from the same area. Other Theban evidence of the early years of the Egyptian state is not easy to come by: an exploration at Karnak in the early twentieth century revealed fragments of ceramic and stone vessels from this very time, and recent work on the so-called Thoth Hill has revealed a possible archaic temple (p. 78).

We should not be surprised to find traces of the Predynastic and Early Dynastic cultures in the Theban area, given that Thebes lay between two of the major centres of power in the years 3700–3000 BC, Naqada to the north and Hierakonpolis to the south. That more material has not survived from this epoch is doubtless due to the phenomenal amount of pharaonic and modern activity on the site.

The Old Kingdom (Third to Eighth Dynasties, c. 2707–2170 BC)

The Old Kingdom, the 'Pyramid Age', is best known for its huge royal tombs in the north, around the area of the capital city Memphis, about 20 km southwest of Cairo, including the necropoleis of Giza and Saqqara. At this time the country was highly centralized for the most part, and, while much is known about the officials and the administration of the northern areas around Memphis, only the occasional glimpse is obtained before the later Fifth Dynasty into how the country was run outside the capital. Management of the resources of Egypt was perhaps the key to the success of the Old Kingdom; Upper Egypt and Lower Egypt were each divided into twenty-two nomes or provinces, and the produce from these areas went to government institutions and temples; some of it was reused to provide income for the estates of the important officials of the day. There must have been provincial notables in charge of the provinces, but they are largely lacking in the archaeological record before the middle of the Fifth Dynasty; the tombs of one or two occur at provincial sites, but they are rare. However, there are two examples at Thebes, the fourth nome of Upper Egypt. The excavations of the German Archaeological Institute in the 1960s revealed two brick-built mastabas of the Third or Fourth Dynasty in the area of Tarif, the settlement dating from the Predynastic and Early Dynastic periods. Tarif was clearly an important part of Thebes at this time, but it is not clear whether there was an Old Kingdom settlement here or not, although its location opposite Karnak may not be coincidental.

From the middle of the Fifth Dynasty onwards (c. 2475 BC), the kings began to show interest in a more active system of government in the provinces. This is reflected in the archaeological record by a steady increase in the number of well-decorated tombs of provincial officials, mainly governors ('nomarchs'). From the size and extent of their tombs, and the different titles which they held, changes can be observed over time in the power and degree of political freedom given to these officials; the number of provincial tombs seems to peak in about the reign of Pepy II (c.2250 BC). A major change is evident in the design of these tombs: while free-standing brick mastabas had been the favoured form until this time, preference was now given to chapels cut into the rock, doubtless partly associated with the availability of prominent sites in the hills on the valley edge; the Egyptians were also never ones to waste valuable agricultural land for tombs.

Although Thebes was not a major centre of later Old Kingdom provincial nomarchs, it does have a small group of tombs from this period. They are located in the area of the necropolis known as el-Khokha, and the officials probably held their offices in the first half of the Sixth Dynasty (c.2350–2250 BC) (p. 140).

The evidence for royal activity in Thebes in the Old Kingdom is much less clear. No buildings survive which are older than the Middle Kingdom parts of Karnak, but the lower part of a statue of Niuserre of the Fifth Dynasty (c.2445–2414 BC) was found in the Karnak cachette early in the twentieth century. This has been shown to join a torso in Rochester, New York, and together they form the only substantive evidence for statuary of this date from outside the Memphite region.

However, indirect evidence from Karnak suggests that there may have been more material there. A statue (probably from there) in the British Museum (EA 870) dedicated by Senwosret I of the Twelfth Dynasty bears one of the cartouches of Niuserre on its belt, and perhaps suggests that Senwosret had to remove or reuse an older monument, such as that we have just mentioned; a similar statue naming Sahure is in Cairo. The famous Karnak king list, now in the Louvre, bears a very limited selection of kings' names, and could be a list of those whose statues or other monuments were removed by Tuthmose III before his constructions in the temple. Seven rulers of the Fourth to Sixth dynasties are named on it (Sneferu, Sahure, Niuserre, Djedkare, Teti, Pepy (I) and Merenre), and monuments of these kings would seem to form the basis of a small but well-developed temple in the Old Kingdom.

Impressive royal monuments of the Old Kingdom are still found in the north from the long reign of King Pepy II (c.2279–2219 BC), but then the centralized state went into rapid decline, and it is likely that the remaining rulers of the Old Kingdom lasted only twenty-five years between them. Many reasons have been put forward for the decline of the highly unified state of the Old Kingdom into the fragmented Egypt of the First Intermediate Period. Among them are low Nile floods and subsequent famine, too much power being granted to officials, and general weakness in the state. It is probably too simplistic to seek one explanation for the decline, and it was probably due rather to a combination of factors. That there was some instability is evident from the rapid succession of rulers in its later stages, and this might indicate systemic weakness. Perhaps the structures of the Old Kingdom were just exhausted, and if there was, for example, at the same time something of an economic crisis caused by the floods not coming in the accustomed manner, then this might just have provoked the fragmentation of the country, particularly if there were problems with the royal succession.

The First Intermediate Period (Ninth to Eleventh Dynasties, c.2170–1976 BC)

The Seventh Dynasty is very obscure, and the Eighth Dynasty kings continued to reside at Memphis, but on its decline we find the new masters of Egypt ruling from Herakleopolis, just south of the Fayum. We have little on which to base our knowledge of these kings other than the occasional small inscribed object or a reference in a papyrus. They are traditionally divided into two dynasties, the Ninth and Tenth following the history of Manetho, although whether there was any real division between them is far from certain.

Egyptologists traditionally tend to see Egyptian history in terms of the classic rises and falls of society – hence the 'high points' of the Old, Middle and New Kingdoms, and the 'periods of decline and disunity' of the intervening Intermediate Periods. Because the Ninth to Eleventh dynasties show Egypt disunited for most of the time, indeed the first time in its history, we call this epoch the First Intermediate Period.

The First Intermediate Period was a turning point in the history of Thebes. While the rulers in Herakleopolis may have held the nominal allegiance of the rest of Egypt for a few years, it was not long before many of the southern nomarchs started to build their own little empires and began attacking and conquering the military forces of their neighbours. We are fortunate that a large number of private inscriptions from this epoch survive from Upper Egypt, particularly south of Abydos, and they tell us something about the achievements of their owners and those whom their owners served. The rulers of the nomes of Koptos, Moalla and Thebes are prominent in these texts; one shows that the ruler of Koptos (fifth Upper Egyptian nome, north of Thebes) conquered the sixth and seventh nomes, and another, the well-known text of Ankhtifi from Moalla (third Upper Egyptian nome, south of Thebes), shows that he took over the first and second nomes as well, but then later encountered a force attacking him from Thebes and Koptos.

Who were the Theban rulers? We are fortunate that we have a great deal of evidence about them, obviously helped by the fact that the Thebans were to triumph at the end of the campaigns. Monuments from the time refer to individuals called Inyotef (Intef, Antef) who clearly assumed kingly titles and wrote their names in cartouches. Our first clues come from various king lists, which mention three kings named Inyotef, respectively with the throne names

Sehertawy, Wahankh and Nakhtnebtepnefer, and before them two rulers, probably nomarchs, called Inyotef and Mentuhotep. The name Mentuhotep ('Montu is satisfied') will become very prominent as our account of history of this period moves on, and it is clear that these men were all part of the same powerful family, who had come into the nomarchy of Thebes at some point at the end of the Old Kingdom. Their existence is confirmed by other monuments; occasionally the nomarch Mentuhotep's name is found in a later cartouche with the epithet 'tepy-aa', meaning 'the first'.

Egyptian inscriptions, which nearly all come from tombs and temples, are usually lacking in the sorts of historical detail the modern reader would like to find. The reason for this is that these inscriptions were not meant as historical records. If intended for a private individual, they were composed with the aim of glorifying the owner, and thus tended to concentrate on his piety,

Relief of a king, probably Wahankh Inyotef II, accompanied by his daughter Iah, probably from Thebes. Iah was the wife of Nahktnebtepnefer Inyotef III and the mother of Nebhepetre Mentuhotep II.
British Museum, EA1819

or how successful he was – describing his personal achievements in battle, for example, was much more important than describing the wider details of the campaign. If the inscriptions belonged to a king, then it was very important that he should be seen conforming to the concept of *Maat*, which can be roughly interpreted as 'the divine order'; thus kings were never shown defeated in battle, and a detrimental effect was never portrayed.

With that in mind, the inscriptions of the First Intermediate Period provide considerably more hints about what was really happening than is usual. Many come from Thebes. From these texts, one of these rulers stands out as perhaps being responsible for developing the Theban 'empire' in Upper Egypt, namely King Wahankh Inyotef II. A well-known stela showing the king with a number of his dogs (Cairo CG 20512) is dated to year 50 of the king's reign (*c.*2053 BC), and indicates that at that time his southern boundary was at Elephantine (Aswan), and his northern in the tenth Upper Egyptian nome (north of Abydos). Djari, an official of this king with a tomb at Tarif, speaks of fighting with his king against the 'house of Khety' (the Ninth to Tenth Dynasty) in the nome of Abydos, and other texts tell similar stories. It is not clear whether King Wahankh began the Theban expansion – that may have been done by his predecessors Mentuhotep 'tepy-a' and Sehertawy Inyotef I – but clearly in his long reign he established and consolidated an important power base in the south of Egypt. We know less about his adversaries, although it seems that the cause of the Herakleopolitan kings was prosecuted by the nomarchs of Asyut, who have left to us a small group of tombs which refer to the northern rulers, and also to conflict with the south.

Wahankh's successor, Nakhtnebtepnefer Inyotef, had a shorter reign (twelve years), and there are no records of conflict in this time. He was succeeded by another Mentuhotep, who took the prenomen Nebhepetre; scholars early in the twentieth century were confused by his use of no fewer than three Horus names during his reign.[1] He it was who was responsible for reuniting Egypt under one ruler, and it seems likely that the changes in his Horus name reflect different phases in his reign corresponding to stages in the reunification process. A rebellion is recorded in the Abydos nome in year 14 (see stela BM 1203, p. 25), at which time he was using the Horus name Sankhibtawy ('he who makes the heart of the two lands to live'); the next name Nebhedjet ('possessor of the white crown') is not dated, and the third form Sem, Sematawy ('uniter of the two lands') is first found in his year 39. It seems likely that these three names indicate respectively Mentuhotep's aspirations, then his securing of control over Upper Egypt and finally his control of the whole country. Unfortunately, the records are silent as to the actual events between years 14 and 39. Thus Egyptologists usually cautiously put the reunification of Egypt as taking place in or about Mentuhotep's regnal year 39, *c.*2007 BC.

Stela of Inyotef dated to year 14 of Mentuhotep II, probably from Tarif. British Museum, EA1203

Strictly speaking, the Middle Kingdom begins with the reunification by Nebhepetre Mentuhotep II, but we shall keep the rest of the Eleventh Dynasty in this section. Nebhepetre reigned for fifty-one years, and then passed the kingship to (probably) his son Mentuhotep, who took the throne name Sankhkare (Mentuhotep III). Little is known politically about his reign and the site of his tomb is uncertain (pp. 93–4). One well-known official from this reign was the chancellor Meketre, whose tomb contained a remarkable series of wooden models. Also belonging to this reign is a fascinating set of documents which relate to a local middle-class family and to the management of their estates. These are known as the Heqanakht papers, and reveal Heqanakht as an irascible man, keeping eyes on his family from afar when business took him to the north. So interesting are these documents that they inspired Agatha Christie to write her Ancient Egyptian murder mystery, *Death Comes as the End*. Research, however, now suggests that many of the officials dated to this reign should be placed a little later.

The dynasty ends with something of an enigma. Our primary source for chronology of the Old to Middle Kingdoms, the so-called Royal Canon of Turin, has seven years 'missing' from the Eleventh Dynasty; whether missing owing to problems with the source, or to suppression of undesirables, is unknown. From the monumental records we have the name of another king

Mentuhotep, this time with the throne name Nebtawyre (Mentuhotep IV); it seems certain that he should be placed after Sankhkare Mentuhotep, and the missing years of the Turin Canon are usually assigned to him. He is known mainly from quarrying inscriptions in the Wadi el-Hudi (Nubia) and in the Wadi Hammamat (north of Thebes, between Qift and Quseir, linking the Nile and the Red Sea). The latter is particularly interesting: a large force of ten thousand men was sent out to obtain a sarcophagus for the king, led by the vizier Amenemhat, of whom more below. The text is famous for the account that the expedition spied a pregnant gazelle who approached and gave birth on the area which had been selected as the area to be used for quarrying the sarcophagus. Ever looking for divine support, the Egyptians saw this as a good omen, and slaughtered the animal! Another inscription records a dramatic rainstorm during the expedition.[2] No tomb has ever been found for Nebtawyre Mentuhotep, nor monuments in Thebes, but he is mentioned in the Karnak king list, which suggests he must have had some monuments in that temple. We have no idea of his relationship to the rest of the Eleventh Dynasty, but he might just provide a bridge to the Twelfth.

The Middle Kingdom (Twelfth to Thirteenth Dynasties, c.1976–1794/3 BC)

The Twelfth Dynasty was the peak of the Middle Kingdom, but with the rise of this dynasty the importance of Thebes as a political centre declined, only occasionally to rise again in later years. The dynasty is composed of kings named Amenemhat and Senwosret, and there seems little doubt that they were a southern family, although whether from Thebes is far from certain – a propagandistic, loyalist, text from the reign of Amenemhat I, the *Prophecy of Neferty*, indicates that he might have come from Elephantine, since he is called the 'son of a woman of Ta-sety, a child of Khen-nekhen'.[3] The central act in the relative decline of Thebes at this time was the decision of Amenemhat I to move his capital to the north, not to the Old Kingdom residence of Memphis but to a new site just north of the Fayum, modern Lisht. However, he may have started to build a funerary monument at Thebes, which was then abandoned (p. 77).

Research has indicated that there might have been more activity in Thebes in the early years of the Twelfth Dynasty than had previously been thought, and that there were some links with the earlier dynasty. We saw above that Nebtawyre Mentuhotep's vizier was called Amenemhat, and it seems very likely that he was the later Amenemhat I (a bowl has also been found at Lisht bearing the names of both rulers); the fact that his father was called Senwosret (the other characteristic name of the dynasty) makes the connection all the more likely. So, did Amenemhat set in motion a *coup d'état* or did Nebtawyre Mentuhotep have no successor and he filled a vacuum? To compound the situation, it is also possible that a group of rather shadowy kings attested from inscriptions in Lower Nubia might belong in this obscure period. Some interesting facts which might question the rights of succession of Amenemhat I are worth pointing out.

Firstly, the stress given in literary texts of the Middle Kingdom to the legitimacy of the dynasty makes it rather clear that it was in fact somewhat questionable. Secondly, Amenemhat I's normal Horus name for most of his reign was Wehemmesut, literally 'repeating of creation', thus perhaps 'renaissance', but for the first few years of the reign it was Sehetepibtawy, 'he who pacifies the two lands'. The earlier name is very much in the style of those of the kings of the Eleventh Dynasty, while the later we will find again in other periods of history, such as at the end of the Twentieth Dynasty, when it indicates some sort of political change or restart. Together this might suggest that Amenemhat took advantage of a difficult situation at the end of the Eleventh Dynasty to advance his own ends, either during Nebtawyre Mentuhotep's lifetime or after his death, and that initially his capital might have been in Thebes. However, it soon became clear that some sort of break (or change in style) from the immediate past was needed, and so he moved north and promoted himself as the bringer-in of a new era.

The departure of Amenemhat for the north of course spelled a major change in the fortunes of Thebes. The centre of activity moved to the north, and this meant that the city lost much of its political power. However, compensation came in the religious sphere, with the promotion of Amun to principal state deity. Amun had of course existed since at least the Old Kingdom, but he had been just one of a number of deities in the region – another prominent god was Montu, who had several cult centres in the Theban area during the First Intermediate Period (p. 42).

Important political issues of the Middle Kingdom also do not specifically touch the Theban area, so they will be mentioned only in passing. There is circumstantial evidence that Amenemhat I was assassinated, and that the heir to the throne, Senwosret I, who had been acting as co-regent with his father for a number of years, had to rush to the residence, perhaps to deal with an attempted coup. The kings of the Twelfth Dynasty maintained a variable policy towards the important local nomarchs in northern Upper Egypt left at the end of the Intermediate period; they were courted by the early kings of the new dynasty, and yet in the reign of Senwosret III they seem to have disappeared, suggesting a reassertion of central government. The kings of the dynasty followed an active policy in Nubia, building a series of forts to protect the trade routes between Egypt and the heart of Africa; they also made some limited incursions into the Near East.

Theban material of this date outside Karnak is rather difficult to find. Senwosret III's veneration of Montu meant that he built at Medamud, and also added statues of his own to Nebhepetre Mentuhotep's mortuary temple at Deir el-Bahari. Allowing for some tombs to be dated later than the reigns of Mentuhoteps Nebhepetre and Sankhkare, there seem to be no tombs which can easily be dated to the main part of the Middle Kingdom, presumably reflecting the migration of the ruling classes to the north. The notable exception is the tomb of Inyotef-iqer (TT60) (p. 141).

The period of the reigns of Senwosret III and his son and successor Amenemhat III was the high point of the dynasty, and indeed of the Middle Kingdom. After Amenemhat, however, things declined. We find the reign of Amenemhat IV followed by that of a Queen Neferusobek, both of whose relationships to Amenemhat III are uncertain, and neither of whom has left any significant traces in Thebes. Evidence of them in Nubia, however, indicates that they kept their grip on Egypt and its southern province.

The Second Intermediate Period (Thirteenth to Seventeenth Dynasties, c.1794/3–1550 BC)

It is much more difficult to draw a line between the Middle Kingdom and the succeeding Second Intermediate Period than it was between the Old Kingdom and the First Intermediate Period. Tradition places the successor to Neferusobek, Khutawyre Wegaf, in the Thirteenth Dynasty, and it appears that this line of kings continued to rule from Lisht with no apparent break or diminution of their power over Egypt. What is astonishing about this dynasty is the number of kings attributed to it. This part of the Turin Canon is relatively well preserved, and we can see something approaching sixty rulers in roughly 150 years; most reigns were about three years in length, but there are others of between four months and thirteen years. The picture from other sources in Egypt is not one of chaos, since the administration continued, and seems to have largely been in the hands of viziers from a small number of families, who seem to have provided the necessary continuity of power.

The major political event of the Second Intermediate Period was the advent of the Hyksos rulers. These people of Syro-Palestinian descent, whose residence was at Avaris (Tell ed-Daba) in the Eastern Delta, may have invaded the north of Egypt, but are far more likely to have gradually settled in Egypt over many years, and then taken advantage of the weakness of the Thirteenth Dynasty to set up their own kingdom. The name 'Hyksos' derives from the Egyptian for 'rulers of foreign lands'. These kings formed the Fifteenth Dynasty, and the only king's name preserved in the Turin Canon, Khamudi (the last), is not written in a cartouche, suggesting that the Ramesside compilers of this list did not regard them as legitimate rulers. But they were not the only kings in the Delta; the Fourteenth and Sixteenth Dynasties of Manetho are thought to have ruled in areas there as well, and there may be further examples. It looks very much as if the political control of the Delta was highly fragmented, as it was also to be in the later Third Intermediate Period.

The political situation in Thebes at this time is not totally clear. Various kings of the Thirteenth Dynasty, primarily those named Neferhotep and Sebekhotep, left statues at Karnak and probably built small structures in the area of the Middle Kingdom temple. The later kings of this dynasty may have had their power centre in Thebes, at which point it becomes very hard to distinguish them from the subsequent Seventeenth Dynasty, and in fact the one may simply be a continuation of the other, with an artificial separation induced in later lists, such as those used by Manetho to compile his history. Clearly the Middle Kingdom continued in spirit; the only monuments of some of the Hyksos rulers found in Upper Egypt are some blocks found at Gebelein to the south of Thebes, and it is not impossible that these were reused there at some later date, so the case for their control of the area is weak at best.

The kings whom we conventionally assign to the Seventeenth Dynasty appear to be exclusively Theban. It can be no coincidence that some of the rulers were named Inyotef, the name which had been so prominent in Thebes in the First Intermediate Period. For the early years of this dynasty, which Egyptologists start in about 1645 BC, we have monuments of some of the kings, and indeed indications of where some of them were buried (pp. 94–5), but it is not until the latter years of the dynasty that we have firm evidence of political events extending beyond the boundaries of Thebes, or at least southern Upper Egypt. At that time the influence of Thebes extended to just north of modern Asyut.

The historical importance of this dynasty is that it began the battle to rid Egypt of the Hyksos kings. It is clear that it was difficult for many to accept the idea of their country – or even a part of it – being ruled for the first time in its history by foreigners, and, while the Thebans might have paid at most lip service to some of these kings, they were clearly anxious to be rid of them. The first of these kings certainly known to have been involved in conflict with the Hyksos was Seqenenre Taa (c. 1560 BC). Both sources we have for this are less than ideal: the first is the Ramesside literary text called the 'Quarrel of Apophis and Seqenenre',[4] which is badly damaged but paints a portrait of the greatest of the Hyksos rulers, Apophis, dwelling in Avaris, and complaining that the noise of the hippopotami in Thebes is depriving him of sleep! We assume that this is an oblique reference to some form of more political conflict. The other evidence is more dramatic, and consists of the mummy of this king, which was found in the Deir el-Bahari royal cache (pp. 98–9). His head bears horrific injuries, and it is conjectured that he met his death in battle, perhaps while on a chariot to judge from the angle of some of the wounds; the most likely opponents are of course the Hyksos, and the axe marks are possibly indicative of a type of Middle Bronze Age II weapon, such as might have been used by the Hyksos.

The sudden death of Seqenenre brought to the throne a king called Kamose, whose origins are far from certain. That he pursued the campaign against the Hyksos is abundantly clear, as we have one of the most detailed accounts of a conflict ever found in Egypt. The main sources were two large stelae erected at Karnak; the first was found before the Second World War and is fragmentary, but the beginning of its text was discovered on the so-called Carnarvon tablet, discovered by Carter and Carnarvon in their excavations at Thebes before they turned their attention to the Valley of the Kings. The second stela is almost complete, and was found inside the second pylon at Karnak in 1954, reused in the base of a statue of Ramesses IV. The stelae seem to have formed a pair, as the text on the second takes over where the first probably stopped. As always with Egyptian royal narratives, it is full of praise for the king; although it must be remembered that the king has to be portrayed in a certain way, being brave, taking the lead and not heeding the caution of his advisers, it is none the less a remarkable narrative, and worth relating in some detail.

The boundary with the Hyksos was at Kusae, about 40 km to the south of Hermopolis in Middle Egypt, and Kamose's first campaign was against an outpost of Asiatics in the town of Neferusy, in the region of Beni Hasan. The next major event was the capture of a messenger travelling through the oases from Apophis, the Hyksos king, to the ruler of Kush.[5] The message from Apophis encouraged the ruler of Kush to help him attack Thebes in a pincer movement, offering him an equitable division of Egypt after a successful attack. Kamose sent the messenger back to Avaris with the aim of ruining Hyksos morale.

From this stela it is clear that Kamose was active in northern Upper Egypt, but it does not indicate that he reached Memphis, let alone Avaris in the Eastern Delta. We also know that he conducted campaigns in Lower Nubia, although whether he had serious conflict with the Kushites is unknown. Kamose did not have a long reign (perhaps three years), and it was left to the next king to complete the expulsion of the Hyksos.

The next king was in fact Kamose's brother Ahmose; despite this family link, Manetho began the Eighteenth Dynasty with Ahmose, but this is to be attributed more to the ushering in of a new era than anything else. The main source for our knowledge of the expulsion of the Hyksos is the biography of a soldier called Ahmose son of Ibana from el-Kab (about 90 km to the south of Thebes). The historical data, as always in Egyptian texts, are almost incidental in this biography, since what was important is his own personal bravery, and the rewards he received from the king.[6] None the less, we learn that he fought with kings from Ahmose to Tuthmose I, and the most important part is that which relates to the capture of Avaris. He reports a naval battle and other fighting around the Hyksos residence, and then the sack of the city; following this, the Hyksos were chased into Sharuhen in southern Palestine, and there besieged for three years. Determining the date of these events is difficult, since there are few dated monuments from the probable twenty-five-year reign of Ahmose, but they probably took place in the latter part of the reign, perhaps between years 18 and 22. The long pause between the campaigns of Kamose and Ahmose is probably to be explained by the fact that Ahmose was quite young at his succession, as his body, found in the Deir el-Bahar cache, is probably that of a man aged between thirty and forty years. He may thus have spent the first two-thirds of his reign growing up, perhaps preparing himself for the conflict which was to come, and consolidating the areas conquered by Kamose in Upper Egypt and Nubia.

The New Kingdom (Eighteenth to Twentieth Dynasties, c.1550–1070/69 BC)

Once again a Theban family was in control of the whole of Egypt. Although it is conventional to date the start of the New Kingdom from the accession of Ahmose, only once the Hyksos were removed from the land can the new era be said to have really commenced. The New Kingdom is in many ways the best documented period of Egyptian civilization, and we cannot hope here to do more than touch on the major historical events, since most of them took place away from the Theban region.

The Eighteenth Dynasty (c.1550–1292 BC)

Domestic affairs: At the beginning of the dynasty the royal residence was obviously in Thebes, but, as always, it was not easy to maintain the country from a southern centre, and Memphis became the capital, although exactly when is still debated – we lean towards the early part of the dynasty, although others want to see the move as late as the reign of Tuthmose IV.

The reign of queen, or rather 'female king', Hatshepsut is one of the more intriguing episodes. A daughter of Tuthmose I and wife of Tuthmose II, she became regent for the six-year-old Tuthmose III on his succession, but after seven years in this role she took on kingly aspects and titularies. While not denying Tuthmose's kingship, she was the senior partner, ruling Egypt (it seems) with the support of a group of high-ranking officials who probably owed their promotion to her favour – officials such as Senmut and Hepusoneb. She built widely in Thebes, notably her temple at Deir el-Bahari (pp. 80–1).

Once she died, full control passed to Tuthmose. At some point in his reign, perhaps the last fifteen years, he appears to have organized a campaign to obliterate part of her memory. One of her shrines in Karnak was dismantled, and in many other places her figures were recut, and her names were replaced

Karnak, block from the dismantled 'Red Chapel', showing Hatshepsut and Tuthmose III before the barque of Amun

with that of Tuthmose III, and even sometimes with those of Tuthmose I and II, which led one scholar to put forward a case for a civil war between these three rulers.

Egypt seems to have reached a peak of prosperity in the reign of Amenhotep III (1388–1351/50 BC), during which time there was little military activity and much building, especially in Thebes. Amenhotep's son was the well-known Amenhotep IV, who subsequently changed his name to Akhenaten, moved his residence to el-Amarna, and instigated a new religious cult. The period of Akhenaten's changes (c.1348–1330) is usually referred to as the 'Amarna period'. The essence of Akhenaten's belief was the promotion of the Aten, the physical disc of the sun, to be the supreme and only deity; the temples of Amun were closed, and the names of Amun and some other deities were hacked out all over Egypt. In some cases even the plural 'deities' was removed! An unusual, some say 'realistic', art style was developed to cope with the new beliefs. All sorts of reasons for the changes made by Akhenaten have been put forward, including breaking the power of the priesthood; a fascinating theory developed in the 1990s suggests that the cult of the Aten was in fact the cult of the deified Amenhotep III.

Akhenaten began by building temples to the new god in Thebes (p. 59), and there are a few tombs of the early part of the reign (p. 163), but, after his move to Amarna, activity in Thebes dropped to almost zero. Subsequent to his death, problems with the succession seem to have lead to a period of relative political weakness. He seems to have been succeeded by a King Smenkhkare, about whom little is known, and who was followed by Tutankhamun. This young king, probably a son of Akhenaten, died without issue, and the throne was occupied in turn by two senior figures of the time,

Ay and then Horemheb. The changes made during the Amarna period began to be reversed; while many of them date to the reign of Tutankhamun, Horemheb later tried to usurp responsibility for them, and certainly placed his name on many monuments of Tutankhamun and Ay.

Foreign affairs: Many rulers pursued vigorous foreign policies, in both Nubia and the Near East, and the start of this can be seen right at the beginning of the dynasty. Ahmose son of Ibana relates a Nubian campaign in the reign of Ahmose, followed by others under his successors Amenhotep I and Tuthmose I. The Egyptians campaigned actively against the kingdom of Kush at Kerma, and soon controlled the Nile valley at least as far south as the fourth cataract. Indeed Nubia was never really a major problem for most of the New Kingdom.

The expulsion and pursuit of the Hyksos into southern Palestine seems to have presented the Egyptians with the basis of a ready-made sphere of influence in the Near East. Tuthmose I (1504–1492 BC) seems to have been the first king actively to campaign there and, in his relatively short reign, he extended a measure of Egyptian control over a relatively large area, although the records of this are sparse. His grandson, Tuthmose III, always considered as Egypt's 'warrior pharaoh' *par excellence,* left much more in the way of annalistic records of a series of campaigns which he waged in the first twenty years of his sole reign (pp. 54–5). He extended the empire further, fighting against the new local power of Mitanni, and perhaps went even as far east as the River Euphrates, and put in place an administration designed to maintain

Battle-scenes of Ramesses II in the Ramesseum

Egyptian control there. Tuthmose's successors continued to campaign in the Near East, although there was a definite lessening of activity in the second part of the dynasty, which coincided with the rise of the Hittites, who began to chip away at Egyptian control in the Near East. Some military campaigning seems to have restarted in the reign of Tutankhamun to reassert Egyptian control in this area.

Thebes: All these events are reflected to some extent in building and burial activities in Thebes, and the present-day prominence of many of these monuments means that many of them will be covered in other chapters of this book. The tombs and mortuary temples of almost all of the kings, as well as the burial places of many of their officials, still exist, while the temples of Karnak and Luxor speak volumes for the efforts expended to glorify the god Amun.

The Nineteenth Dynasty (c.1292–1186/5 BC)

Domestic affairs: Conventional chronology puts Horemheb as the last king of the Eighteenth Dynasty, but in many respects he belongs in the Nineteenth Dynasty. Horemheb began the dismantling of monuments of Akhenaten, which was continued with a vengeance by his successors. He had no children, and appointed his senior general Ramesses to be his successor. The latter only reigned two years, but allowed a settled succession which would permit Egypt to rebuild from the relative instability of recent years. His son, Sety I, and his son, Ramesses II, were the two great rulers of the dynasty. Early in the reign of the latter the royal residence was moved from Memphis to a new city at Qantir in the Eastern Delta, quite close to the old Hyksos capital of Avaris. It is thought that the dynasty's family origins lay in the Delta, and that this had much to do with the choice of site; this city is the Piramesse of the Bible.

After the successful first hundred years, including the reign of Ramesses' son Merenptah, the end of the dynasty is really rather confused. At the root of it were squabbles about the succession. Either of two kings may have succeeded Merenptah, either the enigmatic Amenmesse – some say he was a viceroy of Nubia, although this is also disputed – or Merenptah's son, Sety II. Amenmesse could also have temporarily ousted Sety II, at least in the south, but Sety appears ultimately to have regained control. He was succeeded by Siptah, whose origin is also uncertain. He was in all probability quite young, and his affairs were guided by Tawosret, the widow of Sety II, and the obscure chancellor Bay, both of whom constructed tombs in the Valley of the Kings (pp. 110, 171). On Siptah's death Tawosret took the throne, continuing the regnal years of her predecessor, and modified her tomb to reflect her new status, while often also erasing references to Siptah, which suggests that she regarded him as no true successor to her husband.

Foreign affairs: Sety I and Ramesses II certainly campaigned in Nubia, mainly reasserting Egyptian control south of the second cataract. Far more time was spent in the Near East, where Sety and Ramesses were faced with the growing threat from the Hittites, and had to reassert Egyptian control over a number of territories which had been in the Egyptian sphere of influence since Tuthmose III. The conflict with the Hittites culminated in the Battle of Qadesh, on the river Orontes in Syria. The details of this conflict are well known, thanks to Ramesses' many accounts in his temple inscriptions, but there is also Hittite evidence. Put simply, the result was a stalemate, with no great advantage to either side; the Egyptians had been driven back and then recovered, although ideology required that it be presented as a great victory in Ramesses' inscriptions. In the reign of Merenptah we find the first references to the so-called 'Peoples of the Sea', the population movements in the Mediterranean, some of whose groups were clearly trying to settle in force in Egypt, but who were repelled by the king.

Thebes: Thebes remained basically a religious and burial city. Kings came to visit on special occasions, but it was becoming more and more remote for rulers who dwelled in the Eastern Delta and who had no ancestral connections there. The great temples of Thebes benefited from the programmes of building work of Sety I and particularly Ramesses II. The kings of this dynasty also built some important mortuary temples, and of course lavish tombs in the Valley of the Kings. The area now known as the Valley of the Queens began to receive decorated tombs of the royal spouses. Officials were still buried in Thebes, but there is certainly also considerable evidence for the burials of officials in the Memphite region, at Saqqara.

The Twentieth Dynasty (c.1186–1070/69 BC)

Domestic affairs: Sethnakht, the first ruler of this dynasty is often compared with Ramesses I, as his short reign ushered in a new family after a troubled period. Things are very confused at this time, and it is quite likely that Sethnakht set himself up for a while as a rival ruler to Tawosret, since an important stela of his from Elephantine says that it was only in the second year of his (three-year) reign that he finally dealt with interior and exterior factions. Inscriptions of his son and successor, Ramesses III, indicate that Sethnakht felt that he legitimately succeeded Sety II, ignoring the three other rulers; he certainly adopted the tomb of Tawosret as his own (pp. 111–13).

Ramesses III was the last great pharaoh of the New Kingdom, and it appears that he fell victim to assassination. Various references exist to what may have been a harem conspiracy, perhaps related to the succession to the throne. Whatever the cause, he was followed after his reign of thirty-two years by his son Ramesses IV, and then seven further monarchs called Ramesses, most of whose reigns are relatively obscure. Source material for this period is almost totally Theban, and inevitably events are seen more and more from a Theban perspective (see below).

Foreign affairs: The Egyptian involvement outside the Nile valley was relatively minimal in comparison to the previous periods, and most of it concerns Ramesses III. That king did maintain some presence in the Near East, and probably campaigned there, but against a background of the Egyptian empire having declined to very little. He was also subject to attacks on the boundaries of Egypt, from the Libyans and the Peoples of the Sea. These attacks were repelled, and Ramesses recorded his victorious campaigns in his temple at Medinet Habu; the Sea Peoples were not a problem again, although Libyan settlement in Egypt did not cease, and it was not long before those of Libyan ancestry took the throne. Egypt seems to have maintained control over Nubia until almost the end of the dynasty.

Medinet Habu, temple of Ramesses III: king smiting an enemy

Karnak, Eighth Pylon: scenes showing the high priest Amenhotep

Thebes: The kings continued to reside in Piramesse, and their involvement with Thebes was again primarily with the temples and their places of burial. The temple of Ramesses III at Medinet Habu and the royal tombs are the major monuments of the time on the West Bank. At Karnak the temple of Khonsu is largely a construction of this dynasty, as well as other smaller structures.

The records from the workmen's village at Deir el-Medina are numerous and important for all sorts of reasons in the Twentieth Dynasty. Relevant to the wider history, for example, are the references we find to incursions from Libyans in the area, which might be put down to a knock-on effect of the successful campaign of Ramesses III against them in the north, which forced them south, through the oases, to Upper Egypt in search of somewhere to settle.

We also find a series of papyri later in the dynasty, from the reign of Ramesses IX on, which deal with tomb robberies and report the inquiries into them (pp. 184–5). These tell us much about some of the local politics, and occasionally wider history. In the reign of Ramesses XI there are a number of political events which were to have momentous consequences for Egypt. The first concerns a high priest of Amun called Amenhotep. The high priests of the cult in Thebes must have been very important individuals, and Amenhotep, who was in power in the reigns of Ramesses IX–XI, was particularly so, and had himself portrayed on the walls of Karnak in a manner and on a scale which his predecessors could hardly have imagined. Normally, the most a high official would expect in a temple such as Karnak was to be able to erect a statue of himself. At some date in the reign of Ramesses XI, Amenhotep was temporarily removed from his position or 'suppressed'.

Also in this reign we hear of a very powerful official named Panehsy acting as the viceroy of Nubia, but basing himself in Thebes. He had designs on even more power: still in favour with the king in Ramesses XI's year 17, in year 19 he was spoken of as an enemy of the state. Amenhotep seems to have been officially reinstated, and a recent theory suggests that Panehsy was the devil of the piece, who was subsequently driven back into his viceregal territory of Nubia, where the Egyptians were still fighting him ten years later, and where he was buried, having presumably stolen Nubia from the Egyptian crown.

Year 19 of Ramesses XI is also important for another reason, since in that year the Egyptians started another Wehemmesut era ('repeating of births' – commonly called 'renaissance'). We noted the use of this phrase at the start of the Twelfth Dynasty; perhaps its employment at this late stage in the Twentieth Dynasty was supposed to indicate that internal dissent had been silenced, and a new path to glory was to be instituted. At Thebes at least, it became the preferred way to date documents by saying 'year *n* of the "renaissance" '. Ramesses XI remained most of the time in the Delta, which meant that the most prominent figure at Thebes, Piankh, was extremely powerful.

It seems improbable that the high hopes of the 'renaissance' were fulfilled. When Ramesses XI died, it seems unlikely that he was buried in the tomb cut for him in the Valley of the Kings. With him the family line came to an end, although dating to the 'renaissance' era continued at least until its year 10, when Piankh was still in charge in Thebes.

The Third Intermediate Period (Twenty-first to Twenty-fifth Dynasties, *c.* 1070/69–714 BC)

Historians tend to start yet another intermediate period at this point, although it is very debatable whether the usual criteria of political disunity really appear until some point in the Twenty-second Dynasty, and perhaps the term 'post-imperial epoch' is preferable in some ways. Our account of this complex period will be almost exclusively from a Theban perspective.

The Twenty-first Dynasty (c. 1070/69–946/5 BC)

The throne of Egypt passed to a ruling family from Tanis, whose first king was named Nesybanebdjedu, or Smendes. The residence at Piramesse was abandoned, and Tanis was used as the burial ground as well as temple and residence – the only intact royal burials other than that of Tutankhamun have come from the temple precinct at Tanis.

For most of the Twenty-first Dynasty Thebes seems to have existed almost as an independent province, although there may have been marriage alliances with the rulers in the north. The chief official was still the high priest of Amun, who was often also the army commander. Most significant of all, three of the high priests seem to have taken to writing their names in cartouches. The first of these, the well-known Herihor, used to be placed in the reign of Ramesses XI, but is perhaps better now dated to the early years of the new dynasty; that he was a contemporary of Smendes is shown by the famous 'Report of Wenamun', describing an eventful visit to the Lebanon to obtain wood for the Amun temple in Karnak.[7] Herihor wrote his name in cartouches only in the temple of Khonsu at Karnak, using 'high priest of Amun' as his second cartouche name, but his successor (and possible son) Panedjem I seems to have used them more wicely, at least for the second half of his reign.

We know that the high priests' area of control extended as far as el-Hiba (just south of the Fayum), and Panedjem I is attested in the area of the first cataract. Hints exist of internal conflicts in the south, with references to people sent into exile in the oases. The best-known activity of these priests, however, is attending to the reburials of their New Kingdom predecessors in the Valley of the Kings (pp. 98–100). Conventional robbery used to be blamed for this, but it now seems more likely that the reburials under the high priests of the late Twentieth and early Twenty-first Dynasty had more to do with deliberate state-sanctioned recycling of the wealth of the tombs to support the Theban economy than with the thieving nature of the inhabitants of Thebes.

The Twenty-second to Twenty-third Dynasties (c. 946/5–750 BC)

The Twenty-first Dynasty gave way to a new line of rulers originally of Libyan descent. They were perhaps from Tell Basta in the Delta, but moved their capital to Tanis. The first of these kings, Sheshonq I, did not wait long before asserting control over Thebes, binding it to his dynasty by placing his own men in the top positions, and by arranging marriage alliances with the major Theban families. Sheshonq is the biblical Shishak, and was the first Egyptian ruler for many years to be involved in the Near East. He undertook building work at Thebes, in particular the court in front of the second pylon at Karnak (p. 63).

Although none of his successors in the first part of the dynasty was as prominent as Sheshonq, matters were at least stable, but in the second half of the dynasty things became far more chaotic. In the reign of Osorkon II (875–837 BC), the king's cousin Harsiese, the high priest in Thebes, gave himself royal status and titles rather like Panedjem in the previous dynasty.

Osorkon did reassert his control over Thebes after Harsiese's death, and continued building at Karnak. In the 830s and 820s BC there appears to have been a civil war of sorts, concentrated in the south, known from the text *The Chronicle of Prince Osorkon,*[8] and ultimately much of the south slipped from the control of the kings in Tanis. Slightly later, in the reign of Sheshonq III, a crisis in the Delta caused the kingship to be divided, with a new Twenty-third Dynasty ruling from Tell el-Muqdam (Leontopolis) in the central Delta. This new line of kings seems to have been accepted by the Thebans, probably as much to rid themselves of the Twenty-second Dynasty as anything else. The Twenty-third Dynasty kings seem to have continued the practice of putting their family members into the priesthoods of Thebes; it has even been suggested that the dynasty was not one coherent line of kings but that different rulers governed from different places at different times, and one of those places was Thebes. Takelot III (776–755 BC) was paramount among these rulers.

The Twenty-third to Twenty-fifth Dynasties (c.750–714 BC)

So by around 750 BC Thebes still owed allegiance to the Twenty-third Dynasty in the north. At around this date, however, a new power came on the scene, that of the Upper Nubian kingdom of Napata, which had its base at the city of that name in the region of the fourth cataract. This African kingdom, which used many Egyptian iconographical and architectural forms, began to extend its influence northward, and Kashta was the first of its kings to be attested in the south of Egypt, at around 750 BC. We term them the Twenty-fifth or Nubian Dynasty. His successor, Piankhy or Piye, certainly extended Nubian control over the Theban region by about 740 BC, perhaps restricting the influence of the Twenty-third Dynasty to the area north of Herakleopolis, just south of the Fayum. Later in his reign (c.728 BC), Piankhy began to push northwards to gain control of the whole country, as we learn from a large stela now in the Cairo Museum. He achieved his aim, and mentions the various rulers of the Delta on his stela, but he left no presence in the north, and so the most prominent of the Delta rulers of this time, Tefnakht from Sais, reasserted himself locally and took on kingly attributes; he and his son Bakenrenef formed the Twenty-fourth Dynasty, but their power was purely in the north. In 715 BC Piankhy died and was succeeded by his brother Shabaka, who reasserted the dynasty's claim to all of Egypt, and established full control over the whole country. Thus by 715 BC it can be said that the Third Intermediate Period had really come to an end.

The Late Dynastic Period (Twenty-fifth to Thirtieth Dynasties, 714–332 BC)

There ensued a period of peace and relative prosperity, well reflected in Thebes where there were building works and a clear increase in the wealth and prestige of the local officials. The main threats to stability came not from within but from without, as the reign of Shabaka's successor but one, Taharqa (690–664 BC), coincided with the expansion of the Assyrian Empire. In 674 Esarhaddon attempted to invade but was repelled; in 671 he drove Taharqa from Memphis. The Egyptian king clearly fought back from a southern stronghold, since Esarhaddon was on the way to quell an uprising when he died in 669. His successor Ashurbanipal re-established Assyrian control of Egypt in 667/6, driving Taharqa to Thebes, where the latter died, passing the kingship on to Tantamani. Tantamani very soon re-established control over Egypt to the Delta, prompting Ashurbanipal to return in 664/3, which resulted in the sack and looting of Thebes. Thereafter Tantamani retired to Nubia, leaving Thebes as almost an independent entity, since only the Delta was under the control of Psamtek I of Sais, who had been appointed as a vassal ruler by Ashurbanipal.

Power in Thebes over the later part of the Twenth-fifth Dynasty had moved away from the high priest of Amun, and resided mainly with the mayors of the city and also the fourth priests of Amun. The most prominent of these

The Assasif as seen from above Deir el-Bahari. Visible are the mud-brick superstructures of the tombs of Pabasa (TT279) and Montuemhat (TT34)

was Montuemhat, who was in charge of the city after the departure of both the Assyrians and the Nubians. Religious power resided with the Divine Adoratrices of Amun (see pp. 136–8), and further practical power was in the hands of the officials who administered her domains – all this we can see reflected in the large and impressive funerary monuments built by these officials (see pp. 152–3).

After a few years, Psamtek I moved to add the south to his overall domain. He did this in the now time-honoured fashion of putting his own people into important positions in Thebes, the most significant of which was the establishment of his daughter Nitocris as the future Divine Adoratrice in 656 BC. Henceforth the centre of political activity shifts away from Thebes to the north of the country. The Twenty-sixth Dynasty, also known as the Saite period from its home city Sais, continued the artistic and architectural revival just mentioned, but also saw internal disputes, and eventually gave way to the Persian invasion of Cambyses II in 525 BC; the Persians are numbered as the Twenty-seventh Dynasty. Egyptian rulers reasserted themselves in about 404 BC, and the Twenty-eighth to Thirtieth Dynasties then lasted until the second Persian invasion in 342 BC. In that period there was a considerable revival of building activity in the temples of Thebes, firstly under Hakor (Twenty-ninth Dynasty, 393–380 BC), and especially under Nectanebo I (Thirtieth Dynasty, 380–362 BC). These Persian kings, sometimes referred to as the Thirty-first Dynasty, were never popular in Egypt, and it is said that the populace of the country welcomed Alexander of Macedon when his conquest of the Persian Empire brought his armies to Egypt in 332 BC.

The Post-dynastic period (332 BC onward)

The area of Thebes became less and less important during the Post-dynastic period, and most of the major political events, apart from certain uprisings, took place in the north, where Egypt came into real contact with the Mediterranean world. Hence the following survey is not particularly Theban.

It seems unlikely that Alexander the Great visited Thebes, although a sanctuary in Luxor Temple and various small constructions in Karnak attest work carried out in his name. He left Egypt in 331 BC under the command of the satrap (a Persian title meaning viceroy) named Cleomenes. When Alexander died in 323 BC, his generals very rapidly divided up the great empire he had won in the course of his Persian wars, and Egypt was claimed by Ptolemy, son of Lagos. In theory, Philip Arrhidaeus, the half-brother of Alexander, was ruler of the empire; he left his mark in Thebes with a new sanctuary in the temple of Amun at Karnak, and he was succeeded by his son Alexander IV of Macedon. But the real power in Egypt remained with the satrap, and Ptolemy maintained his official viceregal status until 306 or 304 BC, when he set himself up as an independent king. He maintained an active foreign policy, and Ptolemaic control at its height extended east and west of Egypt and included Cyprus.

Various Ptolemies visited Thebes, and it remained essentially a religious city, even though the Greek name for Upper Egypt, 'Thebais', was clearly based on its name. In fact the Ptolemaic power centre in the south was at Ptolemais, not far from modern Sohag. There was one major revolt in Thebes against Ptolemaic rule, in the first twenty years of the reign of Ptolemy V (204–180 BC), and some minor rebellions took place in 132/1 and 88 BC.

The family of Ptolemy maintained control of Egypt until 30 BC. Gradually the foreign lands were lost; this was not always helped by internal intrigues in the family. As time went by, Rome rapidly became the important player in the region, and ultimately Octavian, soon to become Emperor Augustus, took over when Cleopatra VII committed suicide after the Battle of Actium in 30 BC. The Ptolemies had been sensitive to many aspects of Egyptian customs, such as observing festivals and building temples, although this Cleopatra is reputed to have been the first of the line of rulers to have learned to speak Egyptian. This was of course politically expedient, although it is questionable as to how much change was noted locally.

The change to Roman control was relatively straightforward. Augustus developed a slightly different system of government for Egypt when compared with other provinces, in that it had its own prefect, rather than being controlled by the Senate. The importance of Egypt to Rome was economic, and the country supplied the imperial state with a considerable part of its grain supply. The effect of Roman control was to depoliticize the country, and this helped to expand the economic value of Egypt. A Roman garrison was stationed in Thebes after the Roman takeover, but was withdrawn by AD 23; shortly after that a revolt broke out, which was suppressed by the prefect by AD 29.

None the less, there were occasional revolts against Roman rule, often inspired by troubles elsewhere in the Empire, and these became somewhat more frequent in the third century AD. A new Roman camp was established in Thebes around AD 300. With the conversion of the Empire to Christianity under Constantine, and the shift of allegiance of Egypt to that emperor's new capital at Constantinople after AD 330, there were major changes, both economic and cultural. The importance of Alexandria was to decline, and the cultural influence of Christianity was to change many of the factors which had been so definably Egyptian for the previous 3,500 years. The situation changed further with the Arab conquest in AD 642.

Further aspects of Christian and Islamic Egypt will be considered in the final chapter of this book.

THE TEMPLES OF KARNAK AND LUXOR

The two major sites on the East Bank of the Nile at Luxor, which almost everyone travelling to Luxor will visit, are temples: Luxor Temple, which lies beside the river in the heart of the town, and the complex of temples at Karnak to the north. Both are associated with the cult of the local pre-eminent deities, Amun-Re, his wife Mut and their son Khonsu, although other deities are also represented there.

The deities of Thebes

The original local god of Thebes was probably Montu. He is known to us as a warrior god, called 'lord of Thebes', temples dedicated to whom have been discovered at Armant and el-Tod to the south of Luxor, and Medamud to the north. Whilst the Mentuhotep kings of the Eleventh Dynasty incorporated Montu in their names, the Twelfth Dynasty kings called Amenemhat showed reverence for the god Amun in the same way, indicating a shift in influence away from Montu at the period. Although from this time onwards he was a less significant god, Montu remained popular and Senwosret III seems to have had a particular devotion to him; in addition to some modest building at his temple in Armant, he seems to have established a cult centre closer to Thebes at Medamud, 8 km north-east of Karnak. Senwosret's veneration of this deity might also explain his attention to the memory of Nebhepetre Mentuhotep: when Naville was excavating the latter's mortuary temple at Deir el-Bahari, he found in the debris several statues of Senwosret III, some of which are on display in the British Museum; these can best be explained by Senwosret's reverence for his predecessor. In Ptolemaic times at the temple at Medamud a cult grew up involving worship of the so-called Buchis bull, which was the living personification of Montu on earth. The mothers of the bulls selected were worshipped in their own right at a temple at Armant to the south, and the Buchis bulls were also buried there.

The god Amun makes his first appearance in the pyramid texts, where he appears in association with his sister Amunet. As a pair they represented the hidden elements of chaos. Exactly how they came to be associated with Thebes is still unclear. Amun's importance nationally grew during the Middle Kingdom, particularly in the Twelfth Dynasty, and the associations of the kings of this era with the Theban area (p. 26) meant an increase in his standing at Thebes and a consequent decrease on the part of Montu in the area. Amun was soon established as the pre-eminent deity, in a form combined with the sun-god Re, known as Amun-Re, the king of the gods. The sun-god had previously been the pre-eminent deity in his own right, and it is very likely that the combining of Amun with Re was done to incorporate the old pre-eminent god with the new.

Amun was depicted in many forms, most characteristically as a man wearing a crown topped with two long plumes. His skin was frequently shown as blue, representing lapis lazuli. He could also be represented as a ram with curled horns, as a goose, and as a male figure with erect penis, particularly when associated with the ancient fertility god of Koptos called Min. In this form he was often referred to as Amun-Kamutef, literally 'Amun, the bull of his mother', in which he took on the attributes of one of the primordial creator gods who created himself by impregnating his mother, in this way becoming his own father. This concept was important for the cult of the king, as each king was really his own father, reborn to new life, and, since the father of the king was a god, the king himself was also a god.

His consort was the goddess Mut, usually depicted as a woman with a vulture head-dress, or wearing a crown, either the white crown of Upper Egypt or the double crown of Upper and Lower Egypt. She was particularly known as a war-goddess. Their son was the god Khonsu, who was very much associated with the moon, in token of which he is often shown with a crescent moon on his head. He is also very frequently shown as a standing mummiform figure with a sidelock of hair, by which the Egyptians signalled youth.

Together, Amun, Mut and Khonsu form the so-called Theban triad worshipped throughout the area. The temples of Luxor and Karnak were dedicated in various ways to this triad.

Temple architecture

Before considering any Theban temple, it would be wise to become familiar with the traditional form of an Egyptian temple and the religious and cultural concepts which underlay that form, as well as some of the terminology regularly used in describing temples.

At the entrance to the buildings of a typical Egyptian temple there was usually a large gateway formed of two towers with sloping sides, and a gap between. Such a gateway is usually referred to by the Greek term *pylon*. The main temple at Karnak had several pylon gateways as a result of its extension over the centuries by various kings, whereas the temple dedicated to Khonsu within the same complex had only one pylon. Behind the pylon was usually an enclosed courtyard open to the sky, often with a colonnade at either side. Beyond this could be a further pylon or else the beginnings of the roofed parts of the temple. One of the first such parts tended to be a hall containing many

Karnak: scene in the Hypostyle Hall, showing Ramesses II with the Theban triad

pillars supporting the roof, sometimes lit by clerestory windows, or else by light coming in through the wall beside the open courtyard which was complete only up to about two-thirds of its height. Such a pillared hall is often also called a *hypostyle* hall, from the Greek words *hypo* meaning under and *stylos* meaning pillar. Beyond the hypostyle hall (or halls – some temples had more than one) lay the completely closed-in parts of the temple, usually consisting of a *pronaos*, which served as an antechamber to the sanctuary, and the sanctuary or *naos* itself, often referred to by the Egyptians as *djeser djeseru*, the 'holy of holies', although in Thebes this phrase was used particularly in connection with the temple of Hatshepsut at Deir el-Bahari. Around the sanctuary there was often a corridor from which other rooms could be accessed, which seem to have served as chambers for other deities, either visiting from other temples or simply the consort and child of the principal god.

Outside the main temple buildings were large storerooms and areas for food preparation, and usually also a sacred lake from which water for rituals was taken, and where the priests could purify themselves. Certain ceremonies also seem to have taken place at the sacred lake itself. Surrounding all of this was a large enclosure wall pierced at various points by gateways. Unlike the temple buildings, the enclosure walls were constructed of mud bricks which were laid in such a way that the courses did not run horizontally but rather rose and fell in a wavy pattern.

The principal form of transport in ancient Egypt was the boat. To travel north, one simply went with the current, which flows at an average of 6 km per hour; this could be assisted by rowing to increase the speed at which one travelled. Going south, one could hoist a sail and travel with the prevailing wind from the north. Deities too travelled by boat; even when crossing areas of dry land they journeyed within a barque carried on the shoulders of priests. Special resting places, called barque shrines, were erected by kings where the god's boat could rest temporarily. At the point at which the temple reached the Nile, or a canal leading down to the Nile, there would usually be what is normally referred to as a quay. This term implies that the function of such a place was as a point were boats tied up and possibly where the deity of a temple could embark on his or her boat. However, it is more likely that the quay served as a formal point of termination of the main axis of a temple.

Symbolism

Egyptian culture has always been strongly influenced by the flow of the River Nile, which is not surprising since the country essentially lies within a desert. Until the modern damming of the Nile, the level of the river would rise, in most years, at the end of the summer and water would cover all the flood-plain. As the flood receded, patches of ground would emerge from the water and, if left to their own devices, soon be covered over with a flush of new vegetation. This annual reappearance of life had a profound influence on the religious beliefs of the ancient Egyptians, and, in the various myths of creation that they composed, the primordial mound which emerged from the waters of chaos was portrayed as the location where the god responsible for creation resided and carried out his work of creating the world.

The temples of Egypt represented, in their design, this mound of creation. The floor level, rising as it did towards the inner sanctuary, signified that the sanctuary, on top of the mound itself, was the location in which the deity of the temple, who was conceived of as the local creator god, performed the act of creation. The columns of the hypostyle halls and colonnades represented the plants growing on the mound as the waters receded, and the wavy courses of brick in the enclosure walls may have been intended to symbolize the waters of chaos from which the mound had emerged.

The architecture of the temples also reflects a strong connection with the life-force of the sun. Most temples were aligned so that their central axis lay at 90° to the course of the Nile. Since the river runs approximately from south to north throughout most of Egypt, this meant that such temples had in theory, if not always in practice, an east–west alignment and that the sun would pass along the axis of the temple each day. Symbolic of this was the regular depiction of the sun, endowed with wings, flying along the axis of the temple. The sun rising or setting between the two towers of the pylon gateway formed the hieroglyph *akhet* ☒ 'horizon'.

The house of the deity

It is important to remember that access to the temples was restricted, and that they were not the general places of worship that, for example, western churches are. The underlying reason for this is to be found in the fact that the temple was the 'mansion' where the deity lived and the priests were servants; the Egyptian term *hem netjer,* usually translated 'priest', literally means 'servant of the god'. The main part of the daily ritual involved tending to the deity's needs, albeit in magical and symbolic form. Thus, in the morning, food was prepared for the deity, who, once it was ready, was ritually woken up, fed and dressed for the day.

In the same way that all and sundry did not have access to the court of a king, access to the temple was restricted. It has been shown that, for example, at Luxor Temple members of the local populace were allowed and indeed possibly encouraged to enter parts of the temple, in order that they could witness some of the rites of the Opet Festival (pp. 67–9). However, the areas they could visit there seem to have been limited to one side of the two open courtyards. Additionally, certain private individuals were permitted to place statues of themselves within the precincts of a temple. It is most likely that they were eminent people who had in any case some connection, either actual or of a purely honorary nature, with the cult of the deity in question. Such statues could themselves be the focus of something akin to a cult, as for example in the case of a man called Amenhotep, son of Hapu, who may have been the architect of Amenhotep III's constructions at Luxor, and whose statues within the precincts of various temples came to be regarded by the ordinary populace as intermediaries between themselves and the deities. None the less, the innermost areas were the private apartments of the deity and remained out of bounds to ordinary mortals.

Further emphasis to the feeling of privacy and mystery of these rooms is lent by the fact that the chambers of the temples become increasingly dimly lit and enclosed as the sanctuary area is approached where the deity resided. This was achieved by raising the floor level of successive areas and at the same time progressively lowering the ceiling height. At the rear of the temple there were relatively few openings to allow in daylight, whereas nearer the open courtyards the hypostyle halls seem to have had more apertures for light.

The complex of temples at Karnak

The temples at Karnak form one of the largest religious complexes in the world. Here a number of temples are enclosed within the perimeter wall of the main one which is dedicated to the god Amun-Re, including temples dedicated to Ptah, the principal god of the capital at Memphis, to Khonsu and to

Cube statue of the overseer of seal-bearers, Senneferi, probably from a Theban temple. British Museum, EA48

Karnak, Open Air Museum: the reconstructed kiosk of Senwosret I

Montu, as well as numerous smaller shrines, each of which would be regarded as a temple in its own right elsewhere. An avenue of sphinxes links this complex to the nearby temple of Mut, and another, still visible in places, led from the Karnak complex all the way to Luxor Temple.

The early temple of Amun

There is some evidence[1] that a temple stood here already in the Old Kingdom, but the oldest remains still visible date to the reign of Senwosret I, when the temple was apparently already dedicated to Amun. The core of the Middle Kingdom building lay in the heart of the current temple, behind the sanctuary, and it is very difficult for the non-specialist visitor to envisage the structures of that period that stood there. The walls of the Middle Kingdom temple were constructed of limestone, which was later removed for use elsewhere. Hence, the location of this phase of the temple is marked by the now virtually empty space between the sanctuary and the Festival Hall of Tuthmose III, denuded of its limestone structures, with little visible other than the granite thresholds and the alabaster base on which the image of the god probably resided at that period. However, a fine example of the craftsmanship of this period is to be seen in the small shrine, probably originally from this area, erected by Senwosret I, which is now on display in the Open Air Museum.[2]

Several kings of the Thirteenth and Seventeenth Dynasties are named in the

Karnak king list (p. 21), which suggests that they may have erected some structures there; there are also some surviving monuments of the period, including a flood stela (p. 64) and a number of statues from the Karnak cachette. The Second Intermediate Period closed with the successful exploits of the Theban ruler Kamose and his brother, Ahmose, who was revered as having finally expelled the Hyksos from Egypt and who was the founder of the Eighteenth Dynasty. Kamose, who succeeded in driving the Hyksos out of Middle Egypt, dedicated his victories to the local patron god, Amun, by setting up two large stelae, recording his actions, in the precincts of Karnak (p. 30). During the New Kingdom, as we have said, the kings of Egypt retained a strong association with their home town and promoted the local god, Amun, to the status of national god in the form Amun-Re. From this time on, the temple precinct of Karnak became a focus for building projects to demonstrate loyalty to Amun-Re.

Initial expansion – the early Eighteenth Dynasty

This process had begun certainly in the reign of Amenhotep I, the successor of Ahmose, and the remains of some of his constructions can be seen in the Open Air Museum, including a fine alabaster barque shrine and the remains of a gateway erected on the south side of the main temple. His successor, Tuthmose I, seems to have enclosed the Middle Kingdom temple with a large stone wall. The entrance to the temple proper at this time was through the pylon now known as the Fourth Pylon, which stood before a pillared hall. Beyond this was the fifth Pylon, also erected by Tuthmose I, which led into the sanctuary. An obelisk of the same king is still in place outside the Fourth Pylon and probably stood within a courtyard outside the temple. To the north of the central area Tuthmose I expanded a structure already begun during the reign of his predecessor designed to house the treasures of the expanding temple. This Treasury lies just outside the later enclosure wall of the temple, at the north-east corner of the complex. It is likely that there was a sizeable administrative area nearby.

Although no traces of it remain *in situ*, a large number of limestone blocks have been recovered from the interior of the Third Pylon which show that Tuthmose I constructed a 'Festival Courtyard' at the front of the temple. This was to be the last work carried out in limestone at Karnak. Outside the courtyard he erected a pair of obelisks of which only the bases remain. There are also indications that he may have erected a structure behind the Middle Kingdom temple area in the space now occupied by the Festival Hall.

With the accession of Hatshepsut to the throne there seems to have been a new impetus to the development of the temple of Amun-Re. She undertook a large project of reworking the area around the sanctuary, which was designated in the texts as the 'Palace of Maat'. The rooms either side of the sanctuary that were originally decorated by Hatshepsut were later reworked by Tuthmose III, who erased or plastered over her figure wherever it appeared within the reliefs. Also in the sanctuary area she built a barque chapel of red quartzite which is now displayed in the Open Air Museum (the 'Red Chapel').[3] The scenes on it show that she also constructed six resting places, or way stations, for the barque of Amun on its journey via land to Luxor Temple.

Hatshepsut erected two obelisks between the Fourth and Fifth Pylons, originally intended to be of gold, although in the end only their very tops were covered in gold leaf. The positioning of these obelisks is rather unusual: it was normally the case that obelisks stood outside the main entrance to a temple, and it may be that Hatshepsut was trying to draw attention to the work she had carried out in the inner parts of the temple. It is indeed likely that their positioning was of considerable symbolic importance because Tuthmose III attempted to hide them by building walls around them. The northern obelisk is still in place, surrounded by the remains of Tuthmose's wall, which ironically protected it from damage, including that perpetrated by the followers of Akhenaten; the top of the southern obelisk lies near the sacred lake.

Hatshepsut's building activities at Karnak were prolific, and it is very likely that she was keen to legitimize her position as king by showing great loyalty to the main god. It seems that it was she who began work on a formal side axis that branched off to the south towards Luxor Temple, although remains of an earlier gateway of Amenhotep I (now in the Open Air Museum) were found in the first court of this lateral axis, suggesting that there was already a recognized temple approach from this direction. Here she began the construction of the Eighth Pylon, which was taken over and completed by Tuthmose III. Until this time the processional axis of the temple had been at an angle perpendicular to the flow of the Nile, extending from the shrine at the centre of the temple down to the quay, where the temple reached the canal leading up from the Nile.

To the south of the temple, and on the lateral axis, lies the temple of Mut. Here Hatshepsut may have renewed an older building that stood on the site. Certainly she was responsible for the temple of Amun-Kamutef which lies close by, although Tuthmose III later erased her name wherever it appeared, and replaced it with his. The barque shrine erected opposite it, just outside the Mut temple, bears both their names and must have been a joint undertaking.

The lateral extension of the temple reflects a major change in that the temple of Amun-Re was no longer a single temple but became part of a complex of temples, and its use became very much bound up with rituals associated with the notions of kingship, in the forms of the Opet Festival and the Valley Festival (pp. 67-9, 78–80). During the reign of Hatshepsut it is clear that the annual Opet procession left the temple through the Fourth Pylon, turned to

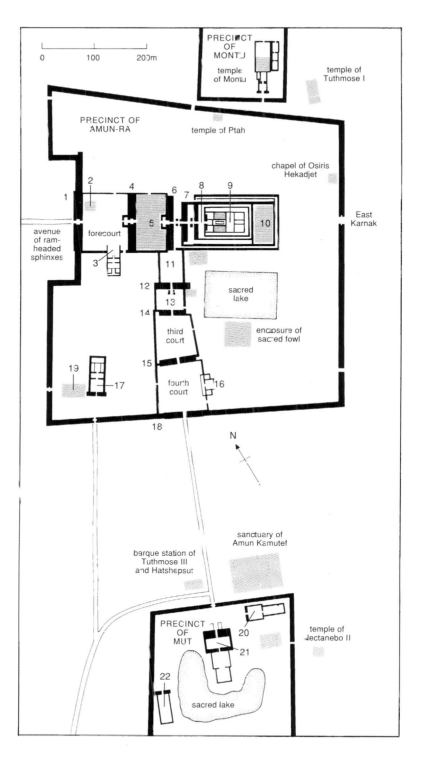

Plan of the temple complex at Karnak

1 first pylon
2 triple shrine of Sety II
3 temple of Ramesses III
4 second pylon
5 Great Hypostyle Hall
6 third pylon
7 fourth pylon
8 fifth and sixth pylons
9 Middle Kingdom court
10 festival hall of Tuthmose III
11 first ('cachette') court
12 seventh pylon
13 second court
14 eighth pylon
15 ninth pylon
16 *sed*-festival temple of Amenhotep II
17 temple of Khonsu
18 tenth pylon
19 temple of Opet
20 temple of Khonsu Pa-Khered
21 temple of Mut
22 temple of Ramesses III

Statues of kings of the first half of the Eighteenth Dynasty on the south side of the Eighth Pylon at Karnak

the south and, passing through the Eighth Pylon, visited the Mut temple. From there it travelled by land down to the area where Luxor Temple now stands,[4] with the barque being provided with resting places en route. The processions of the Valley Festival, on the other hand, would have proceeded straight out of the Fourth Pylon and down to the canal from the Nile, where they would have embarked to be carried straight across the river and up the canal on the opposite side towards Hatshepsut's valley temple, from which they would have been taken up to her funerary temple.

These two axes continued to function from this time onwards. A striking feature is that the kings' statues that were set up on the lateral axis all face along the axis, whereas the statues of kings that lie on the main temple axis all face in towards the axis. It has been suggested that the main temple axis is the divine axis and relates to the god of the temple's association with the sun-god who daily travelled along the length of the east–west axis, whereas the lateral axis is that of the kings.

As we have seen, Hatshepsut's successor and sometime co-regent, Tuthmose III, tried to erase the evidence of her contributions to the Karnak complex. However, he also added to it himself in no small measure, firstly in the area around the sanctuary, where he erected another pylon, the Sixth, between that of Tuthmose I and the sanctuary itself. He also added a series of shrines in the area thus enclosed, removing in the process earlier structures of Amenhotep I. Around the sanctuary he built an wall enclosing the space and had inscriptions carved on it describing his extensive foreign campaigns, usually known as the 'Annals of Tuthmose III'.

On the lateral axis of the temple he completed the work of Hatshepsut on the Eighth Pylon, erected the Seventh Pylon and built a barque shrine between the two. On the north side of the temple he constructed a temple dedicated to Ptah, possibly replacing an earlier structure of mud brick.

His most obvious addition, however, lies behind the sanctuary area and the area of the Middle Kingdom temple: here Tuthmose erected a building which he termed *Akh-menu*, 'the most glorious of monuments', and which is often called the Festival Hall. The structure immediately strikes one as odd on see-

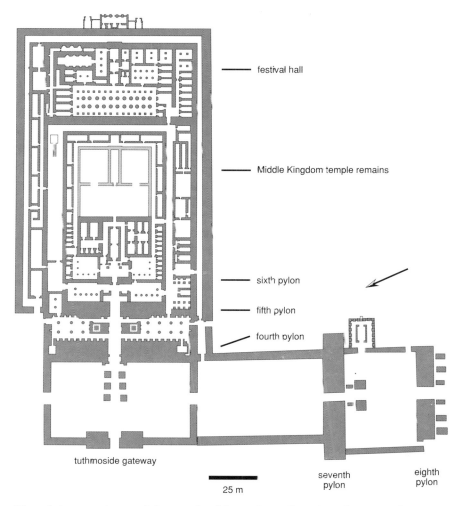

festival hall

Middle Kingdom temple remains

sixth pylon

fifth pylon

fourth pylon

tuthmoside gateway

25 m

seventh pylon

eighth pylon

Plan of the central area of the temple of Amun-Re at Karnak in the reign of Tuthmose III

ing it. One of the reasons for this is the fact that its axis lies at right angles to the main temple axis, and the entrance to the structure lies at the southern end of the west façade and was flanked with two Osiride statues (statues of the king as Osiris). It was originally constructed to celebrate Tuthmose's jubilee festival (Egyptian: *heb sed*),[5] but came also to be used on an annual basis during the celebrations of the Opet Festival.

An important source for the study of Egyptian history was found in this building: a relief, known as the Karnak king list, showing Tuthmose III before some of the earlier kings of Egypt, was found on the wall of one of the chambers close to the entrance of the Festival Hall. The list includes seven kings of the Old Kingdom, seven kings of the Eleventh Dynasty, six of the Twelfth Dynasty and twelve from the Second Intermediate Period. The kings depicted may have been those who, at the time, were regarded as having

Papyriform capitals of the central aisle in the Hypostyle Hall of the temple of Amun-Re at Karnak

built parts of the Karnak complex; an alternative is that this depiction was intended to serve as a means of actually replacing monuments of these kings that Tuthmose dismantled during his building works. If the latter is correct, it implies that there was already a very well recognized cult centre here in the Old Kingdom for which we have virtually no other evidence (p. 21).

The central hall lies along the royal axis, straddling the divine axis. The columns here are markedly different from those found in the rest of the temple, and were perhaps designed to imitate the tent poles used in the earliest Egyptian shrines. It is noteworthy that the column bases either side of the central aisle have all been cut away along the length of the central walkway; the most plausible explanation for this is that, at some time after the construction of the building, a wider barque was used for the god Amun to travel in which meant that the priests carrying it into the Festival Hall would have fallen over the column bases had they not been cut away at one side.

On the east side of the building, at the point where the Festival Hall crosses the divine axis, is a series of three rooms; these form the antechambers to the chapel of Amun, which, rather than lying at the heart of the whole structure, is set in its own suite of rooms off to one side, with no processional way leading towards it. The walls of the chamber in front of the Amun chapel are decorated with the famous 'botanical garden' reliefs. It is probable that the most mysterious part of the jubilee festival took place in this part of the temple, involving the king's mystical rebirth as the offspring of the god.

Against the back wall of the Festival Hall, Tuthmose III also constructed an external temple which probably served as a point of contact between the local populace and the gods of the temple inside.

Almost no structures dating to the reign of Amenhotep II remain, with the notable exception of his own jubilee temple lying at the edge of the courtyard between the Ninth and Tenth Pylons, which was restored by Sety I and Sety II. Similarly very little remains of the works carried out by Tuthmose IV, although it is clear that he embellished the entrance to the main temple, building a porch outside the Fourth Pylon and elaborating the Festival Courtyard of Tuthmose II. The structures were, however, dismantled during the erection of the pylon gateway of Amenhotep III which, in fact, was filled with their blocks; some have been rebuilt in the Open Air Museum.

Enlargement of the temple – the later Eighteenth Dynasty

When Amenhotep III came to the throne he clearly preferred to enlarge the temple complex as a whole, rather than adding to the inner parts of the existing structure. Within the Amun temple he made a radical change by building a new entrance pylon, the large Third Pylon which lies at the point where the lateral axis joins the main axis. In so doing, he effectively incorporated the lateral axis into the Amun temple – Opet processions could no longer proceed

Karnak, temple of Mut: large Sekhmet statue bearing the name of Sheshonq I

directly from in front of the entrance down the processional route of Hatshepsut but now left from behind the pylon gateway. It has been suggested that he may also have added a tall colonnade outside the front of this temple, similar in design to the colonnade which he built at Luxor Temple, and that these tall columns were later incorporated as the central aisle of the great Hypostyle Hall.

South of the temple, he extended the lateral axis by the addition of a pylon beyond the Eighth Pylon. This subsequently formed the base of the current Tenth Pylon, which was put up by Horemheb. Outside his pylon he added two colossal statues of himself, of which only the bases and feet remain outside the gateway of the temple.

To the north of the Amun temple and just outside the current walls, Amenhotep started the construction of a temple dedicated to Montu. The axis of this temple lay in the direction of Medamud, where an older temple of Montu already existed (p. 44).

To the south he built a small temple close to the Mut temple and began work on renewing the Mut temple itself. It is likely that there had been an earlier Eighteenth Dynasty structure there put up by Hatshepsut, which replaced even older buildings. The new temple of Amenhotep III consisted of a colonnaded forecourt, probably with a pylon gateway in front of it, a hypostyle hall and a sanctuary area. The temple was surrounded on three sides by the sacred lake, known as the *Isheru*, which can still be seen today. The many Sekhmet statues in the temple were transported there by later rulers from the mortuary temple of Amenhotep III on the West Bank.

It is also likely that Amenhotep began work on the small temple of Khonsu, to the south-west of the Amun-Re temple, or improved on an earlier structure that was already in existence there.[5] Certainly the avenue of sphinxes that leads from that temple in the Luxor direction was set up by him. An earlier small temple dedicated to Khonsu probably already existed close to that of Mut, and this was later enlarged and modified by Nectanebo I and the Ptolemies and dedicated to the form of Khonsu termed *Khonsu-pa-khered*, Khonsu the child.

The work carried out at Karnak clearly involved the removal of a great many older buildings, the remains of which were placed inside the Third Pylon. If one considers that, at the same time, Amenhotep III was carrying out large-scale building works at Luxor Temple, it is clear that a major programme of expansion on the East Bank was under way.[7] It is likely that this also corresponded with an expansion in the elaborate nature of the religious procedures involved in celebrating the Opet Festival at that period (see below).

The temple to the Aten

The successor of Amenhotep III came to the throne with the name Amenhotep IV, and appears in traditional iconographic manner on the decoration of the side of the porch of the Third Pylon, later completed by Sety I and Ramesses II. The work he undertook just outside the enclosure wall of the temples at Karnak, under his new name of Akhenaten, is much more famous. Here he built a temple to the Aten, very different in form from the traditional temple design in that the emphasis was on open-air worship rather than the dark seclusion of rooms in the heart of a normal temple. The structure was built of small blocks of stone, known as *talatat*,[8] which were much more manageable to cut and manoeuvre than the usual large blocks employed by the Egyptians, and this meant that the new structures could be erected relatively rapidly.

The new temple lay immediately to the east of the temple of Amun, and it may be that this location was significant in that the Aten temple received the life-giving rays of the newborn sun each morning before the temple of Amun was brought to life.

Restoration of the cult of Amun

The changes of the Amarna period did not really outlive its founder. Already very early in his reign Tutankhaten chose to replace the element Aten by Amun in his name, suggesting that it was he who was responsible for the beginnings of the restoration of the status of Amun's cult. Unfortunately, it seems that King Horemheb usurped most of his monuments and left very few traces of Tutankhamun's activities at Karnak. One such is a stela Tutankhamun erected showing himself making offerings to Amun and Mut and recording his concern for the neglect of Amun and the other deities, as well as his actions in restoring their cults; the object now bears the name of Horemheb. A number of statues of Tutankhamun were found in the cachette of statues, and a stela on the Seventh Pylon still remains, although all of these again bear the name of Horemheb.

The Ninth and Tenth Pylons are the work of Horemheb himself. It is unclear whether the latter replaced the pylon that had been erected there by Amenhotep III that had fallen into disrepair during the Amarna period, or whether Horemheb merely completed a structure begun by Amenhotep III, since there is evidence that the lowest courses of the pylon belong to the latter king's reign. From the Tenth Pylon he set up an avenue of sphinxes leading in the direction of the Mut temple to the south, work which was later completed by Nectanebo I. On the main temple axis, he began work on the Second Pylon outside the front of the temple, although it is again possible that this had been started in Tutankhamun's reign. In either case the work was completed by Ramesses I. The pylons Horemheb constructed clearly served a useful function for him in providing places to hide away the traces of the nearby Aten temple. Just as the *talatat* had been easy to erect into a temple, they were easily dismantled and, because of their size, could easily be tucked into the inside of these pylon gateways. The side effect of this, however, was that the *talatat* were well preserved inside these structures, and they have been the subject of study for a number of years in an attempt to reconstruct, on paper at least, some of the walls of the Aten temple.

Further enlargement and repair – the Nineteenth Dynasty

The space thus created between the Second and Third Pylons came to be filled with one of the unofficial wonders of the world, the great Hypostyle Hall: a magnificent structure, containing a veritable forest of columns which was begun during the reign of Sety I and completed by his son, Ramesses II. There are 122 very large columns standing to either side of a central avenue of twelve even larger and taller columns, the difference in height allowing high-level windows to admit light. The capitals of the taller columns are in the form of open papyrus flowers, whilst the smaller ones have closed bud capitals. This detail is typically Egyptian; the taller columns represent papyrus plants that are further developed in their growth owing to their being nearer to the daylight, whilst the smaller ones are less well developed through having less access to the light. To the north and south, the area was enclosed with walls, the outside of which, on the northern side, is decorated with fine reliefs showing Sety I waging war in Syria and Palestine. However, the completion here by Ramesses II is relatively crude in comparison. The size of the individual columns and their great number is striking, and the whole structure must have been even more impressive when its roof was in place.

Sety I was also responsible for a programme of restoration work on parts of the temple that had apparently fallen into disrepair, such as the Eighth Pylon, the jubilee temple of Amenhotep II by the Tenth Pylon and the temple of Tuthmose III behind the Festival Hall. The latter work was completed by Ramesses II, who continued the work on the Hypostyle Hall and the Second Pylon and also added an avenue of ram-headed sphinxes from the pylon down to the new quay which he constructed there. Outside the Second Pylon he also added two large statues of himself, facing one another, and probably also an even larger one, although it now bears the name of Panedjem I. On the southern exterior wall of the Hypostyle Hall he carved reliefs of the Battle of Qadesh, which he later covered over with plaster and superimposed with scenes of his campaigns in Syria, like those of his father on the other side.

Like Tuthmose III, Ramesses also built a small temple behind the back of the main temple which would have been more accessible to the populace at large, and which he dedicated to a form of Amun combined with the sun-god called Amun-Re-Horakhty, 'who hears petitions'. At the temple of Mut he carried out a programme of restoration work and erected a large alabaster stela which records his marriage to a Hittite princess.

Subsequent rulers of the Nineteenth Dynasty did not add greatly to the Karnak temples. The most noticeable new structure of the period is the triple barque shrine built by Sety II in the First Courtyard as a resting place for the barques of Amun, Mut and Khonsu, and he was also responsible for the pair of small obelisks erected on the quay.

Consolidation – the Twentieth Dynasty

As elsewhere at Thebes, building activity declined during the Twentieth Dynasty. One of the most significant additions to the temple during that period is the enormous barque shrine set up by Ramesses III outside the entrance to the temple at the time, the Second Pylon. The scale of this monument would make it a substantial temple elsewhere: it has its own pylon gateway leading to an open courtyard with, beyond that, a portico, a hypostyle hall and three sanctuaries. As in his temple at Medinet Habu, Ramesses III caused his names to be carved in very deep sunk relief in order, one assumes, to make it virtually impossible for his monument to be usurped by any of his successors. Another similarity between the two temples is the sixteen Osiride statues found flanking the east and west sides of the courtyard of his barque shrine and in the same position in the second court of his Medinet Habu temple. The same king constructed a similar temple to the south at the Mut temple, also with sixteen Osiride statues in the forecourt.

He and his successor, Ramesses IV, were responsible for major work on the

Karnak: the temple of Khonsu

enlargement of the temple dedicated to Khonsu. However, only the innermost parts of the temple, including the sanctuary, seem to have been completed by the end of the reign of Ramesses IV, because the outer buildings bear the names of later rulers.

His immediate successors, Ramesses V to Ramesses VIII, left very few traces at Karnak: a few statues and inscriptions remain, but that is all, and it does not seem that they carried out any new programme of building work at the temple. Ramesses IX concentrated his efforts on embellishing the lateral axis, adding a wall and ceremonial doorway to separate the courtyard between the Third and Fourth Pylons and the beginning of the lateral axis, a porch on the south face of the Eighth Pylon and the eastern wall between the Seventh and Eighth Pylons. The reliefs here include remarkable scenes of the High Priest Amenhotep apparently usurping the king's role in officiating in the rituals before the god, and he is also shown at the same scale as Ramesses IX (pp. 37–8). This was merely a taste of things to come.

The major building activity seems to have continued at the temple of Khonsu; the hypostyle hall was completed during the reign of Ramesses XI and is decorated with his reliefs, as well as with reliefs of the high priest, Herihor, from the turn of the Twenty-first Dynasty. The same man appears in further scenes on the walls of this temple in the dress of the king, carrying out the ceremonies normally performed by the king and even with his name written inside a cartouche, although it should be pointed out that this is the only place where it has been attested.

The Third Intermediate Period

The beginning of the Twenty-first Dynasty is a time of relative confusion, with a king ruling in the north, and high priests of Amun in Thebes assuming kingly powers. There seems to be little or no evidence of any work at Karnak by the kings, whilst the priest-kings carried out a small number of changes in the Karnak complex. Further work at the Khonsu temple was carried out by Panedjem I, and he also added his name to the exterior of the temple by usurping the statues of the rams in the avenue leading from the quay to the entrance that had been put up by Ramesses II, as well as the large statue of the same king in front of the Second Pylon. Otherwise there is little trace of any activity from this dynasty.

The two succeeding dynasties, often called the Libyan Dynasties, were much more ambitious in their plans for the temple of Amun. They planned to build a new gateway in front of the temple and a colonnade on either side behind it to form a huge courtyard, enclosing the barque shrine of Sety II and the entrance to the barque shrine of Ramesses III. It is not clear how far they proceeded with their plan for the new gateway, as the present First Pylon is much later in date. However, they did complete the colonnades, and between the barque shrine of Ramesses III and the Second Pylon Sheshonq I erected a gateway which was long ago given the grandiose name 'the Bubastite Portal' because the kings of the Twenty-second Dynasty were associated with the Delta town of Tell Basta (Bubastis). The south side of this gateway is decorated with scenes of Sheshonq smiting his enemies in the presence of Amun-Re. The towns he has conquered on behalf of the god are also listed and include many sites in Palestine; this is almost certainly the Egyptian version of the events recorded in the Bible when 'Shishak king of Egypt came up against Jerusalem' (1 Kings 14: 25). The gateway was completed by his son, Osorkon I.

The Late Period at Karnak

We know little of the activities of the later kings of Egypt at Karnak until we reach the Ptolemaic era. However one king in particular stands out for his activities in the complex: Taharqa of the Twenty-fifth Dynasty. The remains of one of his buildings are immediately apparent when entering Karnak: it is the kiosk in the centre of the first courtyard, with a large block serving as a resting place for the barque of Amun-Re in its centre. When this was constructed it was necessary to remove the avenue of sphinxes that had been put there by Ramesses II, and the ram-headed sphinxes were moved to the sides of the courtyard; they are still there today. He similarly added a colonnade at the temple of Montu, as well as a chapel dedicated to Horpre.

Another of his buildings goes almost completely unremarked by the vast majority of visitors to Karnak, although they may unknowingly have spent some time beside it. The so-called 'Edifice of Taharqa' lies between the sacred lake and the outer wall of the sanctuary area of the Amun temple, and the Karnak rest house is now tucked in between the main part of it and the descending staircase to the east. The main building played host to a daily ritual in which the statue of Amun-Re descended into a series of subterranean rooms and entered the realm of Nun, the waters of chaos surrounding the world. There the god was reborn each day with the sun-god in the form of the scarab beetle, Khepri, on the mound of creation, identified in Thebes with the area called Djeme which we now know as Medinet Habu (p. 90). Obviously, in the context of these rituals its proximity to the sacred lake was important, and the steps down to the waters of the lake at this point were either built at the same time or incorporated into the whole structure. The large scarab beetle which now stands at the corner of the sacred lake originally stood in the funerary temple of Amenhotep III on the West Bank; it may have been transported here to function as part of the rebirth rituals performed in this part of the temple.

A famous reference to Taharqa's reign is to be found on the stonework of the quay where the level of the great Nile flood in year 6 of his reign is recorded. The other inscriptions here[9] make it clear that from time to time the river rose sufficiently high to threaten to enter the temple. There is even a stela, dating to the Thirteenth Dynasty, recording an occasion when the Nile actually entered part of the Amun temple of the day.

In the area between the temples of Amun-Re and of Ptah are to be found a group of chapels dating to the Twenty-fifth and Twenty-sixth Dynasties. Several of them are dedicated to forms of Osiris, and one of them at least was erected by a Divine Adoratrice, Nitocris. Other Divine Adoratrices seem to have added similar chapels to Osiris to the north-east of the temple of Amun-Re. It is unfortunately not clear what lay behind this focus of activity on Osiris.

In the Twenty-ninth Dynasty a new barque shrine was erected outside the first Pylon by Psammuthis. This was later usurped by Hakor, who simply inscribed his name over those of the previous king.

The last major change to the temple seems to have occurred in the last Egyptian dynasty, during the reign of Nectanebo I: it seems that it was he who was responsible for adding the First Pylon gateway to the temple that forms the entrance familiar to the many millions of visitors to Karnak since that time. Of course, the pylon was not finished, as is clear not only from the undressed stone of which it is made but also from the remains of the mud-brick construction ramp still visible in the First Courtyard. The enclosure wall around the Amun-Re and Khonsu temples, as well as similar walls around the Mut temple and the Montu temple, were likewise erected during Nectanebo's reign.

Karnak: rear of the First Pylon, showing remains of the mud-brick construction ramp and displaced ram-headed sphinxes

Final additions: the Graeco-Roman period at Karnak

It is wholly to be expected that the Ptolemaic rulers would be active in showing their devotion to the state god of Egypt, and so we find that they were indeed responsible for a number of works in the Karnak complex. In the first place the old sandstone sanctuary of the Amun-Re temple was replaced with a granite one by the brother and successor of Alexander the Great, Philip Arrhidaeus. Otherwise, their major contribution was probably the small temple close to the temple of Khonsu dedicated to the goddess Ipet, normally depicted as a female hippopotamus and who seems to have been considered the personification of motherhood. The main structure of this temple was begun in the reign of Ptolemy VII and completed under Ptolemy XII, although there was almost certainly an earlier structure here because Nectanebo I left a gateway through the retaining wall at this point, and some of the decoration in the crypt dates to the reign of Ptolemy III. The temple apparently served as a focus for the religious concept of the rebirth of the sun through the means of the mother goddess, Ipet, and thus the temple was considered to be the junction between the night, the realm of Osiris, and the day, the realm of the sun-god in the form of Amun-Re. The crypt of the temple is decorated

A reconstruction of the temple complexes at Karnak and Luxor in the mid-Nineteenth Dynasty

with scenes of the Osiris rituals which took place there, some of this decoration having been completed by the Roman emperor Augustus.

Within the remainder of the temple complex the Ptolemies made a number of additions, such as the gateway in the Second Pylon and the restoration of Taharqa's kiosk in the first Courtyard. In the temples of Mut and Khonsu a small gateway was added in front of the pylon; at the temple of Khonsu a chapel dedicated to Khonsu-Neferhotep was added, whilst at the Mut temple the older Khonsu temple was expanded. Major additions were also made to the Ptah and Montu temples. In the area to the east of the Festival Hall the Ptolemies began work on a temple dedicated to Osiris of Koptos, which was completed by the Romans.

The Temple at Luxor

To the south of Karnak, within the heart of the modern city of Luxor, lies another temple, which was known to the ancient Egyptians as *Ipet-Reseyt*, 'the southern Opet', and is now referred to as Luxor Temple. Unlike most other Egyptian temples, its main entrance does not face the river and its most obvious axis is aligned towards the temples at Karnak on the royal axis rather than the divine axis: it was connected to the complex there by an avenue of sphinxes. In fact it seems that this temple had two axes, a north–south axis which is the one most visible today, and an east-west axis which is to be seen only in the southernmost parts of the temple, and which may have been aligned towards Medinet Habu on the West Bank (pp. 90–1).

The temple served as the focal point of the Opet Festival each year and was therefore of major importance in maintaining the role of the king as the divine offspring of the state god. It is likely that there was already a temple in existence in this place in the Middle Kingdom, although the earliest remains found here date to the Thirteenth Dynasty.

The Opet Festival

The annual Opet Festival was one of the main religious festivals of the Theban area. On the 15th or 19th day of the *Akhet* season, the god Amun would leave his temple at Karnak and proceed south, together with Mut and Khonsu, in their own barques, to the temple of Luxor. During the reign of Hatshepsut it seems clear that the processions travelled overland to Luxor and returned via the river. During the reign of Amenhotep III, however, it is likely that the barque of Amun travelled to the temple of Khonsu, from where both gods travelled to the Mut temple, leaving there, now accompanied by the barque of Mut, by boat to the temple at Luxor. The return journey was again probably made by boat.

Luxor Temple from the south-west

A royal barque also took part in the processions and, from the time of Tuthmose III onwards, it is likely that the royal barque resided in the Festival Hall behind the central part of the Amun-Re temple at Karnak. It must be relatively certain that the king took part in these celebrations in person, as the ceremonies related to the king's renewal as the divine offspring of Amun-Re.

Depictions of the festivities suggest that there were wide-scale celebrations amongst the populace in Luxor during this festival, with people lining the processional route, perhaps wishing to catch a glimpse of the deities' shrines or the king himself. The ceremonies that took place at Luxor Temple are less well recorded, but it is none the less possible to outline what was involved.

The overland procession would have approached the Luxor Temple along the royal axis and simply continued straight into the temple. A procession coming by river would have arrived at a landing stage, close to that used by the local ferry today, and proceeded to approach the temple from the west until it joined the royal axis from Karnak. During the later part of the reign of Amenhotep III, this point would have been just outside the entrance

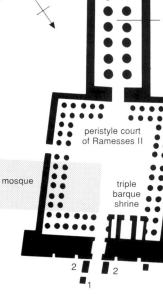

Plan of Luxor Temple

1 obelisk
2 seated colossi of Ramesses II
3 pylon of Ramesses II
4 colonnade of Amenhotep III
5 hypostyle hall
6 first antechamber ('Roman sanctuary')
7 second antechamber
8 'birth room'
9 barque shrines of Amenhotep III and Alexander the Great
10 transverse hall
11 sanctuary of Amenhotep III

0   100 m

to the temple. However, after the addition of the first Courtyard of the temple by Ramesses II, the procession from the river would have entered by a gateway in the west wall of the courtyard.

From here the divine barques were carried into the interior of the temple. The barques of Mut and Khonsu rested in shrines either side of the hypostyle hall, whilst the barques of the king and Amun proceeded further inside. A barque shrine was provided for the king off to one side of the 'Chamber of the Divine King'. Within this chamber the king seems to have gone through a repeat of the coronation ceremonies, after which he moved to the sanctuary of Amun-Re and made various offerings to the god. It is probable that, from here, the king moved to the rear part of the temple, to the part where the axis of the temple changes to a divine axis again and which was dedicated to a primeval form of Amun, known as Amunemopet. Even less is known about the rituals that may have taken place in this part of the temple.

Afterwards the king would re-emerge from the hidden parts of the temple rejuvenated for another year and the processions would return to Karnak via the river.

Development during the Eighteenth Dynasty

It seems that it was Hatshepsut who first began the process of creating a major processional way between the temples at Karnak and Luxor, evidenced by her work on the lateral axis at Karnak as well as by the barque stations she built on the overland route to Luxor; at Luxor Temple itself, blocks bearing her cartouches, as well as those of Tuthmose III and Amenhotep II, were reused during the building work of later rulers, indicating that these kings had been responsible for some of the temple structures. However it was

Luxor Temple: the First Courtyard and colonnade floodlit at night

Amenhotep III who provided the real impetus to the development of the temple. At the same time that he was expanding the temple complex at Karnak, it seems that he decided to renew the buildings of Luxor Temple. The earlier structures were dismantled and the core of a new temple erected, consisting of the cult rooms associated with the Opet rituals, including the chambers of Amunemopet, and a hypostyle hall in front of them.

Subsequently the same king decided to expand the temple northwards by means of an open courtyard with a peristyle on three sides. To the north of this he began work on a colonnade leading to a pylon gateway, with two colossal statues of himself either side of the entrance which faced along the axis of the temple towards the Karnak temple complex. It is not clear how much of the colonnade was completed during his lifetime as, although the bottommost courses of the walls here were erected during the reign of Amenhotep III, in fact most of the decoration in this part of the temple seems to have been carried out by Tutankhamun, and subsequently usurped by Horemheb. The reliefs, which were finally completed during the reign of Sety I, show in great detail the processions of the Opet Festival at this period.

Enlargement by Ramesses II

The colossal statues of Amenhotep III are still present, but now bear the names of Ramesses II and stand in the First Courtyard which was constructed by him in front of the colonnade hall. Even a quick glance at a plan of the temple is usually enough to draw attention to the strange change of axis here. It has been suggested that it was built in this way in order to incorporate an older structure of Hatshepsut, still present behind the pylon; it is, however, likely that, had this been the case, the king would have had the structure dismantled and re-erected in a more convenient location. If one looks carefully, the axis of the colonnade hall was already not quite true to the earlier axis of the temple, and it is possible that this axis was slightly offset to align better with the processional way from Karnak. The more radical change of axis of the First Courtyard may simply be a more extreme result of the same intention. Another explanation may be that the course of the river at the time prevented the temple's being built on a straight axis.

The First pylon gateway is the work of Ramesses II, and statues and obelisks of the same king were erected outside the temple. Again the royal statues face along the temple axis and look towards Karnak. A relief in the First Courtyard shows the exterior of the temple at the time of this king, with flags flying on the flagpoles set in the niches of the pylon. The depiction is relatively accurate, within the traditions of Egyptian art, with the exception of the crowns of the standing figures of the king: the relief shows these figures to have been wearing the double crown, whereas the sole remaining figure is wearing a white crown.

Relief in the First Courtyard of Luxor Temple, showing the façade of the temple in the time of Ramesses II

Later additions

Ramesses III, who seems to have been keen to live up to the reputation of Ramesses II, carried out the next major work at Luxor Temple. He began a programme of decoration of the rear parts of the temple which continued down to the time of the priest-king Menkheperre of the Twenty-first Dynasty.

Subsequently there seems to have been little building activity at the temple until the time of Nectanebo I, who, as at Karnak, constructed an enclosure wall around the temple precincts. The avenue of ram-headed sphinxes from Karnak, dating to the time of Amenhotep III, was replaced at this time at its southern end by human-headed sphinxes. Later the barque shrine within the sanctuary of the temple, which had been constructed by Amenhotep III, was replaced by one of Alexander the Great.

The Roman camp

The final great change for the temple came about during the Roman occupation of Egypt, when the temple formed the core of a military camp (p. 204). Within the temple the Chamber of the Divine King was modified to form a place dedicated to the cult of the divine emperor. A temple dedicated to the worship of Serapis was set up within the old enclosure wall, and later the southernmost part of the temple was converted into a Christian church.

THE WEST BANK TEMPLES

Most of the temples on the West Bank at Thebes were erected by or for individual kings. They contrast strongly with the complex at Karnak, where it seems that almost every king from the First Intermediate Period onwards (and even before) left some impression. The majority of these West Bank temples are in some way concerned with the cults of the kings who built them, and they serve as a counterpart to their burial places in the hills, mostly in the Valley of the Kings. The remainder were devoted to particular local cults on the West Bank. As well as the religious dimension, temples were an important part of the economic structure of Egypt, and information relating to the West Bank temples present us with an excellent opportunity to consider this issue here.

Background and meaning of a mortuary temple

As far back as the First Dynasty, tomb complexes had two clear functions. There was one place for the burial of the body, and another for the cult of the dead ruler, one of the major elements of which was the making of offerings to his spirits. In the earliest royal tombs, those of the First Dynasty at Abydos, the burial places were in the desert in a location now known as Umm el-Qa'ab. Associated with these burial places, but much nearer the edge of the cultivation, were large walled structures, some of which have been known about for many years, but others of which have been found only in the late 1980s. These structures are usually called 'funerary enclosures', and are thought to have been where the cult of the dead king was celebrated, and where offerings were made to him. By the time of the Third Dynasty, the two elements of a royal mortuary complex were integrated, as in the Step Pyramid of Djoser. This unity of tomb and temple continued until the New Kingdom, although at the beginning of the Fourth Dynasty an additional structure, the so-called 'valley temple', was constructed close to the edge of the cultivation, and was connected to the rest of the complex by a causeway. However, from almost the beginning of the New Kingdom, the Egyptians resumed the separation of the two main parts of the mortuary complex; the burial places were usually in the Valley of the Kings at Thebes, and the cult centres, or mortuary temples, were placed between the bottom of the hills and the cultivation, also on the West Bank.

The term 'mortuary temple' does not equate to any one Egyptian expression, but is a modern phrase which attempts to stress the difference between these structures dedicated to the well-being of the deceased king and those great state temples (such as those in the Karnak complex) which are more concerned with the well-being of the deities and the state.

The function of mortuary temples exhibits changes over the millennia, but it seems clear that they were not involved with the actual burial rites of the kings who built them. In the Old Kingdom such temples were very much concerned with perpetuating the power and undying nature of the king as both human and divine ruler, both by attending to the physical needs of his spirits and by the use of magic. Deities were not usually depicted in the buildings, although the afterlife was conceived of as being associated with the sun-god and Osiris. Beginning with the Theban funerary monument of Nebhepetre Mentuhotep II of the Eleventh Dynasty, however, these mortuary structures took on the form more of a conventional temple, a place where other deities were attended to by the king, in return for which care they would play their part in ensuring his place in eternity. The central part of the temple would take the form of a chapel to the king as an incarnation of the major local deity (thus it would be Amun in Thebes – at Medinet Habu there was even a local form of Amun, 'Amun united with eternity'), and there would be shrines to other deities nearby. The construction in many of these temples of an almost fortified enclosure wall and a palace for the king adjacent to the temple buildings proper suggest that the Egyptians were aiming almost at a self-contained realm for the king – or perhaps for the deceased king, as it has been suggested that the design of the palaces makes it unlikely that they were seriously to be used by the living (see pp. 194–6 for the possible use of the palace by the living king). In the Ramesside period the close association of the temple and the king is stressed through representations of the personified temple embracing the king.

Egyptian texts refer to these Theban temples by a variety of terms. A very common expression is 'the house of millions of years', but this is not, as often stated, restricted to structures which we identify as mortuary in nature; for example the Temple of Luxor was a 'house of millions of years'. Rather, this term stresses the intended permanence of such buildings. All the temples have imposing names: the Ramesseum is known as '(Ramesses) united with Thebes', and the great temple of Medinet Habu as '(Ramesses) united with eternity'.

The economic role of a temple

All Egyptian temples played an important role in the economy of the country, but the manner in which the Egyptian economy operated is still very unclear and debated by scholars. Much of the evidence available is highly subjective, but from Thebes in the New Kingdom we do at least have a mass of potentially interesting material, mostly deriving from the West Bank. The Egyptian economy was not based on a formal system of money, although the value of items was sometimes given in a standard weight of copper called a *deben*, weighing roughly 0.91 kg. The normal method of acquisition of goods was some sort of barter or exchange, and wages were normally given in terms of grain (p. 186).

Every temple received income in various forms, but perhaps the most apparent was the food designated as offerings for the deity. In some of the larger temples the daily amount could be massive, such as for the temple of Ramesses III at Medinet Habu: 2,222 loaves and 154 jars of beer, as well as fifty other food items.[1] What happened subsequently to these offerings formed the basis of a major part of the Egyptian economic system: they were first placed before the image of the principal temple deity, then before any other divinities and then they were redistributed to the staff and other dependants of the temple, the so-called 'reversion of offerings', where they formed the wages and benefits of attachment. Important sources which describe this process come from all periods of Egyptian history, although many of the best sources are from Thebes.

The extent to which the temple and state economies were linked is still debated. The funerary temples on the West Bank at Thebes were endowed with land by the king at the time of their foundation, but it is unclear to what extent this was removed by later kings. Presumably the fact that several cults did not long outlast their founders suggests that their estates might have been reassigned to other temples relatively quickly. However, although we are reasonably certain that Ramesses III founded his mortuary temple at Medinet Habu by transferring many of the resources of the Ramesseum to it, it is certain that the Ramesseum continued to function for some considerable time. The same is true for the temple of Tuthmose I, which, although it has never been found, is known to have been functioning in the late Twentieth Dynasty.

We can attest the use of the reserves of the mortuary temples as a source of payment for workers other than those in their direct employ. The best examples of this are in the so-called 'strike papyri' (p. 187), mainly from the reign of Ramesses III, in which the Deir el-Medina workmen went asking for supplies to a variety of older temples when the normal supply failed. The fact that this happened in these special circumstances suggests that it was otherwise somewhat unusual, even with the large resources at the temples' command; Kemp has calculated that a fully stocked Ramesseum could have fed seventeen to twenty thousand persons for a year.[2] Thus it can be seen that the temples possessed enormous resources. It seems that they did have a formal relationship with the state, but were perhaps not a mere extension of it. Rather they were private institutions with wider public responsibilities.

Royal temples before the New Kingdom

The amount of information available about the tombs of the kings buried in Thebes is variable, but the variation is nothing to the extremes encountered when we try to learn about their temples. Some were small, some were massive and some are now almost totally destroyed, while others are among the best-preserved remains in Thebes.

The Inyotef kings of the Eleventh Dynasty have left almost no remains of temples associated with their cults, although it does appear that the cult functions were integrated into their funerary complexes. Thus the little evidence which exists is considered below on p. 93. Nebhepetre Mentuhotep II con-

1 Valley of the
  Queens

2 Deir el-Medina:
  workmen's
  village

3 Ptolemaic
  temple of
  Hathor

4 Qurnet Marrai

5 modern houses

6 Sheikh Abd
  el-Qurna

7 Assasif

8 el-Khokha

9 temple of
  Hatshepsut at
  Deir el-Bahari

10 Valley of the
  Kings

11 Western Valley

12 The Qurn

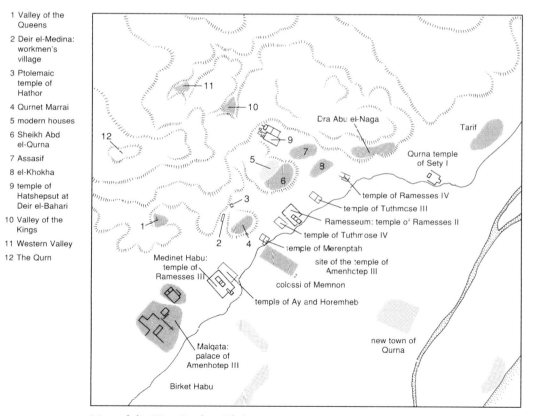

Map of the West Bank at Thebes

75

tinued his predecessors' practice of combining cult structures with tomb, and selected a magnificent virgin site at Deir el-Bahari. His complex, a temple with attached tomb, broke new ground in its architectural features with a ramped entrance, and a colonnade surrounding the central edifice; the colonnades were presumably inspired by the façades of the preceding *saff* tombs. This central edifice has often been reconstructed as a pyramid, but is now thought to have been more in the shape of a rectangular block. This front part of the temple was made of limestone, and seems to have been dedicated to Montu-Re, a form of the sun-god and the pre-eminent local deity of the age, and perhaps a forerunner to Amun-Re (pp. 44–5). The rear of the temple was made of sandstone and was the cult centre for the king. A number of burial places for royal women were incorporated into the structure (pp. 120–1).

The forecourt of the temple complex contained the temple garden, with large trees, several small ones and some flower beds; these are now visible as a series of depressions in the ground. Some of the remains of the trees still in place were identified as sycamore figs and tamarisks. Through the garden and down into the cultivation led a causeway, no doubt influenced by Old Kingdom practice in the north. To one side of the causeway was a dummy tomb, known in Arabic as the Bab el-Hossan, 'gate of the horse', as it was discovered by chance in 1898 when a horse ridden by Howard Carter stumbled on a depression in the surface. Two years later Carter was able to clear it and found not the royal burial he had expected, but the ritual burial of a statue of the king, now in the Cairo Museum, making the structure something of an imitation 'tomb of Osiris'. It appears that the tomb may originally have been cut for the royal burial, but it was later changed; a double arrangement is known from the Old Kingdom (the South Tomb versus the Step Pyramid at Saqqara for example), and there are New Kingdom private tombs with two shafts, one perhaps for burial and the other as a 'tomb of Osiris'.

The principal burial place of the tomb was in fact at the rear of the temple structure, where there is a sloping passage roughly 150 m long leading to a burial chamber with a pointed roof. Many fragments of wooden models, model vessels and so on were found here by the British and German expeditions who examined these passages. It is interesting to compare the relatively crude nature of these royal models with the wonderful quality of those produced for Meketre shortly afterwards (p. 140). Also found here was the earliest known canopic jar lid in the shape of a human head.

Four different building phases have been identified in the temple. The earliest part was a rough wall marking off the building area, and the only constructions which can be assigned to the second phase are the Bab el-Hossan and the queens' chapels. The remaining two phases cover most of the extant building: phase three saw the construction of the final tomb (and probably the sealing-up of the previous one) and construction of the central edifice and

The so-called 'Sankhkare temple', perhaps the original mortuary temple of Amenemhat I

colonnaded courtyards. The final stage was to make the temple even more impressive with the addition of extra colonnades, and the construction of a final series of retaining walls. In the Twelfth Dynasty, Senwosret III placed several statues of himself in this temple, which can be explained only by a particular respect he held for his predecessor, whose name was compound with that of the god Montu, a deity particularly venerated by Senwosret (pp. 27–8).

For many years Nebhepetre's successor Sankhkare Mentuhotep III was thought to have been the builder of an unfinished structure in another natural amphitheatre about a kilometre south of Deir el-Bahari, which appears to have been planned along similar lines to that of Nebhepetre Mentuhotep. It consists of a flat raised platform, a subterranean vaulted tomb at the rear and a causeway running around the south side of the hill of Sheikh Abd el-Qurna down to the cultivation, near what is now the Ramesseum. Research in the 1980s and early 1990s by Dorothea Arnold, using a wide-ranging mixture of epigraphic and archaeological source material, has, however, suggested that it was not Sankhkare Mentuhotep but Amenemhat I who started this temple. He then abandoned it at a relatively early stage of construction when it was decided that it was more practical to govern the country from a site in the north, It'tawy (modern Lisht). This theory has been recently supported by the possible identification of a tomb for Sankhkare Mentuhotep.

A temple certainly of the Eleventh Dynasty is situated on the so-called

'Thoth Hill' at the north end of the site, the highest peak in the region. Known since the early twentieth century, the visible temple was certainly built by Sankhkare Mentuhotep. The site requires a stiff walk of nearly two hours from the area of the Carter house, and has been systematically investigated only in the 1990s. Work by a Hungarian mission has revealed that there is not only a mud-brick temple of Sankhkare at the site, the remains of which are just visible from the cultivation, but also another building of the same king, identified by the excavators as a *sed* (jubilee) festival palace. Further research may reveal whether the constructions of Sankhkare Mentuhotep are perhaps related to a nearby tomb recently discovered and which might belong to him. Perhaps most interesting of all is that a stone temple has been found underneath the brick one, which the excavators believe to be datable to Early Dynastic times, and which would thus be the earliest stone temple in Egypt. The site is thought now to have been dedicated to Horus rather than to Thoth.

No temples are known on the West Bank dating to the Second Intermediate Period. The Seventeenth Dynasty kings buried there (pp. 94–5) seem to have had their cult centres in their chapels,[3] although information is currently very sparse.

Royal temples of the New Kingdom

Although the mummy of the first king of the Eighteenth Dynasty, Ahmose, was found in the Deir el-Bahari cache, no tomb or temple can be assigned to him in Thebes. A strange pyramid-like structure and a temple have been dated to his reign at Abydos, but these may be in some way associated with a cenotaph to himself in the realm of Osiris, rather akin to those built by some kings of the Twelfth and Nineteenth Dynasties. Before we move to the temples of this date in Thebes, we shall consider the major festival on the West Bank, which was celebrated also in some of these temples.

The Beautiful Festival of the Valley

The 'Valley Festival', as we shall call it for brevity, was perhaps the most important of the many festivals celebrated on the West Bank in Luxor during the New Kingdom. Its origins seem to lie in the early Middle Kingdom, and it is thought to be a local variation of a popular Hathor festival probably celebrated throughout Egypt, very much connected with the concept of Hathor of the West receiving the dead into her realm. This festival took place in the second month of the *Shomu* season. Its importance was twofold. Firstly, the major public manifestation was a visit by the image of Amun of Karnak, shrouded in his barque, to the West Bank; from the Nineteenth Dynasty at least, the barques of Mut and Khonsu were also present. The principal target of the procession was the main Hathor sanctuaries on the West Bank, which were situated at Deir el-Bahari, and also the various royal mortuary temples which form so much of the subject matter of this chapter. Many of these temples contained some reference to the festival, but the most detailed scenes are to be found on monuments of Hatshepsut, in particular the upper courtyard of her temple at Deir el-Bahari. Clearly one of the important elements of this aspect of the festival was the reaffirmation of kingship, and in this respect it has affinities with the Opet Festival (pp. 67–9).

The second significance of the festival was the way it related to the non-royal deceased buried in the necropolis and to their families. The living would visit the tombs of their dead, and it appears that a form of reunion between the two would happen. In the Eighteenth Dynasty a number of aspects of the private rituals of the festival were depicted in tomb scenes, such as the making of burnt offerings and the pouring of water, which are usually shown either side of the doorway in the first room of the tomb chapel.

Djeserkaresoneb pours a libation over offerings during the celebrations of the Valley Festival (TT38)

The banquet scenes which are so common in the same period also probably represent celebrations during the same festival, and, with their scenes
of festivity and drinking, heavy in symbolism, seem to reflect one aspect
of the union of the dead and the living. Another, more complex, manner
in which the dead and the living are thought to be united is by their association with the procession of the sun god, the dead praising the procession
of the god as giver of light (and therefore life), and the living taking part
in the real procession. The *ka* of the deceased was also revived by the
presentation of perfumes and flowers from the offerings of the god Amun.

The location of the tomb of Amenhotep I is uncertain (p. 97). A temple
ascribed to him and his mother Ahmose-Nefertari was investigated in the
early years of the twentieth century by Spiegelberg and Newberry and then
by Carter. Today it is unrecognizable, and serves as a rubbish dump in front
of two alabaster factories. There was also a small temple dedicated to this
royal pair at Deir el-Bahari, built in brick, which was dismantled when the
great temple of Hatshepsut was constructed. Little is known about this
temple, although it is likely that it was associated with the local cult of
Hathor and the Festival of the Valley. Its purpose was probably subsumed
into the Hatshepsut/Tuthmoside constructions.

The location of the temple of Tuthmose I is unknown, although it is known
from texts to have functioned well into the Twentieth Dynasty. A French mission working on the area just to the north of Medinet Habu in the 1930s
came upon a number of blocks of a structure of Tuthmose II which was
probably built to his memory by Tuthmose III. There is some disagreement
as to whether this was really a mortuary temple, as it is not in the same area
of the site as other temples of that date and function, but, as there is no real
other evidence for a mortuary temple for this king (it is not mentioned in a
list of temples given by Hatshepsut at Karnak), it is difficult to suggest that it
had anything other than this function, even if it was erected some time after
the king's demise.

The first well-preserved temple of the New Kingdom, Hatshepsut's monument at Deir el-Bahari, was certainly inspired in its design by the adjacent
temple of Nebhepetre Mentuhotep, with its colonnades and platforms. The
unique design of the temple took advantage of unevenness in the valley floor
and the amounts of debris left over from the construction of the Mentuhotep
temple, and part of the design brief was surely to produce an impressive
temple which would fit in with its setting. The important associations of the
site of Deir el-Bahari with Hathor and the Festival of the Valley must have
played a very significant role in the siting and plan of the temple. It was first
excavated by Edouard Naville for the Egypt Exploration Fund in the 1890s.
While it has to be said that the excavation technique left something to be
desired (although it should be pointed out that at this date archaeologists of
Petrie's ability were the exception), there is little doubt that the epigraphic

recording of the temple performed by Howard Carter took the techniques of epigraphy in Egypt to new levels. The temple contained numerous beautiful and well-executed scenes, and these were very well reproduced in the published volumes.

The temple very clearly displays two of the features which characterize New Kingdom funerary temples, namely the aggrandizement of the achievements of the king and his or her personal importance, and also the incorporation into the architectural design of the sanctuaries of deities relevant to the afterlives of the ruler. The second terrace bears on its south side the famous reliefs of the Punt expedition, which Hatshepsut clearly regarded as an important feature of her reign. This expedition went to this exotic foreign land, now normally identified with the Somalia/Eritrea area, to obtain incense trees and other luxury products for the temples, particularly at Karnak. At the north side of the second terrace is the ideologically more important set of birth scenes, the first depiction by a king of the process which had assured his right to the throne. The reason for this first appearance in this temple is not hard to seek, since Hatshepsut's claim to be king was hardly straightforward; it was later incorporated into the scenes sometimes used by kings for whom there was no problem of legitimacy but where it performed the useful purpose of renewal (such as Amenhotep III in the Temple of Luxor). On the same terrace are shrines to Hathor and to Anubis, while on the third terrace (at present not open to visitors) are chapels of Anubis and Amun, and an open courtyard dedicated to the sun-god.

Again following the model of the Mentuhotep temple, a causeway was constructed down through the Assasif to the edge of the cultivation, where a valley temple was built. Such causeways were not necessary for the other temples, as they were immediately adjacent to the cultivation, which was certainly a point of access by water in the inundation season, and possibly at other times of the year owing to the presence of small canals no longer extant.

The work of the construction of the temple of Hatshepsut is ascribed to her prominent official Senmut. He constructed his own chapel overlooking the temple, and his separate burial apartments run right under the open courtyard in front of his queen's temple. Such was his favour and power that he was permitted to inscribe his image in some of the less visible parts of the temple. An interesting sideline on this period is a satirical scene sketched in a cave above Deir el-Bahari, showing a couple engaged in sexual activity. The female figure wears a uraeus, and has been interpreted as a comment on the contradiction inherent on the occupancy of the throne by a woman.[4]

The mud-brick entrance pylon and part of the enclosure wall of the mortuary temple of Tuthmose III still stand prominently by the road along the edge of the cultivation, although precious little still remains inside the enclosure. It was first investigated by the Antiquities Service under Weigall in the early twentieth century, and further studied by Ricke in the 1930s. A false door of the king probably erected in this temple was reused at a later date in Medinet Habu.

There was another very important temple of this king in west Thebes, located between and above the two great mortuary temples at Deir el-Bahari This construction was discovered only in 1962, as it had been destroyed and concealed by a rock fall in ancient times. This temple seems to take the form of a shrine to Amun, and was called Djeser-Akhet, the 'sacred horizon (of Amun)'; there was also a subsidiary shrine to Hathor at a lower level, famously found by Naville after a rock fall in 1905–6, and now in the Cairo Museum. Like the other temples on this site, it possessed its own causeway to the cultivation. The name of the structure again stresses the importance of the annual visit of Amun to the West Bank to take part in the Festival of the Valley. It has been established that this temple was built late in the reign of Tuthmose III, and it is tempting to associate its construction with the perse-

*Deir el-Bahari, temple of
Hatshepsut: figure of
Senmut in one of the niches
on the second terrace*

*(Left)
Reconstruction of the
temples at Deir el-Bahari in
the Eighteenth Dynasty*

cution which Tuthmose seems to have carried out against Hatshepsut in the later part of his reign – in other words, an intended effect of the erection of his own temple for the cult at Deir el-Bahari was to devalue the function of the buildings of his aunt. Hatshepsut and Tuthmose III also carried out work at Medinet Habu, as described later in this chapter (pp. 90–1).

In 1895–6 Petrie undertook a campaign which brought to light the remains of a number of smaller temples on the edge of the cultivation, which had been previously overlooked, published as his *Six Temples at Thebes*. One of these was a ruined monument to the north-east of the Ramesseum, which was identified as the mortuary temple of Amenhotep II. No name was found for this temple (it has not been examined since that time), but other texts mention two structures of this king, called 'joining the horizon' and 'receiving in life'. The temple of his son and successor Tuthmose IV is located just to the south of the Ramesseum, and was first investigated by Petrie in 1895–6. Parts of it were excavated by an Italian mission in the 1970s. The entrance pylon to the temple was made of brick, and inside it most of the decorated surfaces, of which little remained, were made of sandstone blocks; two stelae were also found by Petrie, and two further ones by the Italians in the 1970s. South of the temple enclosure the Italian excavations have uncovered a building which appears to have housed those who built the temple.

Amenhotep III built the largest temple in Thebes, measuring 700 by 500 m, larger even than the temple of Amun-Re at Karnak. However, it seems that the temple had begun to decay shortly after the death of the king, and in the reign of Merenptah it was used as a source of limestone blocks for the temple of that ruler. Much of the blame for this must be placed on the proximity of the temple to the cultivation, and we assume that the structures were undermined by the presence of moisture. All that now remain are the two statues, known today as the Colossi of Memnon, which stood at the eastern gateway, and a large stela which has been re-erected at the back (west). Between them are traces of pylons and various other seated colossi and sphinx statues. The temple has never been properly investigated, although much is at present being learned about its decoration from study of the reused blocks in the Merenptah temple. It is known that, while a considerable part of the temple was dedicated to Amun, one (northern) part was devoted to the Memphite deity Ptah or Ptah-Sokar-Osiris, to whom Amenhotep also built a temple in Memphis. An astonishing feature of this temple was the amount of statuary it seems to have contained, in that Amenhotep attempted to represent in stone the litany of Sekhmet, the avenging goddess who had to be appeased to prevent the destruction of the world. This he did by producing one seated and one standing statue of the deity for every day of the year, which were then placed in this temple, along with many statues of other deities. The quantity of sculpture was so vast that the temple was used by later kings as a source of statuary for their own monuments in Thebes and elsewhere. It is even more remarkable that most of the work done in this temple took place in the last ten years of the king's reign in conjunction with his three *sed* (jubilee) festivals, at which time there was a vast building programme under way in Thebes and the rest of Egypt.

No mortuary temple for Amenhotep IV/Akhenaten is perhaps to be expected at Thebes, as he intended to be buried at Amarna, although it cannot be excluded that he may have begun some structure before the religious changes began in about years 3–4 of his reign. However, there must have been some building activity of his in the area, since mud bricks stamped with his name have turned up in excavations in various places, including our own in TT294. Indeed, work adjacent to the Ramesseum has revealed the floor of a building from the early reign of Amenhotep IV.

In 1931 the Oriental Institute of the University of Chicago discovered a site to the north of the enclosure of Medinet Habu which proved to be a mortuary temple of Ay subsequently usurped by Horemheb. The best-known discovery from here was of two large statues, which are in fact, on stylistic grounds, thought to represent Tutankhamun. One reference to a priest of a temple of Tutankhamun is known, and it does seem just possible that Ay might have taken over a chapel built for Tutankhamun as part of his own funerary monument, in the manner in which it is speculated that he did with

The 'Qurna' temple of Sety I

the royal tomb (p. 104). Ay does appear to have constructed a separate
temple in memory of Tutankhamun, remains of which have been found in
Karnak, but its original location is uncertain.

Ramesses I did not perhaps have time to construct a temple in Thebes, and
instead his son Sety I constructed a chapel for him in his own West Bank
temple. This temple (often called the 'Qurna temple') is the earliest of the
well-preserved examples of what is clearly the standard type of temple, with
open courtyards and pillared halls, and barque shrines to other deities. These
include Ptah-Sokar, Mut, Khonsu, Amun in the form of Sety, and Nefertem-
Osiris, as well as a courtyard dedicated to the sun-god. At the back of the
central sanctuary was a false door of sorts, a feature also encountered at the
Ramesseum. Although rarely visited by tourists, and despite the fact that the
front part of the temple is beneath the adjacent village, the reconstruction
works undertaken by the German Archaeological Institute give an excellent
idea of how such a temple might have looked in the late New Kingdom. The
temple was unfinished at the death of Sety, and was completed, like so many
of his monuments, by his son Ramesses II.

The mortuary temple of Ramesses II, the Ramesseum, is familiar to those
interested in English literature through Shelley's poem 'Ozymandias'; many
are the tourists who have recited this work while standing in the front courtyard of the temple. 'Ozymandias' is almost certainly a classical form of the
prenomen of Ramesses II which we conventionally write as Usermaatre. The
colossal seated statue referred to in the poem was made of granite and
approximately 20 m high; the present French mission excavating and restor-

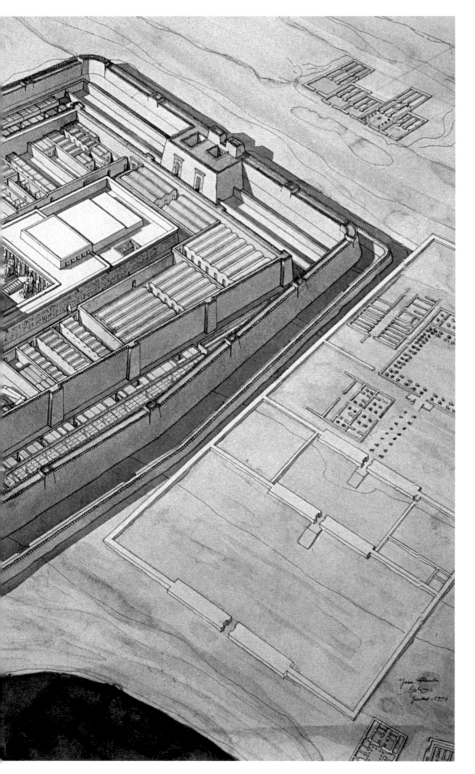

Reconstruction of the temples at Medinet Habu in the Twentieth Dynasty

ing the temple often mentions the possibility of restoring this piece to its former glory, but there are many who would regret the loss of the present romantic aspect presented by the ruins. The same mission has identified the statue body to which the head in the British Museum known as the 'Younger Memnon' belongs; this was removed by Belzoni.

The temple follows the basic pattern of halls and gateways seen in Ramesses II's father's temple, but on a larger scale. The second courtyard is decorated for the first time with a series of statues representing the king as Osiris, clearly seen before on the West Bank only in the temple of Hatshepsut. Inside the hypostyle hall, a small version of its more famous counterpart at Karnak, are scenes from the wars of Ramesses II; an account of the Battle of Qadesh is found on the first pylon, on the edge of the cultivation. One of the most remarkable survivals of this temple is the set of elaborate mud-brick storerooms which were needed to make any such cult centre function; the arches of some of these rooms are still preserved. These rooms were later reused as funerary chapels for burials in the Twenty-second and Twenty-third Dynasties.

It is clear that the now badly damaged temple of Merenptah, first examined by Petrie in 1895–6, was largely constructed from blocks made for the nearby temple of Amenhotep III. Since the 1980s a Swiss mission has been working there, and has been revealing and restoring more of these blocks. It would appear that the temple, smaller in size than that of his father Ramesses II, was not dissimilar in layout to that of Sety I.

The Ramesseum from the north-east

1 first pylon
2 temple palace
3 second pylon
4 hypostyle hall
5 temple of Sety I
6 first vestibule ('Astronomical Room')
7 second vestibule ('Library')
8 third vestibule
9 barque hall
10 sanctuary
11 storerooms and workshops

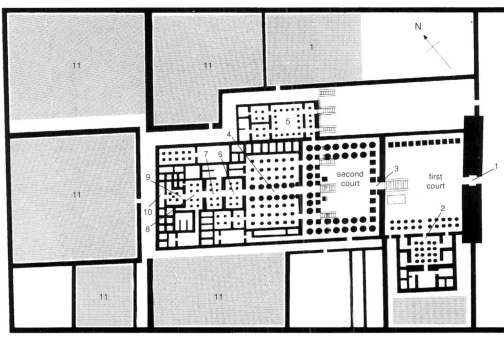

Plan of the Ramesseum

No temples are known for either Sety II or Amenmesse on the West Bank. Petrie discovered a small temple built for Siptah which was subsequently used by Tawosret when she took the throne on her son's demise. No temple has been found for her successor Sethnakht, the father of Ramesses III; he does not appear to have usurped her temple in the manner in which he took over and extended her tomb in the Valley of the Kings.

The last great mortuary temple to have survived is that of Ramesses III at Medinet Habu. The temple itself is extremely well preserved, as is the massive enclosure wall, and gives the visitor the best impression of such a complex at Thebes. Well-preserved courtyards, some with statues of the king as Osiris, lead to a very complex sanctuary area, the part of the whole temple in the poorest state of preservation. Here are chapels for the cult of Amun and a resting place for his barque, along with a series of rooms which seem to have been devoted to the mysteries of the god. Chapels for the king and Ptah are also to be seen, as well as a temple to the Great Ennead. Many coloured scenes are preserved, and the exterior of the temple bears Ramesses' accounts of his great campaigns, notably those against the Libyans and the Sea Peoples.

Medinet Habu also has the distinction of being thus far the best excavated and published temple in Thebes, thanks to the epigraphic and archaeological work of the Oriental Institute of the University of Chicago. The temple area became the centre for the necropolis administration in the Twentieth Dynasty, and remained an important settlement centre right down into late Roman times; the remains of many late structures built into the enclosure walls of the temple can still be seen (p. 203).

There is considerable confusion surrounding structures of the Twentieth Dynasty after Ramesses III. There is no sequence of temples comparable to that of the earlier kings, but there are some structures which can be dated to this period. The clearest are two buildings adjacent to the valley temple of Hatshepsut at the eastern end of the Assasif, examined by Carter and Carnarvon, and then by the Metropolitan Museum. They indicate the presence of a large temple of Ramesses IV, from the foundation deposits which were discovered. This temple appears to have been intended to be even larger than that of his father Ramesses III, although work never in fact proceeded very far. Blocks from this temple inscribed with the names of Ramesses V and Ramesses VI perhaps suggest that these kings took over this temple after its first builder died. There is another temple associated with Ramesses IV north of Medinet Habu, of which even less is known. One possibility is that this king abandoned the large Assasif temple and contented himself with a smaller one elsewhere. Nothing is currently known about temples for the remaining kings of the dynasty.

Other temples

A small number of temples on the West Bank remain to be mentioned. One of these is an important element of the wider cult of Amun and a link with the East Bank, while the others are associated with private individuals.

The small temple of Medinet Habu was a temple of a very different type to most others on the West Bank. It was thought of as built on the mound of creation in Thebes,[5] and housed an image of 'Amun of the sacred place'. The temple seems very much to have been the home of a primeval form of Amun identified with the creator god Kamutef, and may have had its origin in the Middle Kingdom. Texts of the New Kingdom attest the fact that every ten days the image of Amunemopet from Luxor, another primeval form of Amun (p. 69), would come to this shrine. More detail is obtained from texts in the so-called 'edifice of Taharqa' at Karnak (p. 64); there Amun is shown visiting Kamutef and the eight primeval gods of Hermopolis at Djeme, the name for the area of Medinet Habu. Amun was transfigured into a sun-falcon, and rose from a lotus (another reference to creation myths) to become the keeper of *Maat*, the established correct order of the world.[6] Thus revivified, he returned to Luxor.

The entrance to the Eighteenth Dynasty part of the small temple at Medinet Habu

The oldest part of the surviving building was constructed in the reigns of Tuthmose III and Hatshepsut, but, because it was not a sanctuary associated with one ruler but rather a particular cult, it was frequently modified. Extra courtyards were added in the Thirtieth Dynasty and in Roman times, and decorated blocks from earlier periods were often reused, some of which are still visible in the walls.

There are also several small temples worthy of a brief mention, since they are all now more or less destroyed. The high priest of Amun in the reign of Ramesses II, Nebwenenef, owner of TT157, possessed a small chapel at the northern end of the site. Just to the south of the Ramesseum is the small chapel usually referred to that of Prince Wadjmose, a son of Tuthmose I. This temple was among those investigated by Petrie, and in the 1990s it has been re-examined by the French mission working at the Ramesseum. A small chapel with three shrines, it was once thought of as a mortuary chapel to the prince. who did receive some sort of cult in the New Kingdom; however, the current opinion is that it is a chapel dedicated by Wadjmose to local deities, most probably the Theban triad of Amun, Mut and Khonsu.

A more famous individual is Amenhotep son of Hapu, a major character at the court of Amenhotep III, and perhaps responsible for many of his buildings. He was accorded the honour of his own funerary temple, now largely destroyed and excavated in the 1930s, north of Medinet Habu. A very important feature of it was that the first courtyard contained a small sacred lake, surrounded by trees; this has now unfortunately been built over.

The Graeco-Roman temples at Deir el-Medina, Qasr el-Aguz and Deir es-Shelwit are dealt with in Chapter 9.

TOMBS OF THE KINGS

Since classical times the Valley of the Kings at Thebes has been a focal point for visitors to southern Upper Egypt. The valley is only one of the later stages of the development of the Egyptian royal tomb, even though it is one of the best known. An appreciation of the earlier phases of tomb development is thus necessary to understand how the Theban royal burials reached this form.

The tombs of the kings of the First Dynasty are located at Abydos, about 180 km to the north of Thebes. There, in an area of desert not far from the cultivation, known as Umm el-Qaʻab, these kings built tombs which were a cross between tumuli and the mastaba tombs which became so characteristic in the following period. Cult activity for these kings was probably concentrated in a series of large enclosures nearer the fields. The next major development was the innovation of the pyramid structure as a burial place in the Step Pyramid of Djoser of the Third Dynasty at Saqqara, built as a series of mastabas one on top of another, and placed in a large enclosure where the cult rites could be carried out, thus merging the two separate parts seen at Abydos. In the course of the Third and early Fourth Dynasties the concept of the pyramid complex gradually evolved into the large 'traditional' pyramid with an adjacent mortuary temple, linked to a 'valley temple' at the edge of the cultivation by a causeway permitting non-public travel from the fields to the pyramid itself. Decoration, although present in the mortuary temple from the Fourth Dynasty on, appeared only in the pyramid at the end of the Fifth Dynasty, when more ancient texts, known today as the *Pyramid Texts*, were placed in the burial chambers of the kings, so that the magical spells would help to ensure their passage into the hereafter.

Kings at Thebes – the First Intermediate Period

The rulers of the final Old Kingdom dynasty (the Eighth) were still buried in the Memphite region in pyramids, but the situation changed once central control collapsed. Nothing is currently known of the burials of the Herakleopolitan rulers of the Ninth and Tenth Dynasties, but at Thebes by about 2110 BC the ruling local family had declared its leaders kings (the Eleventh Dynasty), and they developed a new type of royal tomb, a thoroughly Theban one, although still basically integrating the burial and cult parts of the royal complex in one linked structure.

The tombs of the three Eleventh Dynasty rulers called Inyotef who preceded Nebhepetre Mentuhotep have survived, but in a rather damaged state. They lie in the contemporary cemetery of Tarif at the north end of the West Bank. A considerable amount of the damage they have suffered is as a result of the development of the modern settlement there which covers much of the cemetery area. Each tomb was a very large example of the *saff* type which developed at this time (pp. 146–8), in front of which was an immense courtyard; the tombs of Inyotefs I–III are today respectively known by their Arabic names of Saff el-Dawaba, Saff el-Kisiya and Saff el-Baqar. Significant parts of each complex were excavated by the German Archaeological Institute in the early 1970s. Each tomb had a long double-pillared façade, off which ran one or more passages with shafts in them, which were presumably the burial places of the kings and their closest relatives. The bad state of preservation of the tombs means that we know virtually nothing about their decoration; only in the Saff el-Baqar can it be ascertained that the walls were lined with sandstone blocks which were decorated to some extent.

In the case of one of these three complexes something more is known about other structures associated with the tomb: at the eastern end of the Saff el-Kisiya, on the edge of the modern canal, are the remains of a mud-brick structure. This perhaps contained a centre for a statue cult, and is reminiscent of some of the valley temples of the Old Kingdom. It was probably the only cult centre in the tomb complex. It was in this building of mud brick that Mariette in 1860 found a stela of Wahankh Inyotef II on which the king was shown accompanied by five of his dogs, and which bears the date of year 50 of his reign. It is particularly interesting that we have an ancient reference to this structure and indeed to the stela, since it was mentioned in the tomb inspections in the Abbott Papyrus, now in the British Museum, in the reign of Ramesses IX: 'The tomb of king Inyotef-aa . . . the pyramid of which has been removed but whose stela still stands in front of it, showing the king with his dog Behkai between his feet. It was checked today and found intact.'[1] The tomb inspectors did not bother to distinguish between the chapel and the tomb itself. Note the use of the word 'pyramid' to describe a tomb which was not of the rock-cut and hidden type found in the Valley of the Kings.

The successor of the third Inyotef was Nebhepetre Mentuhotep II, who is regarded as the founder of the Middle Kingdom, the classical period of ancient Egypt. For the location of his burial he chose a site opposite the temple of Karnak in a bay in the hills, now known as Deir el-Bahari. The tomb he built there was set at the back of its own temple: this structure has been described in the previous chapter (pp. 75–7).

Mentuhotep's successor, Sankhkare Mentuhotep III, was thought for many years to have chosen a similar location for his burial place and mortuary temple, nestling under the cliffs behind the hill of Sheikh Abd el-Qurna. This has been re-evaluated and it is now thought that the temple in question was actually begun by Amenemhat I (p. 77). A Hungarian mission working on a small temple on a hilltop to the north of the site believes it may have discovered Mentuhotep III's burial place in the form of a rock-cut tomb within the same hill. This is, however, highly speculative at present.

Back to the north – the Twelfth Dynasty

Amenemhat I, the first king of the Twelfth Dynasty, abandoned work on his tomb and temple at Thebes as a result of the decision to move the capital of the country further north, to the area near the Fayum called Itjitawy. Once the royal court began to reside again in the north, the rulers resumed using the classic Memphite form of royal tomb, the pyramid. Pyramids of the Twelfth Dynasty in the area south of Memphis tended to be built of mud brick rather than stone, but were essentially similar in concept. The rulers did, however, attempt to make the pyramids more secure than their Old Kingdom models, by introducing more complex passages inside the structures, presumably intended to defeat robbers, who had had few problems penetrating the earlier royal tombs.

The Second Intermediate Period

The next royal burials in the Luxor area were those of the Theban Seventeenth Dynasty rulers, who began the process of expelling the Hyksos rulers from Egypt at the end of the Second Intermediate Period (pp. 29–31). Several tombs belonging to these kings were identified during the excavations of Mariette and others in the early nineteenth century in the Dra Abu el-Naga area. A number of them were found intact and yielded coffins and other burial goods, most of which are now in Cairo or in the Louvre; among them were the burials of Kamose, Nubkheperre Inyotef V, Sekhemre-Wepmaat Inyotef VI, Sekhemre-Herhermaat Inyotef VII, and Sekhemre-Shedtawy Sebekemzaf II. These tombs are mentioned in the Abbott tomb-robbery papyrus as being more or less intact,[2] except for the latest, which was found to have been robbed (p. 185 for a description of the robbery). Unfortunately, their locations have now been completely lost, although in the 1990s three tombs very high up on the side of the hills in this area have been tentatively identified as possible royal tombs of this period. The tombs have a large doorway leading into a single large room, with pillars supporting the ceiling, and a very deep shaft set in the centre of the floor of the room. Above one of these tombs have been found the remains of a mud-brick superstructure in the form of a pyramid. A fourth tomb of a similar design has also been identified fairly high on the hillside of Sheikh Abd el-Qurna. They await further investigation before it can finally be ascertained whether the tombs of the Seventeenth Dynasty kings have been rediscovered. It does appear,

Unusual cone-shaped stela of Sebekhotep from Thebes, bearing the cartouches of King Sekhemre-Shedtawy Sebekemzaf of the Seventeenth Dynasty. British Museum, EA1163

however, that the basic design is not unlike that of contemporary private tombs, which are themselves a development from the *saff* tomb of the First Intermediate Period.

The early New Kingdom

The Eighteenth Dynasty marked the beginning of a new era in Egyptian history, known to us today as the New Kingdom. The first king of the dynasty, Ahmose, built a pyramid-like structure at Abydos, but it is not at all certain that it was a tomb as his body was discovered amongst a cache of royal mummies at Thebes, suggesting that he had actually been buried there. All the remaining rulers of the period, however, apart from possibly during the

The Valley of the Kings from the hills above, with the Nile visible in the background

Amarna period, had burial places on the West Bank at Thebes, and most of these were in the Valley of the Kings. This is, of course, the best-known site in the area and has been a 'tourist attraction' since classical times (p. 205). The name 'Valley of the Kings' is of fairly recent origin and many publications refer to this area as the Biban el-Moluk, an Arabic expression meaning 'the doorways of the kings', or the Wadyein, meaning 'the two valleys', which is a reference to the fact that there are actually two valleys in the hills which were used for burials, the East and the West Valleys. The majority of the royal tombs are in the East Valley.

The rulers of the Eighteenth Dynasty decided to split the burial and cult parts of the royal burial complex. It is possible that this dynasty was more concerned about security than its predecessors, and thus turned from the highly visible pyramid to the concealed rock tomb. It should also be considered, however, that there was no real tradition of pyramid tombs in Thebes, although rock tombs at the site date back at least eight hundred years before.

The valley they chose was in an ideal location for this purpose because although it is hidden from sight, being behind the cliffs which provide the backdrop to the temples at Deir el-Bahari, it is none the less relatively close to the cultivation, which meant that there was little logistical difficulty in getting a workforce on site to carry out the construction work. Although the most direct route is a rather steep climb over the cliffs, there was a much longer, but shallower, access route along the bottom of the valley along which the funeral equipment could be dragged on sledges. It is possible that they were also influenced in their choice by the resemblance of the Qurn, which overlooks the valley, to a pyramid.

The first tomb known to have been cut in the valley is that of Tuthmose I. A tomb belonging to his predecessor, Amenhotep I, is referred to in the inspection of tombs recorded in the Abbott Papyrus, indicating that he was buried in the area. A deep shaft at the top of a small wadi at the northern end of Dra Abu el-Naga was excavated in 1913–14 by Howard Carter, who found in it fragments of stone vessels bearing the names of members of the royal family from the end of the Seventeenth and the beginning of the Eighteenth Dynasties. On the basis of these, and from the description of the location of Amenhotep I's tomb in the Abbott Papyrus, Carter proposed that this tomb was the burial place of that king, together with his mother Ahmose-Nefertari. Arthur Weigall, a contemporary of Carter's, interpreted the location given in the papyrus differently and proposed another candidate for this tomb, KV39 at the very edge of the Valley of the Kings. The tomb was cleared in 1989 but no conclusions can be drawn until the final report of the work is published.

Tuthmose I may have been responsible for establishing the workmen's village at Deir el-Medina (p. 174). We also know, from the tomb of Ineni (TT81), who was Chief Overseer of the Royal Tomb during the reign of Tuthmose I, that he was responsible for excavating Tuthmose's tomb, 'unseen and unheard'. It is not certainly known for which tomb in the Valley of the Kings Ineni was responsible, as there are two possible candidates, KV20 and KV38. The first is the larger of the two and appears to have two burial chambers. When it was excavated by Howard Carter in 1903, it was found to contain two sarcophagi inscribed with the names of Tuthmose I and Hatshepsut respectively. The other tomb, KV38, is much smaller, but was also found to contain a sarcophagus bearing Tuthmose I's name. The current understanding is that the larger of the two tombs, KV20, was the one Ineni constructed for his king. Subsequently, Tuthmose I's daughter, Hatshepsut, who took the throne as a king during the reign of her nephew Tuthmose III, enlarged her father's tomb by adding a new burial chamber where she could rest together with her father.[3] When Tuthmose III regained control of the country, he decided to remove Tuthmose I's body from this tomb and so prepared a new tomb, KV38.

Almost all the Eighteenth Dynasty tombs in the Valley of the Kings are a development of the design of Tuthmose I's original tomb. The tomb is cut in a series of corridors and stairways, separated from each other by door jambs, descending deep into the ground. The corridors run initially to the east, then turn to the south, and then turn again to the west, before culminating in an antechamber and a burial chamber. The antechamber, which has curved walls, was probably the burial chamber in the original design, the pillared hall below it having been added by Hatshepsut. Some decoration was found here in the form of limestone slabs with cursive drawings and writings from the funerary text known as the *Amduat* inscribed in ink on them (p. 117). Like all the early New Kingdom tombs in the Valley of the Kings, this tomb was intended to be hidden from sight, and so the uppermost corridors would have been filled with rubble, and its entrance would have been covered over with further chippings.

The location of the tomb of Tuthmose I's successor, Tuthmose II, is unknown. Several suggestions have been made, but they are all ultimately unsatisfactory. The next king's tomb to be built in the Valley of the Kings was that of Tuthmose III, set high up in the southernmost cliffs. The tomb really crystallized the form of the early Eighteenth Dynasty tomb. Like that of Tuthmose I, its corridors and stairways descend steeply into the ground, changing direction on the way. In this tomb we meet the first occurrence of an enigmatic feature in the royal tombs of the Eighteenth Dynasty, a deep shaft or well, deliberately cut in the floor of the tomb, sometimes having a room off to one side at the bottom. Various suggestions have been made as to the purpose of this well – as a rain catchment point, or as a decoy to tomb robbers. However, the fact that there is often decoration present at this point of the tomb even when it is lacking in other parts indicates that it had more than just a practical significance for the Egyptians, and it has been suggested that it may have been a symbolic burial shaft, perhaps associated with the god Sokar. Beyond the well is a pillared hall, again a regular feature in subsequent royal tombs, which in this tomb leads directly into the burial chamber. Tuthmose's burial chamber, which has four small side rooms lying off it, has curved walls, like the original burial chamber of KV20, and is similarly decorated with *Amduat* texts. In this tomb, however, the wall decoration is particularly striking; one has the impression of being encircled by a large funerary papyrus. The burial chamber, as well as the antechamber, in this tomb has pillars which are also inscribed, including a notable depiction of the king being suckled by Isis in the form of a tree.

The royal mummies

Although Tuthmose III's sarcophagus, in the shape of a cartouche, still lies in its tomb, no mummy was found there. The king's body, together with many of his predecessors in the Eighteenth Dynasty, was discovered in a remarkable cache of royal mummies found in a tomb close to Deir el-Bahari which contained the bodies of some of the most famous kings of Egyptian history.

The cache had been discovered in the 1870s by the Abd er-Rassul family, who lived locally, and plundered by them on a regular basis; objects of clearly royal origin would appear on the antiquities market from time to time. In 1881 a member of the family went to the authorities to reveal the site from

Valley of the Kings, tomb of Tuthmose III: a section of the fifth hour of the Amduat showing the secret cavern of Sokar

which the antiquities were coming. Immediately Emile Brugsch came down from the Antiquities Service in Cairo to investigate the tomb, which he found full of mummies and coffins from the Second and Third Intermediate Period as well as those of many members of the New Kingdom royal families.

The tomb in which they were found belonged to the family of Panedjem II, whose coffins and mummies were not in the disturbed state of the objects of earlier date. Some of the coffins still retained gold decoration, and so Brugsch at once set about clearing out the tomb, rather than leave it unguarded and risk its being further despoiled. The contents of the tomb, including the royal mummies, travelled in short order down to the Nile and from there were shipped north to the Egyptian Museum, an event magnificently dramatized in the Egyptian film *The Night of Counting the Years*.

Seventeen years later, when Victor Loret was excavating the tomb of Tuthmose III's successor, Amenhotep II, he made a further remarkable discovery. Not only was Amenhotep's body within its sarcophagus, albeit much disturbed and reburied inside a replacement coffin, but in the side chambers of the tomb he found the mummies of other kings whose bodies had been placed here apparently for safe-keeping. Between them, these two remarkable caches have yielded the bodies of almost every king of the New Kingdom, and some of them may be viewed in the Cairo Museum. It is always possible that a third cache existed, containing the mummies of the few New Kingdom rulers that have not been discovered yet; the tomb of Horemheb may have served this purpose (p. 106).

Like the cache near Deir el-Bahari, the bodies of the kings found in the tomb of Amenhotep II were extensively damaged, with all valuables very roughly removed, and placed into coffins frequently not their own. Recent re-examination of evidence relating to such reburials suggests that, rather than the royal mummies having been ransacked by tomb robbers and being carefully reburied by the priesthood led by Herihor and Panedjem I of the Twenty-first Dynasty, at the end of the Twentieth Dynasty the royal burials, and possibly those of private individuals, were systematically looted by General Piankh to fill the state coffers. The mummies found in the tomb of Amenhotep II seem to have finally been placed here during the 'restoration work' of Panedjem I, which may, in fact, have been no more than a continuation of the same practice.

Further development of the royal tomb

The design of Amenhotep II's tomb is very similar to that of his predecessor, Tuthmose III, but with a number of modifications. The burial chamber is rectangular rather than curved and has two distinct parts: the first part has six pillars, and between the last two pillars are stairs leading down to the other, lower part of the burial chamber, where the cartouche-shaped sarcophagus lies. There is evidence that a wooden door hung between the burial chamber and the preceding corridor, perhaps symbolizing the entrance to the underworld proper, as depicted in the wall decoration. The wooden door continued to be used from this time onwards in the tombs of the kings of the New Kingdom.

Although the decoration is very similar to that in Tuthmose's tomb, with scenes from the *Amduat* drawn in the same schematic way, there is, however, a new detail here: on the pillars of the first part of the burial chamber, fully formed, rather than cursive, figures of the king are depicted before individual deities, and this motif continues to appear in subsequent tombs in the Valley of the Kings.

The tomb of his successor, Tuthmose IV, seems to have been structurally complete, although the walls of the burial chamber were left completely undecorated, devoid even of a plaster finish; this allows us to see how well cut the tomb was. However, the antechamber and the well room were decorated and show a series of depictions of the king before deities. The figures in these scenes are fully coloured, unlike those in his predecessor's tomb, which had simply been left as unfilled outlines.

The major design change in this tomb is the addition of a longer corridor and an antechamber between the pillared hall and the burial chamber. Another slight difference is at the junction between the antechamber and the burial chamber, where the axis of the tomb makes another right angle.

Tuthmose's burial must have been disturbed already in the reign of Horemheb, eighty years later, because there is an inscription in hieratic on the wall of the antechamber, dated to year 8 of the reign of Horemheb, which records the 'renewal' of the burial of Tuthmose IV by an official called Maya, and a second inscription names Maya's assistant in this work as

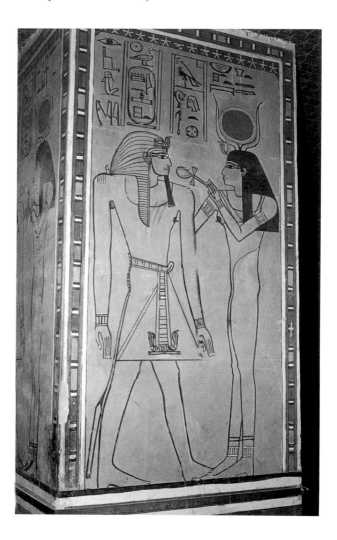

Valley of the Kings, tomb of Amenhotep II: Hathor of Thebes embracing the king

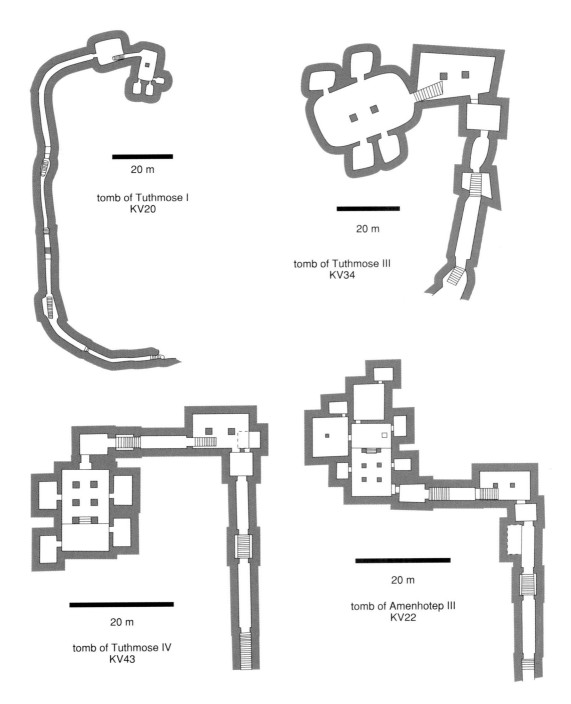

20 m

tomb of Tuthmose I
KV20

20 m

tomb of Tuthmose III
KV34

20 m

tomb of Tuthmose IV
KV43

20 m

tomb of Amenhotep III
KV22

Plans of early to middle Eighteenth Dynasty royal tombs

Djehutymose. The despoiling of this tomb may have happened during the Amarna period, when tomb building activity moved away from this area, and the Valley of the Kings was devoid of the usual activities of the Deir el-Medina workmen. At a later date the body of the king was removed and placed in the tomb of Amenhotep II.

When Amenhotep III came to the throne, he seems to have brought great energy and purpose to royal building projects: at Thebes alone he undertook a huge programme of works, taking a radical approach to the design of the Karnak complex. For his tomb he chose a different location in the hills, known as the West Valley. The design of the tomb is once again a development of its predecessors, with the most obvious change in the orientation of the burial chamber and also in presence of additional rooms, of some considerable size, lying off the burial chamber. These side chambers are presumed to have been provided to hold the burials of the two queens of Amenhotep III, Sitamun and Tiye, although it is not clear that either of them was ever actually interred here. The king's body was found in the tomb of Amenhotep II, and there too was found a female body with long flowing hair, often referred to as the 'elder lady' and also often identified as the remains of Queen Tiye (p. 128).

It is possible that this tomb had originally been started in the reign of Tuthmose IV, as the remains of a foundation deposit containing an inscribed plaque of that king was found outside the entrance to the tomb. However the decoration of the tomb identifies it as the burial place of Amenhotep III. The burial chamber was decorated with the familiar text of the *Amduat* with its cursive figures, whilst the decoration in the well room and the antechamber showed the king before deities. Once again, the figures are more elaborate than those of his father's tomb, and the texts accompanying these figures are much more detailed.

The Amarna period and its immediate aftermath

The successor of Amenhotep III was his son Amenhotep IV, who, as is well known, subsequently changed his name to Akhenaten. It is highly probable that, when he first became king, a site for his burial place in the Valley of the Kings was chosen and a plan compiled, and an unfinished tomb in the West Valley (WV25) may be the site that was begun for him. However, when he departed to Amarna, we know that he set up another workmen's village near the new capital and that a tomb was constructed for him in the so-called 'Royal Wadi' at Amarna. The design of that tomb is clearly based on that of the tombs in the Valley of the Kings, but with two immediately apparent differences: the tomb has an approximately straight axis, and it has a separate suite of rooms off to one side of the second corridor.

One must assume that Akhenaten was indeed buried at Amarna, although it has been suggested that his body, together with that of his mother Tiye, was brought to Thebes at the time of the return to religious orthodoxy and the reinstatement of Amun as principal god in Egypt. If so, it is possible that both were re-interred in a small tomb close to the entrance of the Valley, KV55. Here were found the remains of Queen Tiye's funerary equipment and a mummy in a coffin from which the names had been expunged. Whether this body is that of Akhenaten is still very fiercely debated, and it might be doubted whether the body of a king who was later considered so heretical would have survived at all. Another possible candidate for the body found in KV55 is Akhenaten's successor, Smenkhkare. No tomb has been identified for Smenkhkare at Amarna, and it is likely that he would have been sufficiently reviled as a participant in the Amarna period for his coffin to be deliberately mutilated.

Whatever the uncertainties of the location of the burial of Smenkhkare, that of his successor Tutankhamun is, of course, famous and the story of its discovery by Howard Carter needs no retelling. As all visitors to the tomb will have observed for themselves, this tomb is extremely small in comparison with the other kings' tombs in the Valley of the Kings. It seems likely that the shortness of the reign of the king, who came to throne as a very young man but died in the tenth year of his reign, took everyone by surprise. Instead of finishing off a tomb which had presumably been begun for him in the West valley, a tomb perhaps intended for a non-royal burial in the main valley was modified for his burial. The decoration of the burial chamber is unusual in that it shows a scene from the *Amduat*, depictions of the king before deities and scenes of Ay, his successor, performing the opening of the mouth ritual.

It is hard to imagine how the huge quantity of burial equipment found inside the tomb was ever placed inside this small space. In fact, traces of gold leaf have been found on the walls of the burial chamber, leading to speculation that the workers erecting the nested gold shrines in this tiny space had rather a struggle to complete their task.

The tomb that was used in the West Valley for the burial of his successor Ay is possibly that originally intended for Tutankhamun. Its axis is, like that of the tomb of Akhenaten at Amarna, straight but is otherwise very much like a shortened version of a pre-Amarna tomb in the Valley of the Kings, having a descent via stairs and corridors to a well room, albeit without a well. Perhaps because of the untimely demise of the king, the room beyond the well room is not the pillared hall one has come to expect, but is in fact the burial chamber. The decoration of the burial chamber is very reminiscent of that found in the tomb of Tutankhamun, but it contains the unusual scene of hunting in the marshes. The figures of King Ay were almost all defaced, presumably during the immediate post-Amarna period, and the body of Ay has not been found.

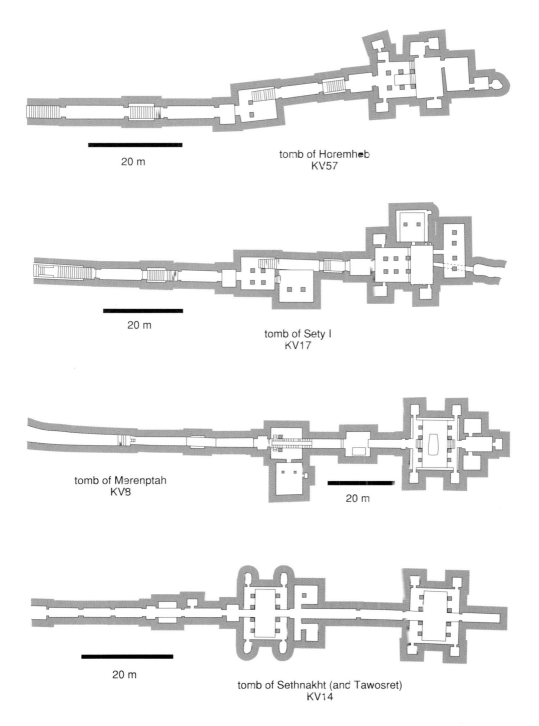

20 m

tomb of Horemheb
KV57

20 m

tomb of Sety I
KV17

tomb of Merenptah
KV8

20 m

20 m

tomb of Sethnakht (and Tawosret)
KV14

Plans of post-Amarna and mid-Ramesside royal tombs

Perhaps to assert his relationship to earlier kings of the Eighteenth Dynasty, Horemheb, who had been a general under Tutankhamun, chose to site his tomb in the main valley. The design of the tomb is very reminiscent of those earlier tombs, but with several modifications. It retains the straight axis of Akhenaten's tomb, and there is no chamber at the bottom of the well. The burial chamber follows the design initiated in the tomb of Amenhotep II, but with an additional staircase to the lower part of the burial chamber where the rectangular sarcophagus stands. The tomb is rather deeper than earlier examples, a feature which recurs in the immediately succeeding tombs. However, the major change in the tomb lies in the decoration, which for the first time was attempted in relief and, perhaps for that reason, is incomplete in many places. The unfinished state of the decoration is invaluable in providing evidence for the techniques in use at the time for producing raised relief. It also provides us with evidence of the importance the Egyptians must have attached to the physical orientation of the tombs: hieroglyphic marks left on the walls by the masons indicate the points of the compass and the tomb lies on an almost perfect north–south alignment. Although the technique used to produce it was new, the decoration of the tomb is generally very familiar, but with the notable introduction of scenes from the *Book of Gates* in the burial chamber (p. 118).

The mummy of Horemheb was not found in either of the two royal caches (pp. 98–100), but within his tomb the dismembered bodies of at least four people were found, together with funerary garlands of Twentieth Dynasty type. A number of graffiti by the entrance to the tomb indicate that it was visited at the end of the Twentieth Dynasty by the scribes responsible for some of the rewrapping of mummies that went on at the time that the caches were established, and it is distinctly possible that the tomb of Horemheb may have been used as a third cache at that period.

The Nineteenth Dynasty

Horemheb's appointed successor was another military man, Ramesses I, the first king of the Nineteenth Dynasty. His reign was only brief and, consequently, the design of his tomb is rather truncated. Similarly, the sarcophagus which is still in the tomb bears painted, rather than carved, decoration which would have been quicker to complete. The steep flights of stairs indicate that, like Horemheb's tomb, it was intended to be a very deep tomb. The king's body has not been found, although the remains of a replacement coffin with an inscription indicating that it was meant to contain his body was found in the Deir el-Bahari cache.

Belzoni's discovery of the tomb of his successor Sety I, and the exhibition he held in London in 1820 of paintings copied from the tomb, created a great interest in the tomb, similar to that associated with the discovery of

Valley of the Kings, tomb of Sety I: one of the 'souls of Hierakonpolis' worshipping a form of the sun-god

Tutankhamun's tomb a hundred years later, and for many years it was 'the tomb to see' when visiting the Valley of the Kings. The design of the tomb is once again a development of earlier tomb patterns, with a number of modifications. Like its predecessors, its steep flights of stairs descend far into the ground. For the first time the tomb includes a side room off the pillared hall, in this tomb aligned on the outer axis of the tomb. The descent from the pillared hall to the remainder of the tomb is offset from this axis, but continues in the same orientation. The burial chamber is again divided into two parts, with stairs to the lower part across the whole width of the burial chamber. Cut into the floor of the lower part of the burial chamber is a steeply descending passage, still not thoroughly investigated, which passes through a stratum of shale, with the remains of stairs and a central ramp. Above this passage Belzoni found the famous alabaster coffin of Sety I, which is now in the Soane Museum in London. Although the passage seems to lead nowhere, it is suggested from time to time that there was another burial chamber at the end of the passageway and that the coffin had been dragged up from there.

Another innovation of the tomb is that it is entirely decorated, from the first passageway down to the rooms off the burial chamber. Furthermore, the quality of the decoration of the tomb was apparently outstanding when the tomb was first found, and most of the scenes, carried out in relief and painting, were completely finished. Unfortunately, soon after the tomb's discovery the walls started to suffer, firstly through Belzoni's taking casts of the reliefs and subsequently through flood damage. The well of the tomb, which had been almost empty at the time of the discovery, was deliberately filled in by Belzoni to make access to the lower chambers easier. When a torrential storm in 1818 brought flood water into the tomb, it rushed unimpeded down to the burial chamber, causing parts of the rock to collapse. Since that time, the tomb has from time to time suffered rock falls, but it none the less remains an awe-inspiring structure.

The additional space given over to decoration allowed for an expansion in the decorative programme. In the first two passages of the tomb a new text was used for the first time, the *Litany of Re* (p. 119). Henceforth, it was regularly positioned in the first corridors of royal tombs, placed, of course, at the closest point of the tomb to the sun's light. Another innovation is to be found on the vaulted ceiling of the burial chamber, which was decorated with astronomical scenes.

Sety was succeeded by one of the best-known kings of Egypt, Ramesses II. Visitors to the Valley of the Kings often expect to find that, in common with his other monuments, his tomb is one of the more impressive examples there. It is, however, in a very damaged state, as it was cut in an area of very poor rock. The tomb has also been flooded on several occasions and the debris which has been swept into the tomb has set almost like concrete. The removal of this fill has caused additional damage to the walls and the decoration on them. The tomb has been worked on since the mid-1990s by a French team, who are not only excavating it but are also consolidating the walls to preserve them. The design of the tomb reverts to the bent-axis tomb, probably because of the poor quality of the rock. The tomb has a shallow entrance, with a decorated lintel, showing the solar disc flanked by Isis and Nephthys, and decorated reveals. This decoration, together with the shallow entrance way, indicates that this tomb was probably never hidden away like the earlier tombs which commence with a very steep descent. There is evidence too that, for the first time, the outer doorway of the tomb was blocked with a wooden door, later modified to a double door, a practice which continued from this time in the Valley of the Kings. Beyond the entrance, shallow stairs with a central ramp lead down into the tomb.

Its design, including the decorative programme used, is very similar to that of Sety I, although, as mentioned above, the axis is not straight. The major design change is in the burial chamber, in which the lower-lying part is set in the middle of the chamber, and this becomes the standard arrangement used in most of the remaining tombs in the Valley of the Kings.

Ramesses II's mummy, like that of his father, was found in the Deir el-Bahari cache, and the two bodies do bear quite a resemblance to each other. According to the hieratic label on it, Ramesses' body had first been re-buried in his father's tomb before being moved again, possibly first to the cliff tomb of Queen Inhapi and finally to the cache (pp. 98–9).

Ramesses II was succeeded by his thirteenth son, Merenptah, whose tomb lies relatively near his father's, but slightly higher, perhaps to avoid the poor stratum of rock into which the tomb of his father had been cut. The axis of the tomb reverts to the straight type. The tomb's decorative programme follows that of its immediate precursors with the difference that the *Amduat* in the burial chamber is replaced by scenes from the *Book of Caverns* (p. 118).

Merenptah's body was found amongst the cache of royal mummies in the tomb of Amenhotep II. It has recently become evident from the studies of Edwin Brock that it was originally buried inside four nested stone sarcophagi, three of red granite and the fourth, the innermost, of alabaster. As there would not have been sufficient space in the burial chamber for manoeuvring these coffins individually into place, the four coffins must have been assembled outside the tomb, and the whole ensemble lowered into position, a mind-boggling task. A singular feature of this tomb is that there are no door jambs separating the different corridors, and the explanation for this adds to one's astonishment at the achievement of the workers on this tomb, for it has now been established that the sarcophagi were in fact too large to pass through the doorways. Anyone who has worked in Egypt can imagine the consternation the discovery of this problem must have aroused at the time! In order to get around this difficulty, the door jambs had to be removed and replacement door jambs, made of sandstone, had to be provided. These became detached over the years, and the remains of several were found in the well of the tomb.

The person who succeeded Merenptah was a man of obscure origins called Amenmesse, who seems to have assumed control of part of the country in place of the legitimate king, Sety II. He began preparing a burial place for himself in the Valley of the Kings, but seems to have been unable to complete it before his death. Although the outermost parts were decorated with reliefs, the design of the tomb is clearly truncated. Whether the tomb was ever used by Amenmesse himself is not certain, but it seems that it *was* used by two royal women named Baketweret and Takhet, whose own decoration was placed over that of Amenmesse, most clearly discernible in the well area and pillared hall of this tomb.

After the death of Amenmesse, Sety II reasserted his right to the throne. It is suggested that he may have begun work on a tomb for himself and his wife Tawosret (KV14), but this was later taken over by King Sethnakht for his own burial, and it was probably the latter king who hurriedly completed an unfinished tomb and installed Sety II's body there. That tomb, KV15, is very abbreviated and does not progress beyond the passage that leads from the pillared hall. The lid of Sety's red granite sarcophagus was found there, but no base has been discovered; his body was found amongst the kings stored in the tomb of Amenhotep II. KV15 is decorated with familiar scenes from the *Litany of Re*, the *Amduat* and the *Book of Gates*, but an unusual feature is found in the well room (which lacks the well itself): here are painted scenes showing figures of the king in shrines in various manifestations, such as on the back of a panther and on a papyrus skiff. Objects just like those represented here were found amongst the burial equipment in the tomb of Tutankhamun and can be seen in the museum in Cairo.

It is likely that Queen Tawosret took control of the country after the death of her husband until his young successor, Siptah, was old enough to ascend to the throne. Siptah's tomb, KV47, is complete in terms of its architectural design, but it was cut into very poor-quality rock, and the burial chamber lies within a seam of shale which must have made it impossible to decorate. Consequently only the first three corridors have any remaining inscriptions. The design is slightly unusual in that there is no suite of rooms off the burial chamber, but this may have been because the rock was not thought suitably strong for carrying out this work. The king's body was found in the tomb of Amenhotep II. When it was examined, it was found that Siptah's left leg was shortened, perhaps as a result of polio, and his foot had obviously become distorted during his lifetime.

The Twentieth Dynasty – late Ramesside tombs

As we have already described, Sethnakht, who succeeded Siptah and founded
the Twentieth Dynasty, chose to use as his burial place the tomb that had
perhaps been prepared as the joint tomb of Sety I and Tawosret. The reason
for this may lie in the fact that he had started work on a new tomb, KV11,
but, after the first two corridors had been cut, the tomb collided with the
tomb of Amenmesse. He then abandoned this tomb and began modifying
KV14 for his own use. In so doing, he did not take over the chambers which
had been prepared for its previous owners, but rather added his own to
the end. The original tomb probably originally ended in a suite of rooms
beyond the burial chamber, which Sethnakht modified by extending a
corridor through them which led to his vaulted burial chamber, with its own
side rooms. The axis of the tomb is completely straight throughout and the

*A harper in the
tomb of Ramesses III
in the Valley of the
Kings*

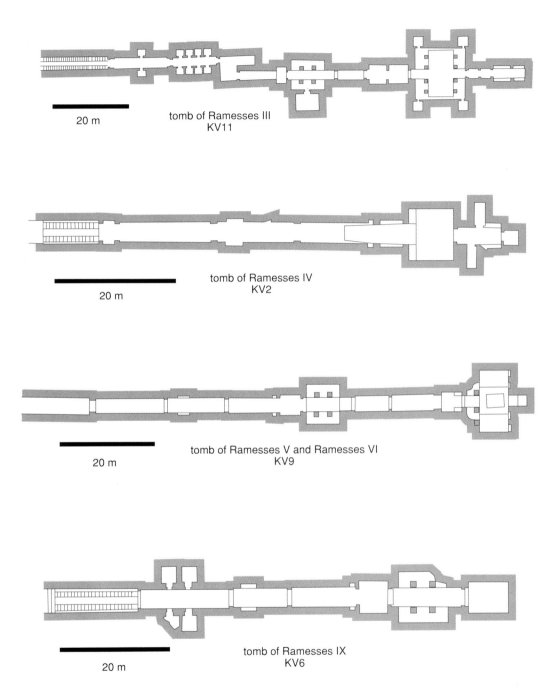

20 m

tomb of Ramesses III
KV11

20 m

tomb of Ramesses IV
KV2

20 m

tomb of Ramesses V and Ramesses VI
KV9

20 m

tomb of Ramesses IX
KV6

Plans of late Ramesside royal tombs

slope of all the corridors is noticeably gentle. The first part of the tomb contains extracts from the *Book of the Dead* and scenes of Tawosret before deities. Otherwise the decoration of the tomb is unremarkable, except for the fact that there are of course two burial chambers, both of which have astronomical ceilings. A coffin of Sethnakht was discovered in the tomb of Amenhotep II and so it is likely that his body was transferred there at some time. It may be that a mummy found stuck to a model boat in that tomb is that of Sethnakht.

The tomb originally intended for Sethnakht, KV11, was taken over by his son Ramesses III. He left Sethnakht's decoration in place, and adapted the tomb by expanding the third corridor to the right to avoid the collision with Amenmesse's tomb. The remaining axis of the tomb continued with an offset from this point.

It is likely that it was this king who added the eight small side rooms off the second corridor which contain unique depictions of, for example, jars, bows and arrows, and snake-goddesses. One of these rooms contains the well-known harpers which were seen by James Bruce on his visit to the tomb in 1768 and became famous because of his reproduction of the scene in his travel memoirs, for which reason the tomb is still sometimes known as 'Bruce's tomb'. Apart from these small chambers and the tomb's change of axis, the main difference between this tomb and its immediate predecessors is the change from one antechamber, followed by a corridor leading to the burial chamber, to two antechambers. The decoration of the burial chamber of the tomb is rather damaged but seems to consist of scenes from the *Book of Gates*, by now a regular feature in the royal tombs, and a new innovation, scenes from the *Book of the Earth* (p. 118).

The base of the king's sarcophagus is now in the Louvre and its lid is in the Fitzwilliam Museum in Cambridge. Ramesses' mummy was recovered from the cache in the tomb of Amenhotep II and was the basis for Boris Karloff's make-up in the famous film *The Mummy*.

The tomb of Ramesses IV lies close by the entrance to the Valley of the Kings and was probably one of those most frequently visited by travellers of all periods, as shown by the numerous graffiti it contains. A papyrus, now in the Turin Museum, contains an ancient plan of this tomb, including the Egyptian designations of the various parts of the tomb.[4] The entrance way and the first two corridors, which are decorated with the *Litany of Re*, are missing from the papyrus; the next corridor is designated 'the fourth passageway of the god'; the well room, which seems to have served as the antechamber in this tomb, is called 'the hall of waiting'; and the burial chamber is called 'the house of gold wherein one rests'. The rooms beyond the burial chamber also have names: the main room is called 'the passageway of the god which is the shabti-place' and the niche in its northern wall is 'the resting place of the gods'; the northern room lying off it is 'the left-hand

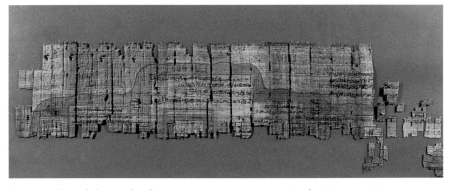

Ancient plan of the tomb of Ramesses IV on a papyrus in the Egyptian Museum in Turin. Cat. no. 1885

treasury', and that to the west is 'the treasury of perfection'; the third room is missing from the plan.

The tomb itself is an abbreviated one, having no pillared hall and no lower corridors, and it appears in the same form on the papyrus. However, the papyrus also refers to the decoration on the walls of the tomb, for example 'the hall of waiting ... being drawn in outlines, engraved with the chisel, filled with colours and completed'. Since the decoration at the west end of the tomb does not conform to the description in the papyrus, it must be supposed that the plan was drawn up after the cutting of the tomb was complete, but before the decoration had been finished. An innovation in this tomb is the replacement of the astronomical ceiling with scenes from one of a group of texts known as the *Books of the Heavens*, which show the progress of the sun-god through the sky (p. 118).

Ramesses V and Ramesses VI appear to have shared the same tomb, KV9. The outer parts of the tomb, the entrance and the first three corridors, have the name of Ramesses V inscribed on them, with no sign of their having been altered, but the remainder of the tomb bears Ramesses VI's name. The tomb is relatively large, and the reigns of both kings were rather brief. Perhaps, therefore, on ascending the throne, Ramesses VI decided to continue the work on his predecessor's tomb and use it as a joint burial place, rather than to finish off hurriedly a short tomb for Ramesses V and then have to commence on his own. The difficulty with this explanation is that it implies that the latter king knew his reign would be only short. Papyrus Mayer B, now in Liverpool, records the robbery of a tomb thought to be KV9, probably during the reign of Ramesses IX, only twenty years after the death of Ramesses VI. However, it was the construction of this tomb that saved the tomb of Tutankhamun from a similar fate, since the huts built by the workmen constructing this tomb covered the entrance to Tutankhamun's burial place until Howard Carter uncovered it in 1922.

Valley of the Kings, tomb of Ramesses VI: *scenes from the* Book of the Earth, *including the re-emergence of the sun from the earth*

Valley of the Kings, tomb of Ramesses IX: *the king before the sun-god, from the* Book of Caverns

The tomb of Ramesses VII is very truncated in length and the king's body has not been found. The decoration that exists is similar to that of Ramesses VI's tomb, but with differences in accordance with the constraints of space. Thus we find the *Book of Gates* and *Book of Caverns* in the corridor, the *Book of the Earth* in the burial chamber and the king before Osiris in the room beyond. Instead of a sarcophagus, the tomb contains a depression in the floor of the burial chamber into which the body would have been placed. An inverted base of a sarcophagus had been provided as a lid. No tomb of Ramesses VIII has been found, although it is possible that a tomb was begun for him in the valley while he was still a prince with the name Sethherkhepeshef. This tomb, KV19, was later completed and used for the burial of another prince, Montuherkhepeshef (p. 134).

The tomb of Ramesses IX is one of the easiest of access in the valley, the slope of the floor being almost non-existent until the descent from the pillared hall. At this point the tomb descends directly into the burial chamber, with no intervening corridors, and it is likely that this represents a modification due to pressure to complete the tomb, as the cutting of the pillared hall is incomplete. Furthermore, the quality of decoration is very good at the beginning of the tomb and deteriorates thereafter. The king's body was found in the Deir el-Bahari cache having been, according to its docket, re-wrapped at Medinet Habu in year 7 of Siamun's reign (*c.*971 BC, approximately forty years after burial). The decoration of the tomb seems at first glance to follow the familiar pattern, but there are several unusual features. The *Book of Caverns* is found in the first corridor together with the *Litany of Re*, the second corridor has an astronomical ceiling and is decorated with, as well as scenes from the *Book of Caverns*, scenes from the *Book of the Dead*. The same decoration appears in the third corridor together with unique scenes of the king and various deities, perhaps from an otherwise unknown funerary text. The burial chamber is decorated with the *Book of the Earth*, the *Book of Caverns* and the *Amduat*, whilst the ceiling has the now familiar *Book of the Heavens*.

Very little is known about the tomb of Ramesses X, KV18, of which only the first passage seems to have been excavated, and the king's body has not been recovered. His successor, Ramesses XI, chose a tomb design very similar to that of Ramesses IX. The main divergence from this design is in the burial chamber which has a shaft cut in it. Most of the tomb is undecorated, and the cutting of the burial chamber itself is not completely finished. No sarcophagus was found here and it seems unlikely that the king was ever buried in this tomb. Remains of burial equipment of other kings in the shaft suggest that this tomb could have been used for the stripping of the royal mummies at the end of the Twentieth Dynasty (p. 100).

The burials of kings of the Twenty-first and Twenty-second Dynasties

Faint traces of a cartouche at the entrance to the tomb of Ramesses XI reveal that there may have been an attempt by a priest 'king', Panedjem I, to use the tomb for his own burial in the Twenty-first Dynasty, but it is unclear whether he was actually buried within this tomb. His body may actually be that found inside the coffin of Tuthmose I in the Deir el-Bahari cache. Panedjem succeeded to the high priesthood held by Herihor, who was the first of this line to attempt putting his name in a cartouche (p. 39) Herihor's mummy has never been located, and attempts to find his burial place in the Theban hills have not met with success.

Another high priest of Amun of the Twenty-first Dynasty, Menkheperre, sometimes wrote his name in a cartouche, and although remains of linen and pieces of coffin so inscribed were found in the tomb known as the Bab el-Gasus (p. 143), his burial has also not been found. Perhaps this 'king' was indeed interred amongst his fellow priests. The last 'king' to be buried in the Theban area was also a high priest, a man named Harsiese, in the reign of Osorkon II of the Twenty-second Dynasty (870–860 BC). He was a cousin of Osorkon who seems to have pushed himself into the role of co-regent; his royal-style burial was discovered in the 1930s outside the large pylon gateway of Ramesses III at Medinet Habu. Amongst the objects recovered was the king's red granite sarcophagus, which had been originally inscribed with the name of a queen of Ramesses II, Henutmire. This was truly the last kingly burial in the Theban area, done in style, and making an association with one of the great pharaohs.

The principal New Kingdom funerary texts

Unlike the tombs of private individuals, the tombs in the Valley of the Kings are decorated with colourful depictions of the gods and the mysterious regions of the underworld. This makes them much harder to understand without knowing something of the background to them

The earliest funerary text found on the walls of the kings' tombs in the New Kingdom is commonly known as the *Amduat*, meaning 'that which is in the underworld', although its original name was 'the book of the hidden room'. This text describes the night-time journey of the sun-god on his barque through the twelve parts of the underworld that corresponded to the twelve hours of the night, detailing the dangers he encountered on the journey. It is found to some extent in most of the kings' tombs of the New Kingdom. The descending corridors of the kings' tombs probably mirrored the descending pathway of the sun-god into the underworld, and the king was thought of as travelling with the god on his journey through the night.

This concept was elaborated and developed in the *Book of Gates*, a regular element after its first appearance in the tomb of Horemheb. It derives its name from the gates which divide the twelve parts of the underworld, each guarded by a snake-deity. These guardians have fearsome names, such as 'the one who spits fire from his eye', and 'the drinker of blood'. The presence of the *Book of Gates* on the walls of the kings' tombs ensured that the owners were able to pass through the gates unharmed by their guardians.

The second of these gates was the actual entry point into the realm of the underworld, and marked the point where the sun-god, travelling on his barque and accompanied by protective deities, actually entered the realm of the night. The inhabitants of the different parts of the underworld, with the exception of the damned, are shown rejoicing as the sun-god passes by. In the fifth hour of the night the sun-god would come close to a particularly mysterious region called 'the secret cavern of Sokar', containing the so-called 'lake of fire' into which the souls of the wicked were cast and from which there was no return; this was an area which the sun avoided. In the next hour, the sixth, the sun god was magically reborn and from there travelled back towards the horizon to re-emerge from the underworld at dawn.

Late in the Nineteenth Dynasty, a new funerary text started to be used, known to us as the *Book of Caverns*, which abandoned the division of the underworld into twelve parts and rather depicted it as a series of oval-shaped caverns, like the burial chamber of Tuthmose III, which contained the figures of deities and the dead who lay awaiting the passing of the sun to bring them back to life. The sun-god is depicted very differently in this text, either as a ram-headed figure called Atum or simply as the sun disc.[5]

Extracts of a new text, the *Book of the Earth*, appear in the tomb of Ramesses III: this becomes a regular feature in burial chambers from the time of Ramesses VI onwards. Again the sun-god's journey through the underworld is described, but, rather than showing the twelve divisions of the night, the text is divided into four sections, the climax of which is the moment when the sun disc is lifted out of the Earth by the arms of Nun, a being representing the primordial waters out of which creation came. This scene is well known from the burial chamber of Ramesses VI.

From the time of Sety I onwards the ceiling of the king's burial chamber was decorated with scenes representative of the sun's passage through the sky. The simplest form of the so-called 'astronomical ceiling' depicted the sky-goddess, Nut, who at the end of each day swallowed the sun and then gave birth to it again at the beginning of the next. Within her body, which stretches across the burial chamber, the sun is shown travelling through the stars. In the tomb of Ramesses IV, and several later kings' tombs, this is replaced by a more formal description of the sun-god's journey, known as the *Book of the Heavens*, in which it is again described in terms of the passage through the twelve hours of the night.

In all these funerary texts the emphasis is on the sun-god, and this is especially true of a different type of text which appears in most tombs of the kings from Sety I onwards. It takes the form of a lengthy hymn to the sun, known as the *Litany of Re*. The hymn is usually found in the first corridor of the tomb, in other words at the point of the tomb that is nearest to the sunlight, and consists of praises to the sun-god in his seventy-five different forms, as well as praising the king in his association with the sun and other gods.

Royal funerary equipment

A surprising amount is known about the burial goods that would have been placed inside the tombs of the kings of the New Kingdom. We are, of course, very fortunate in having a virtually complete example of a burial of a king from Tutankhamun's tomb. However, other evidence exists, not only in the form of decoration, such as that in the tomb of Sety II (p. 110), but also actual remains of the burial equipment which was found in a few of the tombs, particularly in the tombs of Amenhotep II, Tuthmose IV and Horemheb. Of these, the tomb of Tuthmose IV stands out from the rest for the large quantity of funerary goods which survived, including many models.

The main items of equipment were the receptacles for the king's body, usually a coffin, or nested coffins, inside a sarcophagus, or nested sarcophagi, which would have been placed within a number of shrines made of wood covered with gold leaf. Next in importance were the containers for the viscera of the royal mummy, known as canopic jars, which were usually stored inside a special chest. It is likely that these would be placed either near the sarcophagi or within a room off the burial chamber.

Like private individuals, the king was provided with items to enable him to continue his existence in the afterlife in the comfort to which he was accustomed, as well as special ritual items of magical significance in the afterlife. Objects such as furniture were provided for the king's use in the afterlife, some of which would have been made especially for this purpose and others which had obviously been used during the king's lifetime. Other items, such as funerary couches, ritual divine figurines or shabtis, were obviously of use to the king only in the afterlife and would have been specially made. Whether such funerary goods were made locally or further afield is not clear, but one might speculate that the workmen of Deir el-Medina would have been very well placed to carry out such work as well as having the necessary skills.

TOMBS OF THE ROYAL FAMILY

Mention the word 'queen' in the context of Egypt, and Thebes in particular, and readers will think of the Valley of the Queens, and above all of the tomb of Nefertari. However, the visitor to Luxor is often surprised by how few tombs of queens can actually be visited – in the late 1990s the number was two. The two other tombs open in the Valley of the Queens at that time actually belonged to princes. We are often asked where the others are, and the answer is very complex.

The burials of royal wives often have much in common with those of princesses and princes, and thus we shall treat them all together. There is rarely ever in Egypt any systematic organization of burial evident for royal children; only around the Great Pyramid at Giza is anything like a planned cemetery layout known. The question of the location of burials of princes is a particular problem at all periods, and much more research is needed to understand how the Egyptians coped with the paradox of there being siblings of the semi-divine being who held the throne of Egypt.

The First Intermediate Period and early Middle Kingdom

The first Theban kings were buried at the northern end of the necropolis, in the area of Tarif (p. 93). A number of subsidiary shafts are known from these three enclosures, and the name of a Queen Neferkau was found in the tomb associated with King Wahankh Inyotef II, as were fragments which might have belonged to a queenly sarcophagus. Linking this with what is known from the reign of Nebhepetre Mentuhotep, it would seem quite plausible that the queens of the Inyotef kings were buried in their husbands' enclosures, but of the other members of the royal family we seem to have no traces.

A wealth of information is available about the female members of the royal family associated with Nebhepetre Mentuhotep II. A feature of the earlier building phase of his temple at Deir el-Bahari was the inclusion of six small chapels with associated burial shafts for important women of his reign. These chambers were excavated first by Naville, working for the Egypt Exploration Fund in the 1890s, and then by Winlock and the Metropolitan Museum. The sarcophagi of two of these women, Ashait and Kawit, are famous for the elaborate and well-cut scenes they bear on their exteriors, and are now in the Cairo Museum; the tomb of another (Miyt) revealed her to have been a child. The burial of Kemsit also contained wall decoration in the burial chamber; fragments of her chapel and sarcophagus are in the British Museum. The titles they held are of interest, since they are in the chapels called 'royal wife', but in their burials the less elevated 'sole royal ornament' and 'priestess of Hathor'. A 1997 study of these titles has suggested that, as they are called only 'royal wife' in the cult chapel, they were perhaps intended to form a harem for the deified king in his afterlife, and were not queens in his earthly life. The chapels were incorporated into the later building phases, and linen from the burials of Ashait, Henhenet and Miyt can be dated to approximately years 30–41 of Mentuhotep's reign. The interments of many other important women are also in the temple: a tomb for his wife Tem is close to Mentuhotep's main burial place, while the burial of another member of the harem, Amunet, in a triangular court to the north of the main temple, seems also to have contained cloths bearing the names of further women. In addition, the bodies of two nameless women of the period, one of whom was tattooed, were found in other courtyard pits. Another tomb uncovered by the Metropolitan Museum expedition and probably dating to the early part of the reign is that of Neferu, another wife of Mentuhotep. This monument (TT319) was situated just to the north of the main complex, adjacent to an enclosure wall of the temple, and was later built over by Hatshepsut's architects. It was different from the pits just described in that it possessed a more conventional tomb façade leading to a chapel and, via a sloping passage, to a burial chamber. The roughly cut walls of the chapel were originally lined with decorated limestone slabs, many fragments of which were found by the Metropolitan Museum, and which had probably been broken up by later workmen searching for building material. The limestone lining of the burial chamber was in better condition, however, and consisted of friezes of objects and funerary texts, laid out in a manner not unlike that of many wooden coffins of this period. Of all these women associated with this temple, it seems that Tem and Neferu were the true queens of Mentuhotep.

The tomb of Neferu seems to have been an ancient tourist site. After the court of Hatshepsut was built over the entrance to this chapel, the builders constructed a passage from the courtyard above down to the chapel of Neferu, and a number of graffiti of Eighteenth Dynasty visitors found there attest an interest in the past among the people of the New Kingdom.

The Mentuhotep complex contains one of the rare references from the period to a possible prince. Just north of the triangular courtyard mentioned above, underneath the south retaining wall of the temple of Hatshepsut, was a tomb; no items were found which indicate the name of the owner, but a graffito with the name Inyotef in a cartouche was recorded, which is considered to belong to the eldest son of Mentuhotep, who never actually attained the throne.

Relief from the tomb chapel of Kemsit in the mortuary complex of Nebhepetre Mentuhotep II at Deir el-Bahari. British Museum, EA 1450

The uncertainty in the location of the burials of the remaining kings of the Eleventh Dynasty is also true for the interments of their consorts. Nothing which can be identified as a non-kingly royal tomb of the period has been found.

The Second Intermediate Period

We now jump to the later part of the Second Intermediate Period, when the rulers of Thebes again declared themselves kings. One fundamental problem in dealing with the royal tombs of this period is that their specific location in Dra Abu el-Naga is not known (pp. 94–5). Available information about these tombs consists largely of a mixture of objects found and scanty archaeological data, but it is clear that Dra Abu el-Naga at the end of the Second Intermediate Period was not exclusively the burial place of kings. From the surviving objects, Queens Ahhotep (wife of Seqenenre Taa) and Ahmose Henutempet (wife perhaps of the shadowy King Senakhtenre) were buried here; there is also the burial of a Queen Mentuhotep, consort of a King Djehuty, which king might belong in the Thirteenth or Seventeenth Dynasty. The tomb-robbery papyri which relate to the burial of King Sekhemre-Shedtawy Sebekemzaf in fact make it clear that his wife, queen Nubkhaas, was buried with him:

Then we broke through the rubble that we found at the mouth of his recess (?), and found this god lying at the back of his burial-place. And we found the burial place of Queen Nubkhaas his queen situated beside him, it being protected and guarded by plaster and covered with rubble. This also we broke through, and found her resting [there] in like manner.[1]

Diadem of Thirteenth Dynasty Queen Mentuhotep, probably from Dra Abu el-Naga

It thus seems probable that these queens were not buried alone but with kings whose burials have not yet been identified.

The best-preserved tomb assemblage is that of Ahhotep, from which we have a coffin, two gold and silver boats and a number of axes and items of jewellery – a rich burial indeed. A number of items bear the names of her sons, the later kings Kamose and Ahmose, presumably reflecting gifts from both rulers, and ultimately her death and burial in the time of Ahmose.

The royal family of the Eighteenth Dynasty

The New Kingdom royal tombs are often thought of by visitors to Thebes as consisting of those of the kings in their valley, and those of queens in theirs. As almost always in archaeology, however, things are not so simple. We know that, from at least the reign of Tuthmose I, the rulers were buried in the Valley of the Kings, but we have already seen that the situation of the earliest kings of the New Kingdom is not so simple. The situation for queens and other royal women is much more complicated.

In essence the queens of the earlier Eighteenth Dynasty were not buried in any one specific area but rather in concealed tombs spread over the Theban hills. One of the first Egyptologists to recognize this was none other than Howard Carter, who undertook a survey of many of the less famous and more remote valleys in the hills during the winter of 1916–17. Carter summarized the situation admirably: 'On the western side of the mountain above and behind the valleys of Bibân el Malûk we have a necropolis that appears to be the lost cemetery of the royal families – the kings' wives and kings' children – of the Second Theban Empire.'[2]

In the course of his surveying of these hills, Carter noted a number of graffiti, some relevant to our present subject, and many cliff tombs, a handful of which can be ascribed to the royal family members to whom he refers. It thus seems very likely that the anonymous caves (the majority) might indeed have originally contained the bodies of other royal dependants, whose burials were later destroyed or removed. We shall see some possible owners when we look at the non-kingly occupants of the Deir el-Bahari cache.

Let us take two examples to illustrate these tombs. The major part of Carter's paper just referred to is concerned with the tomb of Queen Hatshepsut, the intended resting place of the daughter of Tuthmose I and consort of Tuthmose II, who later declared herself king. Carter located it at the end of the Wadi Sikket Taqa el-Zeid, in the hills approximately 1.5 km to the north-west of the Valley of the Queens – and thus at a considerable distance from the better-known centres of activity on the west bank. The entrance to the tomb was located in the middle of a cliff face 112 m high, 42 m from the top. Carter found this tomb only as a result of a tip-off from

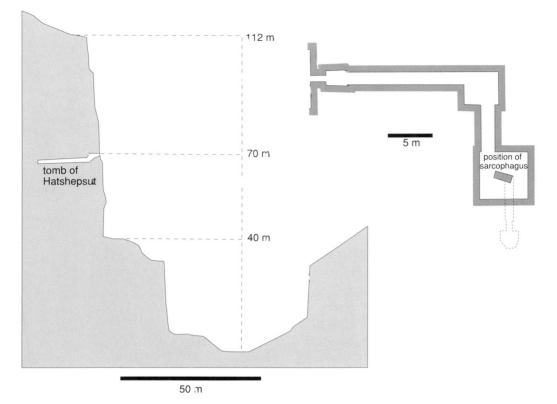

The cliff tomb of Hatshepsut: profile of the wadi showing the location of the tomb, and the plan of the tomb itself

the local inhabitants, and he had himself lowered down the cliff face to confront the robbers who were working in it! Even more remarkable is the feat of installation of the sarcophagus of yellow crystalline limestone which was still found in the tomb. Carter tried unsuccessfully to ascertain whether it had been lowered into the tomb from above or raised from the valley below; he thought he might have identified a route by which it had been brought, but it is no more than, using his own term, hypothetical. Some fragments of pottery were all that remained, and it seems that no burial was ever effected here, consistent with Hatshepsut's later self-promotion.

Another spectacular tomb is the so called 'hanging tomb', known in Arabic as the Bab el-Muallaq, located south of Deir el-Bahari.[3] While this tomb is less remote, it is no less difficult of access. This might be the 'high place of Inhapi', referred to as one of the places in which the royal mummies were stored before reaching their final resting place in the Deir el-Bahari cache (pp. 98–9), but there is no evidence in the tomb itself of its original owner.

Several other tombs of this period must be mentioned, as they have con-

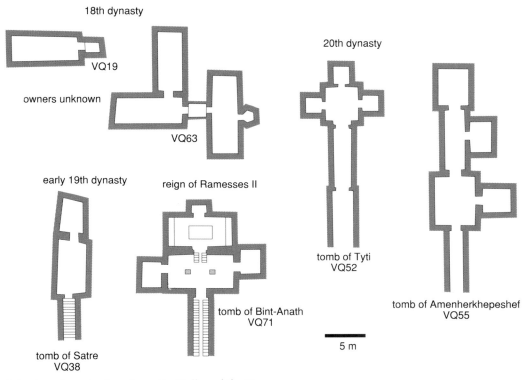

18th dynasty

VQ19

owners unknown

VQ63

20th dynasty

tomb of Tyti
VQ52

tomb of Amenherkhepeshef
VQ55

early 19th dynasty

reign of Ramesses II

tomb of Bint-Anath
VQ71

5 m

tomb of Satre
VQ38

Selection of tomb plans from the Valley of the Queens

nections with royal women and they also illustrate the manner in which the tombs are spread over the necropolis. The first is the possible tomb of Amenhotep I in Dra Abu el-Naga (p. 97), which might also have been the resting place of his mother Ahmose-Nefertari. In a pit near the so-called Sankhkare temple was found the burial of a daughter of Amenhotep I called Ahmose Tumerisy. Also in the remote hills is a tomb which might belong to Neferure, the daughter of Tuthmose II and Hatshepsut.

In broadly the same area of the necropolis is the 'tomb of the three princesses'. This tomb, at the base of a cleft in the rock, was discovered by robbers in August 1916 and emptied of most of its valuable contents, which came into the possession of the Metropolitan Museum. The tomb was briefly examined at the time, and received its first systematic examination in 1988, by Christine Lilyquist of the MMA.[4] This was the burial place of three wives of Tuthmose III who were probably of Syrian descent; it yielded a stunning array of jewellery from the early New Kingdom, showing the wealth available to family members at that time.

The only burial of a queen of this period found intact by archaeologists is that of Merytamun, in a pit adjacent to the temple of Hatshepsut at Deir el-

Bahari (TT358). This tomb had been entered and reused in the Third Intermediate Period, but the original burial had been left intact. There is some dispute as to the date of Merytamun, since, while the burial cannot be earlier than the reign of Tuthmose III on the grounds of its relationship to the temple, it is possible that the queen may in fact be the Ahmose-Merytamun known from the time of Amenhotep I, perhaps reburied at a slightly later date. Lastly, there is tomb 42 in the Valley of the Kings, which might have been cut originally for Hatshepsut-Merytre, a wife of Tuthmose III, whose foundation deposits were found at the entrance.

What of the Valley of the Queens at this date? There are a considerable number of pits which excavators have dated on architectural grounds to this period, although they contained no decoration and are almost all anonymous. They were all of simple design, consisting of a pit and associated chamber, with no evidence of a cult chapel, or anything similar. Only one might have belonged to a queen (VQ47, Princess Ahmose, daughter of Seqenenre Taa of the Seventeenth Dynasty); some objects belonging to a possible Seventeenth Dynasty prince by the name of Ahmose were also found in an adjacent valley. As such, these tombs can probably be grouped with the dispersed tombs of this period around the necropolis. Other tombs of this date in the valley seem to have been the burial places of private officials. A tomb in the nearby 'valley of the three pits' contained a seal impression with the name of Tuthmose III and on a jar inscription was found the words 'king's son'. The other evidence is a cluster of fragments of canopic jars dating to the reign of Amenhotep III, belonging to several women and perhaps one prince; the exact provenance of these is unknown, but the number of individuals could be as high as a dozen.

The impression gained is that the Valley of the Queens and nearby areas were clearly used for court individuals of the early to middle Eighteenth Dynasty. The fact that there are no chapels associated with these burial places indicates that they are to be considered as somewhat different from the contemporary tombs of private individuals in the Sheikh Abd el-Qurna necropolis; perhaps they had separate offering chapels which have yet to be found. It has been argued that remains of small anonymous structures near the large temples could just possibly be the funerary chapels of persons buried elsewhere, and those in the Valley of the Queens seem prominent candidates.

Let us briefly look at the evidence from the royal caches. In the Deir el-Bahari cache were found a considerable number of bodies of queens and princesses, and one prince, all of whom can be probably dated to the first half of the Eighteenth Dynasty. They include Ahmose-Nefertari, the wife of Ahmose (her possible tomb has been noted already), a son of Ahmose named Siamun, Ahhotep (wife of Amenhotep I) and a number of other princesses who were probably contemporaries of those just named. It seems plausible to assume that these individuals were originally buried in the anonymous cliff tombs noted by Carter. The other cache of royal mummies is that in the tomb of Amenhotep II (pp. 99–100). There are a number of anonymous female bodies in this cache, who might well be queens or princesses; one of them, the so-called 'elder lady', has been suggested to be the body of Queen Tiye, the principal wife of Amenhotep III. Another, less well-known, cache of royal women was discovered by Rhind in the early days of Theban archaeology, in a tomb at the foot of Sheikh Abd el-Qurna, and this seems to have consisted of princesses dating to the time of Tuthmose IV to Amenhotep III, who were reburied in the Twenty-first Dynasty.

To set against these mostly female remains, only one other prince's burial of this period has come to light, that of Amenemhat, of uncertain parentage, who died at the age of about one year. There are far more mentions of princes in New Kingdom sources than at earlier times, but few items of burial equipment are known; in the tomb of Amenhotep II were found some canopic jars of Websensenu, either an elder brother of that king or a son. Canopic jars of a Prince Amenemhat were found in the tomb of Tuthmose II. This certainly implies that particular family members who predeceased the king with whom they were associated might have been buried in the royal tomb, and it has indeed been argued that chambers were cut for Queens Sitamun and Tiye in the tomb of their husband Amenhotep III, although they were probably never used, as the king predeceased them. The presence of certain anonymous female mummies, some of which could be royal, in the small tombs in the Valley of the Kings should make us wonder how much of the picture we currently understand.[5]

With the number of wives and concubines which Egyptian kings must have had, it would be logical to expect a considerable number of sons, in addition to the daughters mentioned above. However, we are not aware of royal cemeteries in any other place in Egypt than Thebes at this time. It could be argued that, on an ideological level, the concept of a divine king, the direct descendant of the sun-god and the creator of the universe, sits uneasily with that person having a number of brothers, and with his happening to be the one who was elevated to the kingship. Thus it is perhaps understandable that little is heard about these royal sons and brothers. They would nevertheless surely have been accorded the proper rites of burial after death. So perhaps we just have not found them, have not recognized them or they have been destroyed over the years.

Tombs of the Nineteenth and Twentieth Dynasties

A much more planned and systematic approach seems to have been taken for the burials of female members of the royal family right from the beginning of the new epoch. A tomb was built in the Valley of the Queens for Satre, the wife of the first king, Ramesses I. From this time the Valley had a name, Ta set Neferu, literally 'the perfect place', but which has perhaps has the sense of the 'burial place of the royal harem'. The Twentieth Dynasty Abbott Papyrus refers to 'the great tombs of the royal children and royal wives and royal mothers which are in the perfect place'.[6]

The valley is known nowadays in Arabic as Wadi el-Malikat, a translation of 'Valley of the Queens'; the older form is Biban el-Harem ('doorways of the (royal) women', paralleling the older name for the Valley of the Kings). What was the attraction of the site? Presumably the self-contained wadi appealed to those who were seeking to set up a formal cemetery for queens and princesses. It was not perhaps necessary to choose a secluded site, and the kings anyway seemed to have monopolized the only ones relatively easy of access and at the same time spacious. There may however, be a more subtle religious reason. Just as the shape of the Qurn over the royal wadis may have in some way influenced the choice of those sites for the burials of the kings, it has been suggested that the dramatic rock cleft at the western end of the Valley of the Queens may have played its part. Water pours out of this after a storm, and this may have contributed to its magical impression; it seems

View of the rocks at the west end of the Valley of the Queens

Valley of the Queens, tomb of Tyti: the god Shu

also to have been associated with the goddess Hathor, one of whose functions was to be associated with caves and tombs, and who is often shown peering out of the western hills. Perhaps even the shape of this rock may have suggested the genitalia of this deity.

Some of the tombs have been open since antiquity, although the site does not seem to have been a major tourist attraction in classical times, perhaps because it was also a popular cemetery (p. 202). The site of the Valley of the Queens was known to early Egyptologists and copyists, such as Hay, Wilkinson, Champollion and Lepsius, but it was not until 1903 that systematic excavation took place at the site. The concession was given to an Italian mission from the Turin Museum, under the leadership of Ernesto Schiaparelli. They discovered numerous tombs, among them the famous burial place of Queen Nefertari, and the tombs of Khaemwaset and Amenherkhepeshef, sons of Ramesses III. The publication of this material is nowadays rather inadequate, especially in relation to the archaeology, but it was relatively good for its time. Some further small works were undertaken from time to time, but it was not until 1970 that a fully systematic excavation and survey was undertaken, jointly by the Egyptian Centre of Documentation (CEDAE) and the French National Research Centre (CNRS). This group has investigated all the pits in the main valley, as well as in the subsidiary valleys, and has cleared away the debris of centuries, so that the site looks almost denuded! The identity of many previously anonymous tombs has been ascertained, and much new information has been gained about the architectural development, and also about the history of the valley after it ceased to be a burial place of royalty.

The groupings of many of the tombs of the Ramesside period in the valley indicate a level of systematic planning. The earliest tombs, such as that of Satre, the wife of Ramesses I, are on the southern side, and then Ramesses II (or possibly Sety I, as the tomb of his wife Tawy (VQ80) is here) commenced the construction of a row of impressive monuments for his queens and principal daughters on the north slope. It appears that he began by building monuments for specific persons, such as Nefertari, Merytamun, Nebettawy and Bint-Anath, as well as at least one (Istnofret) which has not yet been located. Then later in his reign, perhaps when building activity in the royal necropoleis was declining, he appears to have ordered the construction of tombs for princesses which were decorated but in which space was left for the names of an owner to be added later (tombs VQ73–5). Recent work in these tombs has been able only to assign early Ramesside ownership to

Valley of the Queens, tomb of Amenherkhepeshef: Ramesses III and Prince Amenherkhepeshef before Ptah-tatenen.

numbers 73 and 75, where the names of the princesses Henuttawy and Henutmire were added later in ink; the other tomb was not used until the reign of Ramesses IV.

It seems likely that the workmen of the royal tomb, or an offshoot of them, were employed building tombs in the valley for the queens (p. 182). There were certainly buildings for workers in the valley, dated to the two main periods of activity, the reigns of Ramesses II and III. It is likely that these structures might be rest houses for the Deir el-Medina workmen, comparable to those above the Valley of the Kings, rather than a separate settlement.

The other major grouping of tombs dates to the reign of Ramesses III: these tombs are relatively close to one another on the southern side of the valley. The valley was possibly becoming rather full by the end of the reign of Ramesses III, and subsequent tombs might have been put into some of the subordinate valleys; six tombs mentioned in a text as being built by Ramesses VI can only have gone in a side valley. VQ74, originally cut in the time of Ramesses II, might have been reused for a Queen of Ramesses IV. We should not forget the tomb of Queen Tyti (VQ52), normally open to tourists, which is extremely difficult to date; she may have been the wife of one of the later Ramesside kings. The Valley of the Queens does not seem to have been exempt from the outbreaks of tomb robbery which were taking place elsewhere: an inspection of the valley in the Abbott Papyrus mentions that the tomb of Queen Isis (VQ5) was found to have been disturbed.[7]

The Nineteenth and Twentieth Dynasty tombs in the Valley of the Queens provide places of burial for many of the principal queens of that period, although they cannot have included all members of the harem. The tombs of some known queens are absent, for example those of the later Nineteenth Dynasty, and many of the Twentieth, and there is at least one tomb mentioned in texts as being in the valley which has not been located. This is the tomb of one of Ramesses II's principal wives, Istnofret, although the resting places of most of his other queens are in the valley. It is of course just possible that some queens might have been buried in their husband's tombs, although there is no strong evidence for this at present: two women named Takhet and Baketweret are shown in the decoration of the tomb of Amenmesse, although their relationship to this king is unclear. For the tomb of Tawosret in the Valley of the Kings, see p. 110.

We learn a little more about the burial places of princes in the Ramesside period than for most other periods of history, but only for the reigns of Ramesses II and III. Ramesses II, with his long reign of sixty-seven years and his many wives, fathered a large number of children, and we do learn about them from monuments and inscriptions of the reign. Distinct burial places of at least two of his sons are known, and are outside Thebes: the well-known Khaemwaset, often called the 'first Egyptologist' after his efforts to restore older monuments in the Memphite region, was buried in or around the

Serapeum at Memphis, while his brother Ramesses-Nebweben was buried at Gurab in the Fayum, near the site of a palace of the harem. The location of the burials of the others is not certain, but it has long been speculated that the large and complex tomb 5 in the Valley of the Kings, with its multiple chambers, was built with this purpose in mind. This tomb is currently being excavated, and what little information is available perhaps confirms this idea.

We also know of the burial places in Thebes of a number of children of Ramesses III. No fewer than five of his sons have tombs in the Valley of the Queens (Pareherwenemef VQ42, Sethherkhepeshef VQ43, Khaemwaset VQ44, Ramesses VQ53, and Amenherkhepeshef VQ55), and there may even have

Valley of the Queens, tomb of Khaemwaset: Ramesses III wearing the red crown

133

been one or two sons buried in the Valley of the Kings, in tombs KV3 and KV13. A formula inscribed on the entrance to the tomb of Amenherkhepeshef ('given as a favour of Ramesses III (for) the great royal children') might mean that it was intended to be the burial place of more than one prince, but it could also just mean that this tomb was one of several set up for individual children of Ramesses. It is too simple to account for this, as one sometimes reads, by saying that these sons died young or in a plague; in fact it seems reasonably certain that Sethherkhepeshef was the later Ramesses VIII, who, while he does not seem to have had a tomb in the Valley of the Kings, perhaps cut another tomb there while he was still a prince (KV19). In the rear of the tomb of Amunherkhepeshef today is a display case containing a still-born foetus, often described to visitors as being that of the prince himself, but the French work in the Valley of the Queens has recently exploded this attractive myth, showing that it is in fact from the so-called Valley of Prince Ahmose, where it was found by the Italian expedition in the early years of the twentieth century.

One other Ramesside prince's tomb is known in Thebes, that of Ramesses-Montuherkhepeshef, a son of Ramesses IX, located in the Valley of the Kings (KV19). This tomb, possibly started by Prince Sethherkhepeshef, is beautifully decorated, and might have originally been designed to be a king's tomb. He must have been particularly special to have received this honour. A son of Ramesses VI might also have been buried in KV13.

Thus, while the situation regarding the burials of some Ramesside princes is somewhat clearer than in the rest of Egyptian history, there are still gaps. We must hope that there is still evidence to be found which will go some way to resolving this problem.

The design and decoration of Ramesside tombs

The earliest Ramesside tombs are quite simple, consisting of a stairway leading to a principal chamber, with perhaps one or two annexes. The tombs of the queens of Ramesses II, so well typified by Nefertari, the best-preserved of them all, are more complex, with one or two wide stairways with a central ramp, and large pillared burial chambers. These tombs, particularly those of the time of Ramesses II, seem to reflect the structure in miniature of the contemporary tombs of the occupants' husbands in the Valley of the Kings, but without the long corridors. A final group, the tombs of the sons of Ramesses III, are more level, elongated and straight, again reflecting to some extent the later Ramesside royal tombs.

The decoration of these Ramesside tombs is both similar to and yet different from that of the kings' tombs, as many texts and some scenes which appear in the Valley of the Kings do not appear in the Valley of the Queens. The tomb of Nefertari serves as the best example of a queen's tomb, as it is so well preserved – its decoration, like its architecture, emulates a king's tomb without crossing into territory reserved only for him. The primary funerary book to appear is the *Book of Gates*, which refers to the gates between the different hours of the night, through which the deceased had to pass. Royal books such as the *Amduat* do not appear, but we do find there, perhaps in compensation, spells from the *Book of the Dead*, which would be out of place in kings' tombs of the period. The queens' and princes' tombs contain many scenes of the owner before the deities with whom they were to be concerned in their passage in the afterlife and indeed it seems that the tombs do represent a model of the progression of the spirit into the afterlife, and, following the rebirth of the individual through his or her association with Osiris, the subsequent ability to return to the earth. These tombs thus stand in a position clearly between those of the Ramesside kings and those of the Ramesside nobles, as one would surely expect from their status.

The Twenty-first to Twenty-sixth Dynasties

A fine line has to be drawn in this period between royal and private persons, since a number of the latter used royal titles in the Twenty-first Dynasty, (p. 39). As some of the consorts and family members of these Theban 'kings' also used royal titles, we can justify mentioning them in this chapter.[8] Their burials have been found in two principal locations.

The burial of Herihor has never been found, but the body of his wife Nedjmet was found in the Deir el-Bahari royal cache. The bodies of Panedjem I and his wife Henuttawy and daughter Maatkare-Mutemhat were also found in this cache, along with at least one daughter of Menkheperre (Istemheb). It seems probable that the Deir el-Bahari tomb was first used at this period for the burials of one of the later high priests (who did not style himself king), Panedjem II, and that the other bodies were added later from a family tomb – possibly even the Bab el-Muallaq cliff tomb described above – along with the New Kingdom royal mummies.

The second location was among the various priestly caches located in the area near the temple of Hatshepsut at Deir el-Bahari. We will mention these caches again on p. 143; for the moment, it will suffice to say that the Metropolitan Museum found in one tomb the burials of Henuttawy, a daughter of Panedjem I, and Henuttawy and Djedmutiusankh, daughters of Menkheperre. Among the burials in the much larger second Deir el-Bahari cache (the Bab el-Gasus tomb) were found the bodies of a number of individuals who may have been linked with the family, although it does appear that the three women above were singled out for special separate treatment.

Once the Twenty-second Dynasty asserted control over Thebes, the local priests no longer took on the titles of royalty. However, certain relatives of the kings of that dynasty were sent to Thebes to cement links between the

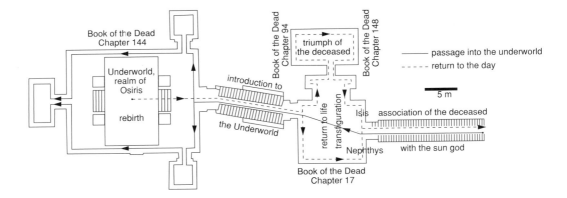

The journey of the queen into the afterlife and subsequent rebirth as suggested by Christian Leblanc

north and south, and it is thus pointless trying to make a somewhat artificial difference between royal and non-royal persons at this time. One exception is Djedptahiufankh, 'king's son of Ramesses', who was one of the last persons to be buried in the Deir el-Bahari cache, and who was related to one of the northern royal families. A coffin fragment of Iuput, son of Sheshonq I, has been found in the Ramesseum area, a popular burial area in the time of the Twenty-second Dynasty.

Later in the period the political situation becomes more confused, and it is likely that some of the Twenty-third Dynasty kings ruled from Thebes. The family of one of these, Takelot III, was extremely extensive, and many of its members were buried in the Deir el-Bahari area (p. 144), although the burial of the king himself has not been found. With the demise of the Twenty-third Dynasty, no more royal persons were buried in Thebes.

The Divine Adoratrices

There is one further group of persons to bring into this chapter, the 'Divine Adoratrices of Amun', also called 'God's wives of Amun'. They can be considered as quasi-royalty in Thebes at least, and their names were usually written in cartouches. The office was not a new one, as it goes back at least to the New Kingdom, when it tended to be held by a queen not necessarily resident in Thebes; during the Third Intermediate Period it was rather different.

As the high priests became more and more involved in temporal as opposed to spiritual affairs, the office of Divine Adoratrice developed into the main focus of the practice of the cult of Amun in Thebes, and, because of the way it operated, became a useful way of cementing relations with the kings in the north. The office of Divine Adoratrice was not hereditary, as the occupants

*Lid of sarcophagus of
Ankhnesneferibre.
British Museum,* EA32

Medinet Habu: the east side of the chapels of the Divine Adoratrices

of the office were not allowed to marry, but rather adoptive: at some point in her life the Adoratrice would adopt a younger woman, who would hold the office as junior partner, and who would become the senior Divine Adoratrice on the older woman's death. A list of the holders in the Third Intermediate Period will be found in the Chronology.

A number of these women built chapels for themselves at Medinet Habu, just in front of the temple of Ramesses III; many tourists pass by them now, but few realize what they are. Into these chapels were incorporated their burial places. The easternmost chapel is dedicated to Amenirdis I, while the other chapel has chambers dedicated to Nitocris, Shepenwepet II, and the mother of Nitocris, Mehitenweskhet. Traces of brick chapels dedicated to Shepenwepet I and Ankhnesneferibre were found east and west of the surviving block of buildings. Two of their sarcophagi were discovered in rock tombs above the village of Deir el-Medina, that of Ankhnesneferibre in 1832 and that of Nitocris in 1885; they are now in the British and Cairo Museums respectively. The tombs in which these sarcophagi were found are sometimes called the 'tombs of Saite princesses', but it seems far more likely that these large stone objects were removed from their original locations at Medinet Habu and transported to Deir el-Medina by people wanting to reuse them for their own burials. In fact, the sarcophagus of Ankhnesneferibre bears an inscription of Pamontu, a priest of the late Ptolemaic or early Roman period, whose brother Montuzaf was buried elsewhere in the necropolis.

TOMBS OF PRIVATE PERSONS

The tombs of private individuals at Thebes are popularly known as the 'Tombs of the Nobles'. These very beautiful and very special tombs will occupy the bulk of this chapter, but before we describe them and their contents it needs to be stressed that they are the burial places of the most eminent individuals of the area, governors, high priests, administrators and their like. These people were very much the elite of the periods in which they lived – hence the term 'nobles' – and we know very little about where the ordinary Egyptians of pharaonic Thebes were buried. We shall, however, consider this difficult subject briefly at the end of the chapter.

Private tombs figure prominently in almost any account of ancient Egypt. The amount known about tombs and burials means that it is often stated that the Egyptians were obsessed with death, but this is not really true. They were very much concerned with life, but wanted to be sure that when they died they were well prepared for it, with an adequately equipped tomb. A tomb had several functions. It served, of course, as the burial place of the owner, and perhaps his closest relatives. But it was also the place in which his spirits resided after death and as such also served as a place for their cult, where offerings would be made and rituals carried out for his benefit. A good tomb also helped to perpetuate the memory of the deceased, and at some periods it also became a cult place for the worship of certain deities favoured by or relevant to the dead person.

The changing locations of the tombs

The Old Kingdom

The oldest recognizable tombs in Thebes date to the Third or Fourth Dynasties, and unfortunately are anonymous; one of them contained an intact burial, but there was no inscriptional evidence to give any idea of the identity of the occupant. They are located in the area known as Tarif, the site of the earliest settlements. These tombs are built of mud brick in the form of a mastaba, a rectangular shape more usually associated with the rows of Old Kingdom stone tombs in the northern cemeteries of Giza and Saqqara near Memphis. This type of construction is relatively rare in the south of Egypt, although there is another example at el-Kab (90 km south of Luxor). It seems probable that they were the tombs of important Thebans of the time, and these two may be only the remains of a larger cemetery destroyed by later construction.

There are five tombs at el-Khokha from the later Old Kingdom at Thebes. As elsewhere in Egypt, the appearance of these sepulchres reflects an expansion of the administration of the provinces which started somewhere in the mid- to later Fifth Dynasty. Some sites, usually considered as administrative centres, have many such tombs, but the small number at Thebes, even allowing for others which have been lost, suggests that the city was not the most important province at this time.

The First Intermediate Period and Middle Kingdom

The real importance of Thebes began in the First Intermediate Period. The first royal tombs of Thebes, those of the Eleventh Dynasty, were located in Tarif, and a survey undertaken by the German Archaeological Institute in the 1960s showed that there are many private tombs there which can only be of this date. The Tarif cemetery is presumably largely contemporary with the three Inyotef kings and extends into the early reign of Nebhepetre Mentuhotep II.

However, Mentuhotep then began the construction of his mortuary temple at Deir el-Bahari, and the focus of the private burials followed. A number of large tombs of the *saff* type (pp. 146–8) were constructed near the causeway of the temple and in the slopes to the south, and some were decorated. Later in his reign his high officials began to cut their tombs in the northern cliff of the valley of Deir el-Bahari. Many of these officials doubtless lived on into the reigns of Sankhkare Mentuhotep III and Nebtawyre Mentuhotep IV, and they may even have continued into the early years of Amenemhat I of the Twelfth Dynasty.

The best-known tomb from this period is that of Meketre, discovered by the Metropolitan Museum in 1920, which overlooks Amenemhat I's temple. This tomb is famous for the wonderful collection of wooden models it contained, including workshops, the tomb owner at work, and all sorts of other activities. But there are many other tombs of the late Eleventh and possibly of the early Twelfth Dynasty in Thebes, almost all of which lie close to either of the two temple sites of the period which we have just identified. The vast majority of them are undecorated. One tomb worthy of mention was found by the Metropolitan Museum expedition; it contained the anonymous bodies of a number of men of this date who had clearly lost their lives in battle and who had been hurriedly buried. These men are often thought to be some of those who fought with Nebhepetre Mentuhotep in his campaign to reunite Egypt.

A few large Eleventh Dynasty tombs were also built on the east face of the hill of Sheikh Abd el-Qurna. Among these is the latest Middle Kingdom Theban tomb, usually called that of Inyotef-iqer ('Antefoker'; TT60), who was a vizier in the reign of Amenemhat I or Senwosret I. He also had a mastaba tomb in the new cemetery of the royal capital at Lisht, and it is now thought most likely that it was his mother Senet who was buried in the tomb at Thebes, as she is actually much more prominent in this tomb.

The late Second Intermediate Period and New Kingdom

The private tombs of Thebes are above all associated with the New Kingdom, but let us look briefly at their Seventeenth Dynasty forebears. The area of Dra Abu el-Naga has been identified above as the necropolis of Seventeenth Dynasty royalty (pp. 94–5), and recent research has identified a number (perhaps no more than twenty or so) of undecorated tombs there and at Sheikh Abd el-Qurna as possibly belonging to the later part of this dynasty.

The rather localized nature of the necropoleis which we have identified in the earlier periods came to an end in the New Kingdom, when tombs were built on all parts of the West Bank from Qurnet Marrai in the south to Dra Abu el-Naga in the north. None the less, certain trends can be observed. The prime location for the tombs of the most important officials in the first half of the Eighteenth Dynasty was on the hill of Sheikh Abd el-Qurna, although some of the very earliest chapels are found in the area of Dra Abu el-Naga which had been popular in the preceding dynasty. Tombs of the Eighteenth Dynasty lower down the hill of Sheikh Abd el-Qurna tend to belong to the second half of the dynasty, and the area of el-Khokha also became popular at this time.

Ramesside activity was concentrated on the area between el-Khokha and Dra Abu el-Naga. Some smaller tombs of this period are found at the bottom of the hill of Sheikh Abd el-Qurna, but on the hill itself Ramesside chapels are almost unknown. For the whole of the New Kingdom the Assasif presents an interesting picture: only a handful of tombs are known, all on the south side of the valley, and they are an extension of the el-Khokha necropolis. The tomb of Samut Kiki (TT409), open to tourists until closed for restoration in the 1990s, is one example. The reason for this must be associated with the Deir el-Bahari temples and their links with the Valley Festival (pp. 78–80); presumably the Assasif was holy ground, and the overseers of the necropolis, whoever they were, must have forbidden the construction of tombs on it.

There is most definitely a reduction in the number of tombs of private officials as the New Kingdom proceeded, as the following very approximate figures show:

Eighteenth Dynasty	350	'Ramesside'	100
Nineteenth Dynasty	80	'New Kingdom'	95
Twentieth Dynasty	55	Also many undatable examples.[1]	

It seems likely that some of the decline in numbers starting in and around the Amarna period is taken up by the expansion of the New Kingdom cemetery at Memphis, but it is currently unclear where many of the tombs of the officials of the later New Kingdom are located, including those who are well known from other Theban sources. The number of Theban private tombs which can be dated to the Twentieth Dynasty is particularly low, and the number from the very last years of that dynasty is almost zero. One of this tiny group is the elaborately decorated tomb of Imiseba (TT65) in Sheikh Abd el-Qurna, itself usurped from an official of the reign of Hatshepsut or Tuthmose III called Nebamun.

The Third Intermediate Period

The Twenty-first Dynasty marks a major change in the approach to making tombs, in that the construction of painted or carved rock tombs simply stopped, with a few notable exceptions. Let us briefly deal with these exceptions first. A number of brick chapels have been found in the areas west of Medinet Habu, west of the Ramesseum, and at various places in the Assasif, all dating to the Twenty-third to Twenty-fifth Dynasties. Further examples appear to have been constructed in the forecourts of older private tombs.

Better known are the large temple tombs with their impressive substructures and superstructures in the Assasif, visible from Deir el-Bahari, and, to a much lesser extent, to the west of the Ramesseum. The earliest is the tomb of Harwa (TT35), which can probably be dated to around 680 BC. Slightly later is the very large tomb of Montuemhat, mayor of Thebes at the end of the Twenty-fifth Dynasty (TT34). There are then found a series of large tombs, mostly but not exclusively belonging to officials in the administration of the estates of the Divine Adoratrices, the religious and cult focus of the time (pp. 136–8). Such tombs are those of Padiamenopet (TT33, the largest private tomb in Egypt), Ibi (TT36), Pabasa (TT296), Ankhhor (TT414) and Sheshonq (TT27). That of Sheshonq is the last such tomb to be built, and is also in the easternmost location; the older tombs were built much further to the west, near the temple of Hatshepsut. That temple and its causeway seem to have been very much a focus for these tombs, and this is evident in their orientation. There is no clear evidence of any cult activity in the temple at this date, but, as some of these tombs employ scenes which in the earlier New Kingdom are associated with the Valley Festival which was always centred on Deir el-Bahari, it is possible that this festival might have been revived to some extent. This orientation may also reflect the holiness and significance of the location of Deir el-Bahari as much as anything else.

Whether because of the economic conditions, a desire for concealment or some other reason, the elite of the Twenty-first Dynasty, the priests of Amun and their families, as well as people of less elevated status, preferred to be buried in (normally) unmarked pits, shafts or caves without any associated offering chapel as had been the case for so many years. Coffin decoration in the Third Intermediate Period, particularly the Twenty-first Dynasty, is very elaborate, and perhaps went some way to take over the role of the decorated chapel.

We have already mentioned the use of queens' tombs of the Eighteenth Dynasty for the burials of some of the high priests, which places were also used for the reburials of the New Kingdom royal mummies. Many of the other priests were buried in a corridor tomb known in Arabic as the Bab el-Gasus, near the temple of Hatshepsut. These burials, fortunately intact for the most part, have revealed a wealth of information about the individuals of the time, and their highly decorated coffins now grace many museums.

The majority of burials of other individuals seem to have been made by reusing the earlier private tombs of all periods, and this practice continued throughout the Third Intermediate Period and beyond. A question which is currently unanswered is what happened to the earlier tomb owners and their occupants. The inspection in the Abbott tomb-robbery papyrus blames robbery in the New Kingdom:

The tombs and chambers in which rest the blessed ones of old, the citizenesses and citizens on the West of Thebes, it was found that the thieves had violated them all, dragging their owners from their inner coffin and their outer coffins so that they were left on the desert, and stealing their funerary outfit which had been given to them together with the gold and the silver and the fittings which were in their inner coffins.[2]

However, so few remains of burial assemblages have survived from tombs of the Middle and New Kingdoms (some exceptions will be mentioned later) that one cannot help but wonder whether something along the lines of the systematic clearing and recycling of royal burials (p. 100) also happened to the tombs of the nobles. There is, however, no archaeological material relating to this, no labels on mummies indicating their places of origin. The impression is indeed that none of the 'respect' (and we use that term carefully) accorded to the divine kings' bodies was paid to the nobles, whose bodies were simply cast away after robbery.

The number of people whom we know to have been buried in Thebes during the Third Intermediate Period is really rather large. Some tombs were used over and over again, but we are usually unable to tell whether by the same family or by several families. Other tombs were reused perhaps only once, and we have seen both possibilities in the excavations we have conducted in Thebes.[3]

The preferred locations for these new burials kept changing: the area of Deir el-Bahari was definitely favoured during the Twenty-first Dynasty, while in the Twenty-second there was a move towards using the area around the Ramesseum. Here a large number of new pits were cut, and small shrines

Late Third Intermediate Period burials on the second terrace of the temple of Hatshepsut at Deir el-Bahari

were often built above these pits, mostly in the area of older mud-brick structures, which presumably served as the backdrop for the new constructions. As time moved on, the area of the temple of Deir el-Bahari itself became favoured for the burials of some of the great families of the later Third Intermediate Period, of the later Twenty-third and early Twenty-fifth Dynasties. Burials were actually effected in the debris which at this time covered the temple, and can be seen in the photograph above, taken during the excavations by the Metropolitan Museum. In addition, burials of small family groups were made inside some of the shrines themselves, subsequently rediscovered by Mariette, Vassalli and Naville.

We assume, in the cases of tomb reuse or burial in temple debris, either that there was minimal cult function for the new occupants or that the tomb chapels and temples themselves served as the places where the living would leave offerings to their dead.

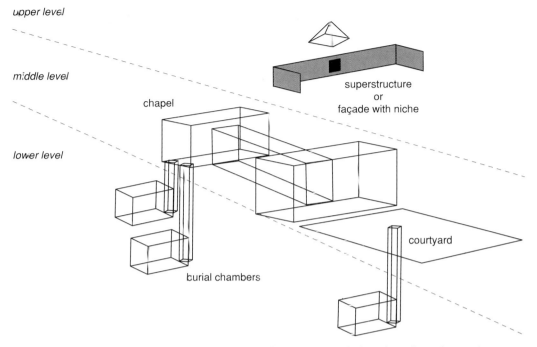

upper level

middle level

lower level

chapel

superstructure
or
façade with niche

courtyard

burial chambers

Schematic diagram of an Eighteenth Dynasty tomb, based on that of Senneferi (TT99), showing the three different conceptual levels

Tomb design

The different parts of a tomb

Visitors to the Tombs of the Nobles tend to visit the chapels, where the painted or carved decoration is normally to be found. However, it is important to realize that this is just one part of a tomb complex, and in fact is not the place where the owner would have been buried. The chapel served as the place where the living could go, where rituals and prayers for the deceased would be spoken and festivals performed, and it also formed the link for the spirits of the dead between their world and that of the living. Their bodies were placed in chambers at the bottom of vertical shafts or sloping passages, almost always below the level of the chapel. The symbolism of this is not hard to find: as the chapel represented the world of the living, the underground area was the world of the dead, the realm of the god Osiris.

From the New Kingdom on, a third level, a superstructure, is often found. A number of tombs of this date have been found to have some sort of structure above them, and in the Ramesside period (if not before) this coalesces into the idea of a brick pyramid above the chapel. The pyramid was a solar symbol for the ancient Egyptians, and it seems that the increasing tendency of the Egyptians in the New Kingdom towards syncretism, or the merging and deliberate reconciliation of different religious ideas, meant that the sun-god was now playing his own role in the Egyptian noble's concept of the hereafter. The sun-god's role in death was originally confined to the afterlife of kings, but, like so many concepts which originated at the top of society, it gradually permeated and affected burial beliefs some way further down the social structure.

The basic division of a tomb into several functional parts goes back to the beginning of the historical period in Egypt: the kings who were buried at Abydos physically separated their cult places, large enclosures on the edge of the desert, from their actual brick tombs, while many officials of the First and Second Dynasties possessed cult niches on the outside of their free-standing mastabas. These niches contained small offering stelae, while in the body of the mastaba there was a vertical shaft. This pattern continued into the Old Kingdom, and already in the Third Dynasty in the Memphite region we find painted decoration in tombs, soon to be followed by relief, which was then expanded to fill offering chapels in the course of the Fourth and Fifth Dynasties.

The Old Kingdom

The typical form of a provincial tomb in the later Old Kingdom is the rock-cut chapel, a frequent feature in the valley cliffs from the Fayum to Aswan, and at Thebes the group of tombs in el-Khokha conforms to this pattern. The earliest is the chapel of Ankhwenis (TT413), who, as the cartouche of the king in his name suggests, probably lived at the end of the Fifth or the early part of the Sixth Dynasty. Only two further tombs are well documented, those of Khenti and Ihy (TT405, 186), and they date to the Sixth Dynasty. The chapels have a simple rectangular design, with one or more sloping passages leading off to the burial chambers.

The First Intermediate Period and Middle Kingdom

A new form of tomb design makes its first appearance in this cemetery, one which would influence the design of the Theban private tomb until well into the New Kingdom. This is the *saff* tomb, so called because it seems to be derived from an Arabic word meaning 'full of holes'; it is characterized by a façade consisting of a series of pillars with a transverse hall behind, which from the exterior gives the impression of a series of holes. Two examples are the tombs of Inyotef (TT386) and Dagi (TT103) in the Assasif. Beyond this hall a long passage runs into the rock, ending in a small rectangular or square chamber, from which the burial shaft or sloping passage descends. The earli-

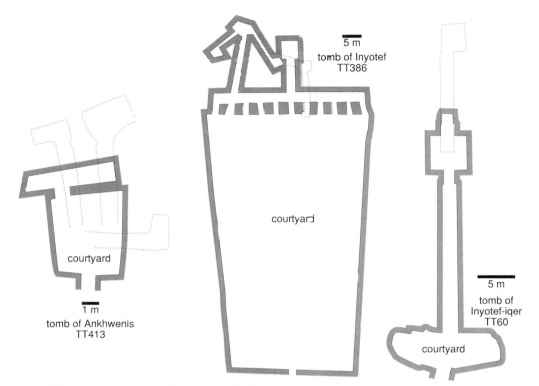

tomb of Inyotef
TT386

5 m

courtyard

courtyard

1 m

tomb of Ankhwenis
TT413

5 m

tomb of
Inyotef-iqer
TT60

courtyard

Plans of Theban tombs of the Old and Middle Kingdoms. Dotted lines indicate underground chambers

Façade of a saff tomb of the Eleventh Dynasty in the hill of Sheikh Abd el-Qurna

est examples of this type of tomb, those in the Tarif cemetery, are not decorated, and virtually nothing is known about burials in them.

Later in the reign of Mentuhotep II, perhaps in the last twenty years of his
reign, his officials began to adopt a different style of tomb. It is very closely
related to the *saff* but the pillared façade and the hall behind it disappeared,
and the passage into the interior of the tomb was lengthened. Most tombs of
this type were excavated into the northern cliff at Deir el-Bahari: these were
the burial places of the important officials of this latter part of the reign of
Mentuhotep (one example is the tomb of Khety, TT311). The latest tombs,
such as that of Inyotef-iqer (TT60), continue to conform to this same basic
plan.

The late Second Intermediate Period and New Kingdom

Although Seventeenth Dynasty tombs are few in number, the effect they had
on the ensuing tomb designs of the New Kingdom proper was immense, since
it is in these chapels that we find the earliest examples of tomb plans which
have long been thought of as typical for the Eighteenth Dynasty.

These Seventeenth and Eighteenth Dynasty designs very much continue the
line of development from the Eleventh Dynasty *saff* tombs. A pillared façade
was still used, but the area behind it was becoming increasingly important
and the pillars less so. The passage to the rear of the tomb became less elongated than before, and the rear room was expanded. The minimizing of the

Tomb of Hepusoneb (TT67), showing partially blocked spaces between the columns

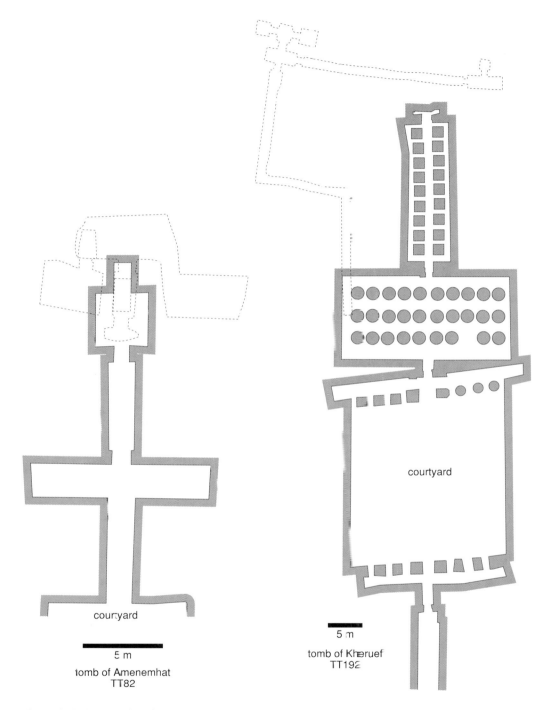

courtyard

5 m

tomb of Amenemhat
TT82

courtyard

5 m

tomb of Kheruef
TT192

Plans of Theban tombs of the Eighteenth Dynasty. Dotted lines indicate underground chambers

pillared façade is particularly emphasized by a number of tombs of the early Eighteenth Dynasty, such as those of the architect Ineni (TT81) and the high priest of Amun Hepusoneb (TT67). Both these important officials used tombs which had already been started in earlier periods as tombs with pillared façades: that of Ineni was probably originally a Middle Kingdom chapel, and that of Hepusoneb Middle Kingdom or Seventeenth Dynasty. The areas between the pillars were partially filled in by their new owners, leaving an impression of a series of small apertures near the top. The almost contemporary tomb of Senmut (TT71), probably the most important person in the reign of Hatshepsut, was actually cut from the rock in such a way as to leave these small 'windows' in the façade.

In this way the enclosed front broad hall developed, and thus the most characteristic form of larger private tomb of the Eighteenth Dynasty, the T-shaped tomb, so named from its similarity to an inverted letter T; one of the best examples is the famous tomb of Rekhmire (TT100). As always with rock-cut tombs, there is a wide measure of variation, some of which may perhaps have to do with the means or status of the tomb owner. However, most Eighteenth Dynasty tombs before the Amarna period can be seen as based on this form, with the rear room and passage compressed to varying degrees, with the result that sometimes all the functions of the T-shaped chapel were incorporated into not much more than one small room (for example, Nakht (TT52) and Menna (TT69)).

At the beginning of this section we mentioned that superstructures became a feature of the New Kingdom private tomb. The evidence for pyramids over these chapels in the Eighteenth Dynasty is ambiguous, although one possible such structure has been identified over the lower tomb of Amenuser (TT131). A few tombs have some sort of small shrine in the rock above them, and in the case of Senimen (TT252), the brother of the better-known Senmut just mentioned, a statue group was cut above his chapel. But the idea of the superstructure as a solar dimension was not yet fully developed, and many chapels possessed simply a small niche in the upper part of the façade of the tomb which probably served the same purpose.

The underground apartments, the realm of the dead, are usually composed of a vertical shaft or a sloping passage, which lead to one or more irregularly cut rooms in which the deceased and his wife, and perhaps even other members of his family, were buried. As far as we can tell, these rooms were not normally decorated, but we are relatively ignorant of the underground apartments, as they have been studied so much less than the chapels of the tombs. Of the few decorated burial chambers known to exist, the most spectacular is far and away that of Sennefer (TT96), mayor of Thebes in the reign of Amenhotep II, one of the tombs usually open to tourists (often called the 'tomb of the vines').

From approximately the reign of Amenhotep III a newer type of tomb was

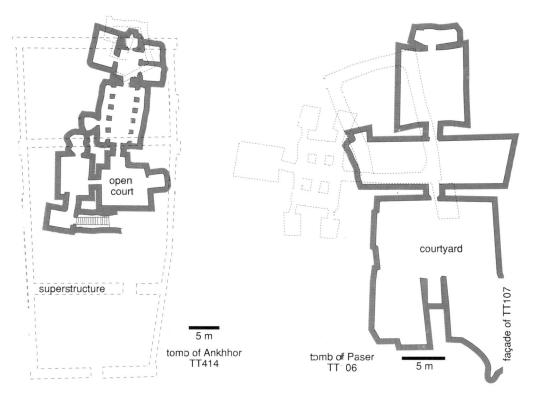

5 m

tomb of Ankhhor
TT414

tomb of Paser
TT 106

5 m

façade of TT107

Plans of Theban tombs of the Nineteenth and Twenty-sixth Dynasties. Closer dotted lines indicate underground chambers, wider ones the superstructure of the tomb of Ankhhor

adopted by some of the highest officials, characterized by its large size, and use of several courts and pillared halls (for example, Amenemhat Surer (TT48), Kheruef (TT192), and Ramose (TT55)). These new tomb types are the precursor of those which were to be seen next at Amarna, and then in Thebes during the Ramesside period, as well as in free-standing form on the desert at Saqqara. The latter are often termed 'temple tombs', from the parallels between their gateways and pillared halls with the similar (albeit much larger) features in the cult centres of major deities.

The Nineteenth and Twentieth Dynasties

Plans of Ramesside tombs tend to be variations on those which had gone before. It is important to stress that there is a marked difference between the largest tombs, of which there are a relatively small number, and the more numerous small to medium-sized chapels, the shapes of which are usually not unlike the small tombs of the preceding dynasty. The large tombs follow on very much from the temple tomb concept noted in the later Eighteenth Dynasty, with one or two pillared halls, and some of them have large court-yards in which were erected a set of brick-built gates, paralleling the pylons in the temples of the gods. A good example of this is the tomb of Djehutymose (TT32) of the reign of Ramesses II; other impressive tombs of this date are those of Paser (TT106), and Nebwenenef (TT157). Pyramid superstructures are common above the larger tombs of the Ramesside period, and the remains of these impressive mud-brick structures can still be seen today, especially in the hill above the village of Dra Abu el-Naga. The larger examples actually have small chapels inside the pyramids, decorated with (now badly damaged) scenes showing Osiris, other deities and the deceased.

One type of burial shaft is particularly characteristic of Ramesside tombs: a sloping passage with two or more right-angle changes in direction. In some cases this shaft is curved. There must clearly be some special purpose in such a design, and a case has been made for these architectural devices to repre-sent the topography of the next world, with parallels in funerary literature such as the book usually known as the *Amduat* (p. 117). This type of tomb shaft, while characteristically Ramesside, is first encountered in the reign of Amenhotep III, and is also found at Amarna. It may even be an attempt to copy the design and symbolism of the royal tomb.

The Third Intermediate Period

As we have described, the majority of burials of the Third Intermediate Period were effected in shafts without chapels of their own. None the less, two new types of tomb were built. The less well known type consists of a small brick structure with an entrance gateway and (usually) three small chapels at the rear, in the floor of which are normally the shafts for the occu-pants. These chapels have been dated to the Twenty-third to Twenty-fifth Dynasties, mainly on the basis of material found in their shafts. Some possible traces of paint have been noted on the mud brick, but no more formal decoration has survived.

The major new monuments are the large tombs of important officials of the Twenty-fifth and Twenty-sixth Dynasties located mostly in the Assasif. They are large and feature a complex mix of symbolic architectural elements, many of which are developments from some of the features we noted in the Ramesside period, as well as others, such as the large superstructure, perhaps inspired by architectural forms going back as far as the Old Kingdom. The tombs are on three levels as before. The brick superstructure with its pylon gateways emphasizes the 'temple tomb' aspect, but also includes elements within its architecture which have been interpreted as representing the primeval hill of creation, so important in Egyptian mythology, and also aspects of the Osirian underworld. Some tombs include pyramids with their

associated solar symbolism. The second level consists of the cult rooms –
often large and complex – which usually include an open court which contained plants, doubtless symbolizing the growth and rebirth associated with
Osiris. Continuing the metaphor of the temple tomb, parallels can be drawn
between these rooms and (for example) royal mortuary temples of the New
Kingdom. The third level is the burial chambers which are often complex,
and here it appears that much of the inspiration might have come from the
tombs in the Valley of the Kings, albeit arranged in a less linear arrangement
– perhaps more akin to the twisting Ramesside shafts we noted above. This
is obviously yet another part of the realm of Osiris, and we can thus see connections with this deity at all levels of the tomb.

Decoration

The purpose of decoration and its meaning

The simplest explanation for the decoration of a tomb is that it ensures the
continued existence of the material depicted. We have noted that the offering
chapel would be used for rites for the owners of the tomb, and the most
important among these was the regular provision of food and drink for their
spirits. Such a supply of food is attested in documents from many periods
which show that agreements were drawn up between the tomb owner while
he was alive and his relatives or priests who would look after his tomb and
provide offerings for his *ka*. We can see this in action from the Old Kingdom
right down to Greek times: a fictional, but none the less convincing, portrayal
of such activities is one of the occupations of the family at the centre of
Agatha Christie's novel set in ancient Thebes, *Death Comes as the End*.

While an ancient Egyptian sincerely wished his cult to continue for ever, it
was nevertheless felt that 'insurance policies' should be put in place when the
inevitable happened and the practice of the cult stopped. Presumably the
Egyptians had seen it happen. Therefore we believe that, in the simplest form,
the existence of paintings of offerings and offering rituals on the walls meant
that, in the right circumstances, these would magically come to replace the
real material which was no longer there. Thus the most basic set of scenes in
an Egyptian tomb usually includes an offering ritual. We will see below other
more complex examples where the scenes served a symbolic as well as a
magical purpose.

Magic was very important to the ancient Egyptians – not the sort of illu-
sionism which the term signifies in so many societies at the end of the twentieth century, but real magical power, to be feared and disbelieved at one's
peril. The painted figures of the owner, and also his statues, if he possessed
them, could magically provide a home for his spirit should disaster befall his

physical body in the tomb. The power of these figures is illustrated by the fact that they, or even the hieroglyphs which write an individual's name, were often defaced by enemies intent on destroying the memory of an individual.

Lise Manniche in her book *City of the Dead: Thebes in Egypt* gives a good description of what many of these scenes really mean. She stresses how much of the decoration is concerned with rebirth and 'projecting the tomb owner's personality and enabling him to continue his existence beyond the grave'.[4] Thus we can easily understand the role of the depiction of the funeral, and even the pilgrimage to Abydos. In the latter the deceased would be shown travelling to the holy city of Osiris to take part in the god's festivals and subsequently returning to Thebes; the deceased and his wife are always shown in a semi-mummiform fashion, and their boat is usually accompanied by another bearing their coffins. Regardless of whether this trip was actually made in life, it was an important part of the association with Osiris necessary for the afterlife.

The scenes which are harder to understand are many, and include what are usually termed in guidebooks 'scenes of daily life', those showing agriculture, craftsmen at work and so on. Some of these clearly reflect matters related to the owner's occupation on earth – agricultural scenes are often (but of course not exclusively) found in the tombs of granary officials, while viziers sometimes show taxing scenes and other aspects of administration with which they were concerned. Quite a few Eighteenth Dynasty officials are depicted before

Tomb of Hepu (TT64), reign of Tuthmose IV: craftsmen, including chariot-makers and sculptors

Tomb of Nebamun: the tomb owner and his family fowling in the marshes. British Museum, EA37977

the king on the walls of their tombs, and such scenes make it clear that the tomb owner wished to stress how important he had been in this life, since showing the king in a tomb was surely not a privilege granted to everyone. But because we do not find these scenes in every tomb (and not every man came into contact with the king), we must assume that they are just part of the concept of projecting the owner's personality into the next world. These scenes are certainly not there to leave later visitors a deliberate picture of what life might have been like at the time! We can, of course, use these scenes as source materials to deduce how the Egyptians might have dressed, reaped their crops and so on, but they have to be interpreted with a degree of caution.

There are other scenes which are far less obvious in their meaning, and for which scholars have had to search much harder to decode the symbols and suggest interpretations. One such is the common fishing and fowling scene, best exemplified by that of Nebamun in the British Museum.[5] The tomb owner does indeed appear to be spearing fish and throwing sticks at birds. But questions arise when we examine it more closely: why is he accompanied by his spouse in festive dress? Why is there a duck on the prow of the boat? The explanation lies in a complex mix of symbols, mostly of sexuality and rebirth, which are of course in themselves not unrelated notions. Research has indicated that the duck was an erotic symbol, and the concept of a woman in fine clothes, and particularly wearing a heavy wig, has sexual overtones – a woman in a well-known papyrus accuses a man of saying (we paraphrase), 'Put your wig on and let us have a good time together', which clearly classes as an indecent proposal![6] The fish in the centre of the picture is the *tilapia*, known to the Egyptians for its tendency to take its young into its mouth for protection, and to let them out when danger was past; the Egyptians were great ones for seeing parallels between the natural world and their religious ideas, and it is not difficult to imagine that they would see this as a potential symbol for rebirth.

Construction and decorative technique – all periods

Rock tombs were probably constructed in two major stages. Firstly, the chambers were hewn out of the rock by masons. Most of the evidence of this stage is obscured by the decoration, but in many tombs where the plaster has fallen off, we can see various marks on the walls which presumably guided the workmen. In the burial shaft of the Ramesside tomb of Djehutymose (TT32) graffiti exist on the walls giving some indication of the progress made cutting the shaft, while a number of ostraka found near the tomb of Senmut (TT71) of the reign of Hatshepsut indicate that, for example, eleven masons in one day cut an area perhaps 3.9 m wide by 0.65 m deep.[7] Once the desired shape was achieved, the plasterers, sculptors and artists set to work.

Egyptian tombs of all periods are decorated in either painted relief, painted plaster or a combination of both. Painted raised relief was probably the ideal, since it probably was the most luxurious and expensive, but the rock was often of inadequate quality for it to be used. The adhesion of paint to this rock is very variable, and some of the best-known examples have lost almost all their paint. Theban tombs of the Old and Middle Kingdoms are mostly painted, with some relief work. There is more painting than carving in the New Kingdom (largely owing to the poorer rock quality), although the very largest tombs, particularly in the Ramesside period, were executed in relief as much as possible. Sunk relief was used to a limited extent in the Eighteenth Dynasty, and tended to be restricted to architectural elements such as door jambs and stelae; the Ramessides used it more often. The large Twenty-fifth

Tomb of Djeserkaresoneb (TT38): unfinished heads of the deceased and wife, showing grids and outlines (reign of Tuthmose IV)

to Twenty-sixth Dynasty tombs at Assasif mostly employ painted relief, both raised and sunk.

The most common technique was the painting of plaster, and it is this which particularly characterizes Theban tombs. The wall was shaped as well as possible by the masons, and then layers of plaster were used to build up a flat surface. Fragments of limestone were frequently put into the plaster to strengthen it. In many tombs the plaster is lime-based, but mud plaster is quite common, not as strong but probably cheaper. On top of the rough surface was then placed a thin coat of very fine plaster or wash, which provided the base for the artists. On this a draughtsman roughly laid out the figures in red paint, using a system of guidelines and grids to ensure that the proportions were correct. The painters then converted these to the required standard, usually laying out areas of solid colour, and then finished them by outlining the various items in the composition. Finally the background area was overpainted to ensure that the traces of the guidelines and any failed attempts were removed. In many cases either these lines have not been removed or over the years the covering layers have decayed, leaving us with a range of hints as to how the originals were prepared.[8] The ostraka noted above from the tomb of Senmut note the issue of plaster and cakes of colours.

One major problem is the identity of the men who worked on the tombs. In the vast majority of cases the work is anonymous, but there are a couple of exceptions. One Eighteenth Dynasty tomb, that of Amenemhat (TT82), does show the owner making a thanksgiving to his workmen, while in the Twentieth Dynasty a graffito suggests that one of the workmen of the royal tomb might have decorated one of the few known late Twentieth Dynasty private tombs, that of Imiseba. It has indeed often been stated that the workmen of Deir el-Medina might have built the private tombs, but in the busiest period of tomb-building, the Eighteenth Dynasty, it is hard to see how the same men could have achieved this and fulfilled their principal function. The workmen who are mentioned in the Senmut ostraka are not known from elsewhere, but, as there are effectively no records from the workmen's village at this time, we cannot know if there is an association there. Perhaps the royal workmen did play an occasional role, for example when they were laid off from royal work (p. 179), but it seems that there must also have been a community of workmen of whom we currently know nothing.

Decoration of the Old Kingdom

The mastabas in Tarif are undecorated. The art of the group of el-Khokha tombs, made in a combination of carving and painting, is typical of the work produced outside the capital city: it is less refined, but it has a charm of its own. Offering scenes are there, along with pictures of butchers, an essential element in tomb decoration of the Old Kingdom; there are also less common scenes, such as boats in the tomb of Ankhwenis.

Decoration of the Eleventh and Twelfth Dynasties

No decoration has survived from the early Eleventh Dynasty tombs in the Tarif cemetery. However, it seems likely that some of them at least contained stelae and other decorated slabs, since a considerable number of such items came on to the art market in Luxor in the latter years of the nineteenth century, the probable provenance of which is the so-called 'Antef cemetery' of Petrie at Tarif. The British Museum possesses at least two of these, the stela of Inyotef (BM 1203, important for the date on it; see p. 25) and that of Tjetji (BM 614).

In the tombs near the causeway of Mentuhotep II at Deir el-Bahari, and on the south side of the valley there, painted and carved decoration is found. Among these earlier tombs, three particular examples stand out: those of the vizier Dagi (TT103), the guardian of the royal harem Djari (TT366) and chancellor Inyotef (TT386). The decoration is painted on the pillars and sometimes on the walls of the hall behind the pillars. The scenes include those of craftsmen, ships and agriculture, as well as offering scenes. Particularly

*Tomb of Ankhwenis
(TT413), early Sixth
Dynasty: the tomb
owner*

interesting is a scene in the tomb of Intyotef showing the siege of a possible Syrian fortress.

On the north side of the valley a different method of applying decoration was employed, only preserved to any degree in the tomb of the chancellor Khety (TT311). The long corridor or passage towards the burial chamber was lined with limestone slabs decorated in sunk relief, as was the burial chamber itself. The latter reliefs show the sorts of idealized sets of offerings and ritual objects associated with the tombs, and have much in common with the decoration of coffins of that time. We have seen in an earlier chapter (p. 121) that this method of decoration was used in the tomb of Mentuhotep II's wife Neferu, and was either a response to the quality of the rock not being amenable to carving or a exhibition of the ability to command this level of resources. The tomb of Dagi noted above was also modified to include some decoration in this manner, suggesting that he may have received a promotion to vizier late in life and thus felt compelled to 'update' his tomb.

Tomb of Inyotef-iqer (TT60): butchery scene (early Twelfth Dynasty)

In many ways, the most important Middle Kingdom tomb in Thebes is that of Inyotef-iqer (TT60), since it is well preserved, and, most importantly of all, must have inspired the decoration of the subsequent Eighteenth Dynasty tombs. The tomb was published by Norman de Garis Davies in 1920, and includes many of the scene types which become so prominent four to five hundred years later: we see craftsmen and other 'scenes of daily life', dancers, funeral scenes, the Abydos pilgrimage, fishing and fowling and offering scenes, to pick out some of the major categories. The paintings in the tomb are well executed, and possess the rather formal stiffness which is found in most painted scenes up to the New Kingdom, a stiffness which is not quite so evident in the high-quality carved scenes of this date found in Theban temples, and in tombs near the northern capital of Lisht. The tomb of Inyotef-iqer is the last of the great tombs of the Middle Kingdom, since, with the transfer of the capital to the north, lavish tomb-building seems to have stopped.

Decorative programme – Eighteenth Dynasty

Although the arrangement of the decoration of these tombs is still not fully understood, we can make certain generalizations about the location of scenes. We often have to assume that much of the variation is down to the whims of the tomb owner.

The decoration of the front hall of a tomb tends to be of the 'daily life' category, but one or two offering places are usually found there. These offering places are marked by large stelae or that very Egyptian item, a 'false door'. Scenes showing the owner before his king also feature here, most typically on the walls opposite the entrance, where they would be the most visible.

Some scene types are almost completely confined to the Eighteenth Dynasty. One group is related to the Valley Festival, the annual festival when the god Amun travelled from Karnak to visit his shrine at Deir el-Bahari. This was a time when relatives visited the tombs of their family members, and the various deceased tomb owners were thought of as taking part in the festivities. The most common scene related to this is the representation on either side of the entrance, in almost every tomb up to the Amarna period, of the deceased making offerings, especially burnt offerings, to Amun as he passed by in the festival. The god is thus never shown.

Another characteristic scene of this period is the banquet, where men and women are shown seated in their finery, often having consumed food and drink to excess. Manniche has shown that the symbolism of this scene is complex, being associated again with rejuvenation and rebirth, as well as almost always appearing in the context of the Valley Festival.[9]

Depictions of the funeral procession tend to be found in the long passage of the tomb, normally on the southern wall. It consists of rites which ensure the passage of the deceased from one life into the next. This scene contains a number of elements which go back to scenes of Old Kingdom date in the chapels at Memphis, and it is possible that the ancient and less than relevant nature of some of these scenes meant that the composition was ripe for a change, which did indeed take place. The fishing and fowling scene interpreted earlier most usually appears on the wall opposite the funeral, but can appear in other locations.

The rear room, where one exists, served as the major cult centre of the deceased, and is often referred to in the literature as the 'shrine'. In several tombs, indeed, the central part of the ceiling of this room is shaped like the roof of an Egyptian temple naos or shrine, with a profile much like the hieroglyph ⬛. The scenes found here vary somewhat, but idealized offering scenes and lists were located here, since this was presumably the main focus of the cult of those for whom the tomb was built.

The transition to the Ramesside period

It should not be thought that Egyptian tomb design remained static during the Eighteenth Dynasty (or at any time in history for that matter). We can see changes in composition and art style as the dynasty progressed: the formal style of the reign of Tuthmose III gave way to softer, more adventurous forms in the reigns of Tuthmose IV and Amenhotep III. The depiction of the funerary procession also began to change after the reign of Tuthmose IV. Many of the older and perhaps obscure rites were removed, and the paintings concentrated more on the procession and burial itself, with the rites before the tomb emphasized.

The private chapels did not escape the effects of the Amarna period, not least with the excising of many examples of the name of the god Amun in the inscriptions. There are few tombs from this time at Thebes, but we can see

Tomb of Amenmose (TT254): priest pouring oil on to lamp (approximately the reign of Ay)

*Tomb of Roma
(TT 294): painting
of Roma and wife
before Osiris*

witnesses to the changes. In the tomb of Kheruef (TT192), we find both
Amenhotep III and Amenhotep IV shown in relief of the best traditional style.
However, in the tomb of the vizier Ramose (TT55) there is an abrupt change
from the formal style of Amenhotep III to one wall which was decorated in
the more extreme Amarna style. It seems as if the tomb of Ramose was never
finished or occupied, and he may perhaps have moved with his king to
Amarna and been buried there. Other tombs, such as that of Parennefer
(TT188), also exhibit decoration in both styles. There seems then to be a short
period when no tombs were obviously being built in the Theban private
necropolis, but there is a small but significant group of chapels which belong
to the closing years of the dynasty. These tombs clearly show the artistic
influence of the Amarna style, but their scene composition was not dramatically different to those from the end of the reign of Amenhotep III.

The freedoms introduced by Akhenaten are reflected well in the tomb of

Amenmose (TT254), of about the reign of Tutankhamun or slightly later, yet the tomb is essentially one of the Eighteenth Dynasty. However, by the reign of Sety I, a mere twenty or so years later, major changes had taken place, and the decorative features of the tomb had been completely re-evaluated.

Ramesside decoration

Usually the first observation a visitor makes when visiting a Ramesside tomb is the omission of the so-called 'daily life' scenes. Gone is the agriculture, the craftsmen and even the banquet pictures, except in very rare cases. It then becomes apparent that there are far more overtly religious depictions in these chapels than before. The occasional scene of the deceased before Osiris is found in Eighteenth Dynasty tombs, as are pictures of the jackal-god Anubis. However, in a Ramesside tomb, many more scenes of the deceased before deities are seen. The primary deity is Osiris, but there are various others, such as the sun-god, in the form of Re-Horakhty. The banquet scene may have disappeared, but many examples of the deceased and his wife seated at tables of food, or receiving rites from a priest, are found; the funerary procession to the tomb is much more prominent, and there are often other scenes, such as the judgement of the dead, or the spirits of the deceased being attended to by the tree-goddess. The impression is that this is all much more explicitly religious than before, and research into these scenes suggests that the concept of the tomb has become much more focused on the needs of the deceased. For example, the deities shown are not just any selection of gods but rather those to whom the deceased would pay attention in his personal religious activity to ensure him a good reception in the next world; the great state gods are usually nowhere to be seen. The increase in provisioning scenes concentrates on this fundamental need of the deceased. Relevant texts from the *Book of the Dead*, while not unknown in the Eighteenth Dynasty tombs, are found with much more frequency, and ensure by their presence the safety and ritual knowledge of the deceased in his journey to Osiris.

One other interesting feature of Ramesside tombs is the manner in which the wall scenes are laid out. In the Eighteenth Dynasty, walls are composed of a series of major registers with sub-registers for each. Thus one tends to 'read' a wall from top to bottom; in the earlier periods one reads from bottom to top. In the Nineteenth Dynasty, while of course there are still registers, they tend to be much more independent of each other than before, and one reads very much more horizontally than vertically. The German scholar who first pointed this out terms it 'film-strip' style;[10] it may have first appeared in Amarna art.

The Ramesside tomb is generally easier to interpret than its predecessors, since the purpose of the scenes is often more clearly indicated, and can be related to specific texts and rituals, whereas the symbolism of the Eighteenth

The tomb of Nefersekheru (TT296): the solar cycle (reign of Ramesses II)

Dynasty was often more subtle and ambiguous. It seems most probable that the decoration of an Eighteenth Dynasty private tomb, which in essence had not fundamentally changed since the Old Kingdom, was indeed ripe for reinterpretation, and it is indeed possible that the mental shock provided by the innovations of the Amarna period may have been the catalyst for this change, if not the cause of it.

The Third Intermediate Period

We are here mostly concerned with the large tombs in the Assasif. The art of this period is generally of a very high quality and is characterized by a hearkening back to older forms, for which the style of the Old and Middle Kingdoms seems to have been a particular inspiration, although there are other scenes copied from New Kingdom tombs. Particularly interesting is the tomb of Ibi (TT36), in which is a copy of at least one scene from a tomb of another Ibi of the Old Kingdom at Deir el-Gebrawi, some 300 km to the north of Thebes, just north of Asyut.

Most of the scenes in these tombs are overtly religious in nature, with many chapters of the *Book of the Dead* making an appearance. However, far more of the old 'daily life' scenes make their appearance: the tomb of Ibi contains scenes of craftsmen, for example, and there is a very well-known scene of beekeeping in that of Pabasa.

Just occasionally, decoration of the Third Intermediate Period was added to an earlier tomb: two examples are the repainting of part of a doorway in the Eighteenth Dynasty tomb of Minnakht (TT87), and the painting of a stela in a large and otherwise undecorated early Middle Kingdom *saff* tomb near the top of the hill of Sheikh Abd el-Qurna (TT117).

Burial equipment

Burial customs

From the earliest times the ancient Egyptians were buried with grave goods. The Egyptians were by no means the only ancient people to have attempted to 'take it with them', but they took this element of preparation for death very seriously. Much of what we know about burial customs has to come from piecing together the remains of robbed burials, since intact ones have been found only rarely. Fortunately, the sheer quantity of material is of great help.

The central part of a burial was always the container for the body, which ranged from the simple wooden boxes of the early periods to the colourful and elaborate coffins and mummy cases of the Third Intermediate Period. Another essential element which goes back to at least the Old Kingdom is a container in which to place the embalmed viscera of the deceased. These objects are best known in the form of human- and animal-headed canopic jars, each identified with a particular deity. From the later Middle Kingdom onwards, the funerary figurine or shabti became common, appearing individually or in small numbers at first, but then multiplying during the Ramesside period so that there was one for every day of the year, plus an overseer for every ten of them. Truly the organization of life was reflected in death. The purpose of these figurines changed somewhat during their development, but they are most commonly considered as taking on some of the work which the deceased was supposed to perform in the next world.

Pottery containing food and drink for the deceased is ubiquitous, but other types of object vary a great deal according to period. The wooden model boats, workshops and so on much beloved of museum visitors are a feature of burials in the First Intermediate Period and Middle Kingdom – it is possible that they took the place of painted tomb decoration and would magically recreate this world for the deceased. Domestic furniture was quite common until at least the middle of the New Kingdom, but it must be realized that, although many of the items found in burials were used by the deceased during their lifetimes, a considerable number of items were also made specifically for the burial – some show signs of wear, while others do not.

Burial contents of the Old and Middle Kingdoms

No significant find of burial equipment has survived from Old Kingdom Thebes, but a number of intact burials have been found from the Middle Kingdom. Compared with examples of the New Kingdom, the burials were relatively simply equipped; coffins were made of wood, and Theban examples seem relatively plain, especially when compared to those from elsewhere in Egypt. Wooden models were very common although those mentioned as coming from the tomb of Meketre (p. 140) were the apogee of the technique. Most were fairly crude in execution, and this includes examples which have survived from the burial of Nebhepetre Mentuhotep II, showing that even kings needed such goods.

Pottery, jewellery and a small number of funerary figurines and canopic jars are known, although the best examples usually do not come from Thebes. Bodies were mummified, and one characteristic of the mummification technique of this period was the use of vast quantities of linen for the wrapping phases; one burial, that of Wah, probably a retainer of Meketre, used more than 300 square metres of material

Burial goods of the New Kingdom

There is no shortage of items in museum collections which probably originated in Theban tombs of the New Kingdom, but there is a very limited number of burials which have been found intact by archaeologists and which can thus be properly investigated. In the early days of Egyptology the local population was busy ransacking tombs in the search for objects to sell to European collectors, and an enormous amount of valuable context information was lost. It is of course also possible that private tombs were officially cleared at the end of the New Kingdom in the same way as the royal tombs.

More intact burials of the Eighteenth Dynasty have survived than of the Nineteenth and Twentieth. Some of the Eighteenth Dynasty examples come from tombs of non-royal persons buried in the Valley of the Kings (Yuya and

Burial chamber of Kha at Deir el-Medina, in the condition in which it was found

Tuyu, Maiherpri), and thus their burial effects might be expected to be somewhat special (pp. 170–1). It is clear that, in the Eighteenth Dynasty, individuals were buried in coffins accompanied by ritual objects necessary for the afterlife (such as canopic chests), but also with a number of everyday objects, such as jewellery and cosmetic items, pieces of furniture, large quantities of linen and even musical instruments. The most spectacular of these burials was that of the foreman of the royal workmen Kha, buried at Deir el-Medina; his burial, now in Turin, contains burial goods of the highest quality. Another remarkable burial is that of Ramose and Hatnefer, the parents of Senmut (TT71); the finds are now in New York.

Matters are less clear in the Ramesside period, largely owing to the relative lack of well-documented burial assemblages. The much rarer intact burials, such as that of the family of Sennedjem from Deir el-Medina (reign of Ramesses II – objects now in Cairo and New York), seem to show an increasing emphasis on elements such as coffins, canopics and shabtis to the relative exclusion of items of everyday life. This change seems to reach its logical conclusion in the Third Intermediate Period, as we shall see below. It is tempting to relate this change in burial practices to the changes we have already observed in the decoration and layout of tombs in the Ramesside period, which might in themselves have evolved out of a rethink of practices in the later Eighteenth Dynasty.

Burial effects in the Third Intermediate Period

The burial equipment of the Third Intermediate Period very much concentrated on the basic religious necessities. It is too simple to say that this might indicate the declining wealth of the country, since some of the objects (particularly coffins) must still have been very expensive (pp. 187–8). It is also likely that at this time the reduction in funerary equipment which began in

A cartonnage mummy case of the Third Intermediate Period. British Museum, EA6681

the Nineteenth Dynasty reached its conclusion, in that now only objects with a direct relevance to death and burial were placed with the deceased.

We are fortunate that the large number of relatively intact burials from the Third Intermediate Period has allowed us to gain a much better idea of the contents of an elite Theban burial of this period than at any other. A typical burial would consist of one to three coffins, mainly of wood. The use of cartonnage cases around the mummy also became very popular in the middle of this period. It is very likely that the elaborate decoration of most of these coffins was carried out as a substitute for the decoration of a tomb chapel. Also very common were canopic jars, although there was a phase in the earlier Third Intermediate Period when the internal organs of the mummy were reinserted into the body after embalming. Very many examples of different types of amulets are attested for the magical protection of the body, as well as some newer ritual objects, such as Osiris and Ptah-Sokar-Osiris statuettes. Pottery containing offerings for the deceased remained an important element, but all other indications of earthly living more or less disappeared.

Once we enter the sixth century BC there is apparently a marked drop in the amount of funerary material available to us. The latest great tomb in the Assasif dates to about 540 BC, but it is difficult to identify burial goods dating from much after 630 BC. It is quite possible that difficulty in dating the objects means that we just do not recognize the material correctly, since Thebes was still a busy place, and people still had to be buried. A little more material is known from the resurgence of Egyptian independence in the Thirtieth Dynasty, but again the evidence is rarer than before 600 BC.

Nobles in the Valley of the Kings

A small number of privileged private individuals received the rare honour of being buried in the Valley of the Kings. Almost without exception, such individuals possessed tombs which are much smaller than those of any king, and they were not normally decorated. Presumably burial in the royal necropolis was important enough.

Most of these tombs are of Eighteenth Dynasty date, and two of them were found intact. In 1905 the tomb of Yuya and Tuyu (KV46) was discovered by the Theodore M. Davis expedition – this couple were the parents of Queen Tiye, the principal spouse of Amenhotep III, and their special status presumably explains why they were given a tomb in the valley. In one relatively small chamber were found the virtually complete and undisturbed burials of both persons, with coffins, shabtis, chairs and even a chariot. Most of the finds are today on display in the Cairo Museum. A few years before, the first intact burial in the valley had been discovered by Victor Loret, when he located the tomb of Maiherpri, a 'child of the nursery' who (presumably because of special favour of the king) was permitted burial in the valley in about the reign of Tuthmose IV. Small portable items, such as oils and jewellery, were missing from the burial, and this indicates a robbery, probably not long after Maiherpri was buried. In addition to elaborate coffins, he was also buried with a number of arrows, perhaps favourite hunting weapons from his life.

Both of these tombs were undecorated. The other named non-royal tomb (KV13) in the valley belongs to Bay, an obscure individual who reached the rank of chancellor and was perhaps the 'power behind the throne' in the period of the reigns of Siptah and Tawosret at the end of the Nineteenth Dynasty. This long tomb is very similar to the original tomb of Tawosret, and shows scenes with Bay often before deities, a role usually reserved only for the king. We are currently ignorant of whether he was actually buried there, but sarcophagi of two later Ramesside princes were found in excavations there by the University of Hamburg.

There are also quite a number of other small undecorated pits in the valley which may have served similar functions. Most have proved anonymous, but one of them (KV48) is known to have been constructed for the vizier Amenemopet, who began a private tomb in the hill of Sheikh Abd el-Qurna (TT29), but was subsequently sufficiently favoured to obtain a burial in the valley. Another tomb (KV45) was that of the overseer of the fields of Amun, Userhat. Some burial equipment of the mayor Sennefer (owner of private tomb TT96) were also found in tomb KV42.

Tombs of the rest of the population at all periods

We cannot leave this chapter without briefly considering where the rest of the population was buried. The tombs we have been considering are those of the top two to five per cent (maximum) of the population. Little attempt has been made until recently to locate other burials, largely because of the riches to be gained from concentrating on the elite tombs, and also simply owing to the scale of the work to be done in those tombs. In many other cemeteries south of Memphis small graves have often been encountered at the foot of the cliffs which formed the burial places of part at least of the non-elite population at different periods. In so many cases it is very likely that the ordinary people were buried in the least favourable locations and their burials were thus far more likely to be disturbed and indeed recycled. Occasionally an isolated simple burial is found in proximity to one of the great tombs, as if that person were relying on the patronage of a great man, but this hardly accounts for much of the population.[11] An inevitable problem of such non-elite burials is that they would be buried with few goods and even fewer inscribed items which might help to identify them; it is also likely that their burials would be simple and not far beneath the surface, thus rendering them more accessible to animal predators, robbers and of course settlement development.

Third Intermediate Period coffins piled up in the tomb of Khaemwaset in the Valley of the Queens, as they were found

The location of popular cemeteries is unclear in Thebes for the Old and Middle Kingdoms, although the preponderance of tombs from those periods in the region of Tarif would make us suspect that ordinary burials were made somewhere in that area. However, an area at the northern end of Dra Abu el-Naga has been identified as a possible cemetery for the non-elite of the Eighteenth Dynasty. This cemetery probably extended some way to the south of that area, since it almost certainly includes an area examined by an expedition from the University of Pennsylvania in the 1920s. In both locations were a number of small brick chapels which could have accommodated the burials of several thousand Thebans of the Eighteenth Dynasty, and, from what we can tell of those buried there, they were not of high status. Things are less clear for the Ramesside period, and it seems possible that in the Third Intermediate Period the social range of individuals being buried in the sorts of tombs we have just described was much wider than before. For example, some minor functionaries of the temples of Amun ('lotus-bearers', 'perfumers' and so on) were buried in the tombs of some of the sons of Ramesses III in the Valley of the Queens. But, as with all this relatively sparse evidence, it is uncertain whether those buried included the field labourers and others at the bottom of the Egyptian social ladder.

The Ptolemaic period does provide us with a much better-balanced picture of the burial system in Thebes. This will be covered in the last chapter.

LIVING IN ANCIENT
THEBES

Although we are fortunate in the unusual wealth of information about the culture of ancient Egypt, through both the quantity and decoration of its remains and its surviving written records, the bulk of this information relates to funerary monuments, or large state establishments, rather than to the everyday life of the ancient Egyptians. One of the greatest deficiencies in this area is the relative lack of habitation sites which have been thoroughly studied. This lack can be attributed in large part to the fact that the majority of towns and villages lay in the cultivable area of the Nile valley. As a result of the regular flooding of this land, the preservation of material is much poorer than it is in the desert parts of Egypt. Another difficulty is that the local inhabitants are understandably reluctant to have their valuable agricultural land turned into an archaeological site. However, archaeologists cannot escape their share of the blame. If the culture were less rich in funerary remains, far more effort would have been put into trying to trace the remains of habitation sites in the cultivation, and great lengths would have been gone to in order to try to preserve what little remained, no matter how badly it had suffered from decomposition. Be that as it may, we are left with the current sad state of affairs.

The village of Deir el-Medina

In the Luxor area, however, we are fortunate in having a relatively large number of sites containing dwellings of one sort or another. One of the best known of these is the village of Deir el-Medina. Set in a valley in the desert, the buildings of the village themselves are very well preserved, and we are additionally fortunate in having a wealth of written evidence about the inhabitants of the village and the way in which they lived. The inhabitants were artisans, responsible for creating the royal tombs in the Valley of the Kings. They were almost certainly the elite of their professions and it is possible that their lifestyle is atypical of settlements elsewhere in Egypt at that time.

It is not known for certain exactly when the village was founded, but it was at some time around the beginning of the Eighteenth Dynasty. The wall built around the original village still contains bricks stamped with the name of the third king of the dynasty, Tuthmose I (1504–1492 BC). Although it is not certain that the first king of this dynasty, Ahmose, was buried in the area, his successor, Amenhotep I, is known to have chosen Thebes as his burial place. Exactly where he was buried is disputed, but the fact that the inhabitants of Deir el-Medina revered him (together with his mother Ahmose-Nefertari) as virtual patron saints suggests that it was perhaps he who first organized the nucleus of workmen for royal tombs, although his successor may have been responsible for settling the workmen here.

In addition to the archaeological record, the site has yielded a wealth of textual material providing us with information about the way that this group of ancient Egyptians actually lived and worked. In addition to papyri, large flakes of local limestone with fairly smooth surfaces, often resulting from the excavation of the royal tombs, were used by scribes rather like note pads. These limestone flakes, written or drawn on, are usually termed ostraka; the same term is also applied to pottery sherds used in the same way. In addition to being used by the scribes as note pads, ostraka were used in all aspects of life where we might use a piece of paper today, for example for keeping lists, accounts, receipts, and even for longer writings such as excerpts from literary works. They also made good sketch pads on which they might draw sketches of life going on around them, or amusing scenes taken from stories or from their own imagination.

So the site of Deir el-Medina provides us with an insight into the lives of a small group of people in a fairly enclosed environment, over a relatively short time span, as well as revealing the work involved in creating a tomb in the Valley of the Kings.

A vivid depiction of a cockerel on an ostrakon found in the Valley of the Kings. British Museum, EA68539

View over the southern part of Deir el-Medina towards the workmen's tombs

The name of this village, Deir el-Medina, is Arabic and means 'the monastery of the city'. (The monastery refers to a Coptic monastery built here much later, and the 'city' is the nearby site of Medinet Habu.) The workmen referred to their village simply as *Pa-demi*, 'the town' 𓈎𓏤𓂋𓏭𓏥𓊖.

We have little information about the village of the early Eighteenth Dynasty, although one of the most exciting archaeological finds from Deir el-Medina was the discovery of the tomb of the foreman Kha, who died during the reign of Amenhotep III. Although the chapel was in a bad state of repair, his actual burial was found intact (p. 168).

The successor of Amenhotep III, Amenhotep IV, later known as Akhenaten, chose to be buried at his new capital, Akhetaten in Middle Egypt. For this reason he set up a new workmen's village there although it is not known whether he brought the workmen from Thebes to Akhetaten (Tell el-Amarna) to carry out the work. Subsequently the kings of Egypt returned to their former burial site in the Valley of the Kings and re-established the work-force at Deir el-Medina. And it is from this time onwards that we have by far the most information about the lives and personalities of this village.

Layout of Deir el-Medina

Although today the site is usually approached from the south, the ancient entrance to the village was at the north and the normal route between the cultivation and the village would probably have been via the gap between the hills of Sheikh Abd el-Qurna and Qurnet Marrai. Looking at the site today, one can still see the fundamental plan of the village, with a central street which had houses lying on either side. A normal house consisted of four rooms: an entrance hall, a little below street level, including a raised platform; the main room, with a higher roof allowing light in through clerestory windows, and sometimes with cellar underneath; a third room which served as a storage and working area, and was also used as sleeping quarters. The fourth room had no roof and was the cooking area, with an oven for

Deir el-Medina: the interior of a house in the workmen's village; the raised platform in the first room is visible at the left

bread-baking and sometimes another cellar. There was also access to the roof from here. The outsides of the houses were painted white and they seem to have had red wooden doors.

The purpose of the raised area in the first room of many of these houses is still a matter for debate. They consist of a platform of mud bricks, 0.75 m high on average, with steps leading up to them, and they were frequently plastered and decorated. The two principal suggestions as to their purpose is that they served as raised beds or as altars. As beds they are rather small in area, probably not large enough for a couple, despite the depictions of Bes, a god associated with fertility, that have been found on them. Bes is however also associated with childbirth, and it is possible that these structures served as beds for the mother of the household with her newborn child, and possibly even as the place where childbirth took place. It is their prominence in the first room of the house that has lead scholars to suggest as an alternative that they might have been used as altars to the god Bes. In fact the two functions may have been combined.

The lintel and door jambs of the main entrance to the house were often inscribed with the householder's name and this allows us to identify the individuals who lived there. Houses seem to have been assigned to families in the first instance by the government, but they then apparently passed on to family members through inheritance. It is clear that the size and elaborateness of one's house reflected one's status and wealth.

Structure of the workforce

The inhabitants of Deir el-Medina were the workers who were responsible for creating the tombs in the Valley of the Kings, and the written material that has been preserved also provides us with a great deal of information about the processes involved in this work. Unfortunately there are a number of problems associated with our understanding of these records. As with any written material not intended as a historical document, the most frustrating thing is the amount of information that the writers omitted.

The team of workmen was called *iset*, which means 'the gang' or 'the crew', a term taken from the personnel manning a boat. On Egyptian boats this crew was usually divided into two groups, each responsible for work on one side of the boat, so that they were divided into 'men of the left side' and 'men of the right side'. In exactly the same way, the workmen of the royal tombs were divided into two 'sides'. It has been suggested that the Deir el-Medina 'men of the left side' were responsible for work on the left side of the tomb; similarly the 'men of the right side' worked on the right side of the tomb. Another suggestion is that the designation indicated the side of the street their houses occupied within the village. However, neither suggestion seems entirely satisfactory.

Orders about the work in the Valley came at least nominally from the king, usually via his representative, the vizier, who would occasionally come to the site to inspect how the work was progressing; such occasions were noted in the daily journal. Since the vizier could not be there frequently, he appointed a person who acted as his representative, the Scribe of the Tomb, who received the orders about work from the vizier and passed these on to the Foremen of the crew. Of all the jobs connected with the building of the tombs, that of the Scribe must have been one of the most stressful, since he had to keep account of all materials used, note down daily the attendance (or non-attendance) of the workmen, receive the supplies to be issued as wages, then issue those wages and subsequently, one imagines, argue with the work-men about how much they had been paid. Small wonder, then, that at some periods there was more than one Scribe involved.

Directly over the workmen were the two Foremen who were each in charge of one 'side' of the crew. Their responsibility seems to have been to organize the work and direct the workmen of their 'side' according to the instructions from the Scribe. Other important figures were the Deputies (who perhaps deputized on occasion for the Foremen), the Guardians, who looked after equipment, and the Door-keepers, who seem to have been involved in main-taining discipline; all of these were assigned to one 'side' or the other. Most of these posts seem to have been passed on from father to son. In the Eighteenth Dynasty a workman would be referred to as a 'servant in the Great Place', a title which was later changed to 'servant in the Place of Divine Order [*Maat*]'.[1]

The numbers of actual workmen subordinate to these individuals varied considerably, from a minimum of thirty-two, at the end of the reign of Ramesses II, to a maximum of 120, during the reign of Ramesses IV. Some variation in number should probably be ascribed to the progress of the work: for example when beginning excavation of a tomb only a limited number of people could be employed, digging the limestone and carrying it out; but later, when excavation had proceeded further, more people would be required to carry out rubble, while others could be employed in smoothing the walls of completed rooms. It is thought that the exceptionally large number of workmen employed during the construction of Ramesses IV's tomb was due to the fact that the king was rather frail and it was early on decided that the tomb would need to be completed rather rapidly.

Of course, once the actual excavation of the chambers was completed, fewer people would have been required, and records of massive layoffs of the workforce have been recorded by the Scribes: 'Thus says the vizier: place any sixty men that you choose who are here in the gang and let the surplus be sent outside. Instruct them that they should become their serfs who carry supplies for you.'[2] The average size of the workforce seems to have been approxi-mately sixty, with thirty men assigned to each 'side' of the crew.

Once a workman was assigned to a 'side' he remained attached to that 'side' usually until death, or perhaps retirement. Only occasionally did workmen get transferred from one 'side' to another, and this probably happened only when one 'side' had become dramatically understaffed, possibly owing to deaths. In general it appears that the numbers per 'side' were kept even.

Work in the Valley of the Kings

The accession of a new king seems to have been greeted with great rejoicing, probably because it meant a new lease of life for the work on the royal tombs. The first things to do were to find a suitable location in the Valley of the Kings for the new king's tomb and to make a plan of the tomb for the workmen to follow. A few examples of contemporary plans have survived, such as the one on a papyrus kept in the Turin Museum which is readily recognizable as a plan of the tomb of Ramesses IV. To what extent the king himself was involved in the design of his tomb is pure speculation, but almost every tomb in the valley seems to be a development of its predecessor with some minor change. This suggests that people with intimate knowledge of the tombs were involved at the planning stage, and there may even have been a library of tomb plans which were consulted in the process of designing the next king's tomb; the plan of Ramesses IV's tomb may be an example of this, since it is clearly the plan of the tomb once the cutting of it had been completed (p. 114). Once a plan had been agreed and drawn up, the Scribe of the Tomb produced working copies of it on limestone ostraka which the foreman could carry round to check whether the work was progressing properly; several such working copies are in existence today.

Finding a suitable location for a tomb was not always entirely straightforward, since we know that, during excavation of a tomb for Sethnakht, the workmen found themselves breaking into the tomb of Amenmesse by accident and work had to stop. Subsequently this unfinished tomb was incorporated into the design of the tomb of Ramesses III. Similarly, tough patches of rock, such as a seam of flint, formed unexpected obstacles; in the tomb of Merenptah a similar hard boulder was encountered and the workmen simply had to leave it in place and work round it.

The work of excavation was carried out principally using a large copper or bronze spike and a wooden mallet to split the rock apart. Fortunately the limestone in most parts of the Valley of the Kings is soft enough not to have presented too much of an obstacle to progress. The rubble chippings which were produced were removed from the tomb in leather or wicker baskets, and a record was kept of how many basket loads were removed per day. Later these chippings could be used in filling in and hiding the access shaft to the deep-lying tombs. As the workmen at the deepest parts of the tomb continued the excavation of the rooms, a second party of workmen followed on their heels smoothing out and improving the shape of the walls prior to the arrival of the outline draughtsmen who would lay out the decoration of the tomb walls.

The unfinished state of many of the tombs in the Valley of the Kings provides us with illustrations of the techniques used in decorating the tombs. The tomb of Horemheb, in particular, clearly shows how the walls were prepared for decoration in painted relief: the first thing that happened was the arrival of the outline draughtsmen who sketched the rough layout of the scenes and hieroglyphs in red; then a second, possibly master, draughtsman came along and made corrections to the rough sketches in black; the next stage was the cutting away of the background around the designs to produce raised figures in relief and it was at this point that flaws in the rock were filled in with gypsum; this was followed with the rounding out of raised figures; finally the whole scene was carefully painted and in some cases a varnish-like coating was put on. Horemheb's tomb was the first tomb in the Valley of the Kings in which relief rather than paintings on flat walls had been used, and it may be that the tomb was left in such an unfinished state because the workmen were simply not well practised in working fast in this medium.

An important issue is that of the lighting used by the workmen. Of course, it would have been possible, while working on the first room, to use daylight, but once further inside this would have become impossible. Our own experience of using mirrors to reflect daylight into even small tombs indicated that this would have been of limited value. So some form of artificial light was required and it seems to have been provided by linen wicks, soaked in animal fat or sesame oil, which burned in a similar fashion to a candle.

The wicks were apparently made in the village by the women, and then kept in a storehouse, possibly located in the valley itself. They were issued to the men by the Guardians and the number issued was carefully noted by the Scribes. The copper tools, such as the rock-splitting spike mentioned above, were extremely valuable and consequently were in the charge of the Guardians, who issued them to the workmen, and were responsible for looking after them and sharpening them. All this was, of course, also recorded by the Scribes, as for example one notes that six spikes were handed out to each workman, while in another case it is noted that a workman returned five spikes.

In such an environment the death of the King would have been the cause for an even greater stir than usual; the current tomb, if not complete, would need to be worked on at high speed, and a possible redesign of the tomb would have had to be undertaken to try to adapt what had already been completed to meet the difficulty of having to bury the king in short order. Records reveal the intense activity on the completion of the dead king's tomb, including woodworking for the doors, and the sealing of the tomb with chips after the burial was complete: 'the workmen were in the Great Field sealing with the rubble to the top'; 'sealing the entrance in the Valley to the top after the burial was finished'.[3] After a lapse of time the circle would begin again with the identification of the location for the next king's tomb and activity would start again in the Valley.

The working day seems to have consisted of two spells of work which lasted four hours each, and a break of indeterminate length for lunch between. A week consisted of eight working days and two days of rest. The practice of taking a long weekend does not seem to have been unfamiliar to the workmen who from time to time extended their weekend to three days by taking off the first day of the next week. Each month consisted of thirty days (in other words three weeks), which meant that generally they had six rest days per month. Although this may not sound like much time off, one has the impression from the attendance record that the workmen were frequently absent from work for reasons which we might regard as social. The purpose of the daily attendance registers was presumably so that wages could be adjusted to take account of absenteeism. In the registers each workman's name is listed, with days he worked marked in black and excuses for absence noted in red. The registers show what we might consider to be amazing leniency when for example Pendua is reportedly absent from work drinking beer with Khonsu. Frequently when a workman is recorded as being off work celebrating his 'festival', probably his birthday, he is then absent for a subsequent day, and it is probably not too farfetched to suggest that he was recovering from a hangover. Brewing beer for religious festivals occurs frequently as an excuse and the festivals themselves seem to have counted as general holidays on which no work was done. Other absences are more understandable, such as illness (when incidentally another workman acting as physician was often off work too, tending his sick colleague) and also death in the family. In one case it is clear that this is purely an excuse, since one workman actually use the excuse of burying his mother on two separate occasions.

It would be a mistake to assume that once the king's tomb was complete the workmen would be left with no work to carry out, nor would the workmen responsible for completing a particular task in the construction, such as the plastering of the walls, be idle until they were called on to work in the current king's tomb. Clearly there were tombs to be constructed for members of the royal family, in the Valley of the Queens and elsewhere, for which we know the workmen were responsible. It is inconceivable that, with such a skilled workforce to hand, they were not involved in other projects. In fact there is evidence that from time to time workmen would be required to work at other construction sites, such as at Deir el-Bahari and at Karnak. One of the draughtsmen is known from an ostrakon to have been called upon to paint the *neshmet*-barque of Osiris, work which he presumably carried out at the (unknown) temple in question. The Scribe of the Tomb, Neferhotep, is known from an inscription he wrote to have visited the quarries in the Wadi

Hammamat in order to obtain stone for work in the Valley of the Kings during the reign of Ramesses IV, and a map drawn on papyrus, possibly of the same date, records the route to the quarries. There is also a record of an expedition by workmen from Deir el-Medina to Gebel el-Silsila during the reign of Merenptah. All in all, one has the impression that the men were kept busy with a variety of projects. There is also evidence that some of the draughtsmen carried out private commissions (p. 158).

Access to the Valley of the Kings

The route taken by the workmen on the way to work was extremely spectacular. A sloping shoulder of the hillside led from the village up on to a level pathway running along the cliffs from here towards Deir el-Bahari. Shortly before reaching the latter, another rising pathway led up on to a ridge above the Valley of the Kings. Here the workmen had built a series of rest houses (see photograph below).

This was not a really suitable route for bringing tomb equipment; it is surely impossible to imagine dragging a granite sarcophagus up this route, let alone a series of nested stone sarcophagi as found in the tomb of Merenptah (p. 109). Instead funeral objects would surely have been brought up to the valley via the long road which now winds its way up from beside the Carter house, following the route now taken by hundreds of tourist buses. This was

The workmen's huts between Deir el-Medina and the Valley of the Kings

also the official entrance to the valley, the one by which the vizier and other officials came when inspecting the work; for example, a document records that 'the Overseer of the Treasury' and a scribe 'came to the entrance of the Valley with a copy of a letter from Pharaoh'.[4]

Intruders

Scribal records note that there were occasional intruders in the valley. Indeed, there were guards' huts built around the perimeter of the valley to watch for unwelcome visitors, and we have the report of finding a person who seemingly just wandered into the valley: 'The Scribe Amennakht, the official Neferhotep and thirty-two workmen (one being absent) went to the entrance of the Valley and found the donkey which had passed inside, as well as one old man all on his own.'[5]

The latter seems to have been a fairly harmless incident, but from the reign of Ramesses IX we learn of far more serious problems. It was at this time that there seems to have been a personality clash in the area, and one which involved the workmen, in the form of a dispute between the mayor of the East Bank, a man called Paser, and the mayor of the West Bank, called Pawera. Paser complained to the vizier that tombs on the West Bank were regularly being broken into and that Pawera was making no attempt to control the situation. He claimed, moreover, that the tomb of Amenhotep I had even been violated. In light of this accusation, Pawera set out to clear his name by holding a tour of inspection, and we are fortunate that it is recorded in detail in the Abbott Papyrus, now in the British Museum, so that we can virtually trace the footsteps of the commission on its rounds. What really becomes evident is that Pawera attempted to 'whitewash' the situation by taking the commission of inspection to mainly Eleventh and Seventeenth Dynasty tombs (one of which had indeed been robbed). They did, however, inspect the tomb of Amenhotep I and found that it was intact.

They also inspected the tombs of several private individuals and found that they had been pillaged. Pawera seems to have been expecting this to happen and immediately presented the commission with a list of eight thieves, who were arrested at once and interrogated. On the very next day the vizier himself carried out a personal inspection of the Valley of the Queens and found nothing amiss. One of the Deir el-Medina workmen, who had apparently been accused of robbing a queen's tomb, was cleared of this charge. The workmen as a group seem to have been incensed at the accusation against one of their number and they marched en masse to the house of Paser to protest against the unfounded allegations.

Paser was probably disappointed at not proving Pawera's negligence and so complained directly to the king. As a result a great royal tribunal was set up to try the workman in question; he was again acquitted. However, the eight suspected thieves were also tried, and the account of their trial, recorded in the Leopold–Amherst Papyrus, gives us the dramatic account of how these people broke into the tomb of the Seventeenth Dynasty king which the commission had found to have been looted, and stole the gold from the coffins of the king and his wife:

We went to rob the tombs in accordance with our regular habit, and we found the pyramid of King Sekhemre-Shedtawy, the son of Re Sebekemzaf, this being not at all like the pyramids and tombs of the nobles which we habitually went to rob. We took our copper tools and forced a way into the pyramid of this king through its innermost part. We found its underground chambers, and we took lighted candles in our hands and went down. Then we broke through the rubble that we found at the mouth of his recess (?), and found this god lying at the back of his burial-place. And we found the burial place of Queen Nubkhaas his queen situated beside him, it being protected and guarded by plaster and covered with rubble. ...

We opened their outer coffins and their inner coffins in which they lay. We found the noble mummy of this king equipped with a sword. A larger number of amulets and ornaments of gold were upon his neck. His mask of gold was upon him. The noble mummy of the king was completely covered with gold. His coffins were adorned with gold and sliver inside and out and inlaid with all kinds of precious stones. We collected the gold which we found on this noble mummy of this god and on his amulets and jewels which were upon his neck and on the coffins in which he lay. We found the queen in exactly the same state and we collected all that we found on her likewise. We set fire to their coffins. We stole their furniture that we found with them consisting of articles of gold, silver and bronze and divided them up amongst ourselves. And we made into eight portions the gold which we found on these two gods coming from their mummies, amulets, jewels, and coffins, and 20 deben of gold fell to each of the eight of us, making 160 deben of gold, the fragments (?) of the furniture not being included.[6]

The papyrus which records this trial is itself the object of a dramatic story. In 1935, while Jean Capart, curator of the museum in Brussels, was working on some objects brought from Egypt by Leopold II between 1854 and 1864, he came across a wooden statuette inside which was tucked part of a very well preserved papyrus. On it were cartouches which he recognized from a papyrus in the Amherst collection. He then 'had brought from the Library the catalogue of Lord Amherst's papyri ... One can imagine my surprise, indeed my stupefaction, as a single glance at one of the plates of the catalogue revealed the fact that the lower edge of the new papyrus fitted exactly the upper edge of the Amherst.'[7] And this is why the document now bears the name Leopold Amherst.

Other tomb-robbery papyri have survived, and in one of these a later suspect protests: 'I saw the punishment which was inflicted on the thieves in the time of vizier Khaemwaset. Is it likely that I would seek a death like that?'[8] This, of course, implies that the tomb robbers of the Leopold–Amherst Papyrus were put to death.

Investigations the following year found that in fact one of the tombs in the Valley of the Queens, that of Queen Isis, had indeed been robbed, and eight workmen were accused of involvement: stolen goods were recovered from their homes in the village and they were arrested and taken away. As a result new Foremen were appointed to supervise the men, probably reflecting the lack of trust now felt by the administration.

Payments

As wages for their work the inhabitants of the village were provided not only with their homes but with food provisions too. This was calculated according to the number of days worked per month. The main constituent was an amount of grain, in the form of emmer for bread-making and barley for brewing beer. The highest-paid members of the workforce were the Foremen, who received 5.5 *khar* of emmer and 2 *khar* of barley per month, and the Scribe, who received approximately the same. The basic workmen were generally paid at a lower rate, 4 *khar* of emmer and 1.5 *khar* of barley per month.[9] Four *khar* of emmer is approximately 300 litres of grain, which comes to 10 litres per day. By comparing this with the grain allowances known from other cultures we find that the workmen of Deir el-Medina seem to have received approximately seven times more grain than a Roman workman and ten times more grain than was consumed by Europeans from the mid-sixteenth to early eighteenth centuries AD. One assumes that these wages were intended to support the families of the workmen too.

The grain ration was further supplemented by supplies of fish, vegetables and wood (presumably for cooking purposes). Supplies of other commodities were also received from time to time, including some special types of cake (probably supplied at the time of religious festivals), dates and, most importantly of all, water, since the village was out in the desert and had no water supply of its own. Taking into account that the crew received housing from the state, one is led to conclude that these workers were not badly off. It is this that must have differentiated them most from the majority of the rest of the local West Bank population, other than those working in the temples.

In addition they seem to have been provided with a group of slave women who worked in rotation in the houses of the village, in particular grinding the emmer to produce the bread for each household. As well as regular visits from the water man, they were also provided with a pottery delivery man. It is understandable that without water it was hard for the villagers to make their own pottery, and so from time to time a man came round bringing jars to replace those that had broken in the meantime.

Wages were usually expected on the 28th day of the month, but delays in deliveries seem almost the rule rather than the exception. On an ostrakon now in Chicago a scribe wrote to the vizier that the workforce was in a bad state: 'it is not easy shifting stones around! The six measures of emmer have been taken from us and we are given six measures of earth instead. Please do something my lord so that we receve our payment. We are almost dead and can hardly stay alive.' One should bear in mind that the last statement is almost certainly an exaggeration. However a little later during year 29 of the reign of Ramesses III the workmen stopped working on the king's tomb in order to protest against this state of affairs. The events are recorded in some detail in the so-called Turin Strike Papyrus. When their patience ran out the whole workforce left the village complaining of hunger and they held a sit-down protest at the temple of Tuthmose III. They were pacified and returned to work until, again upset, they made their way to the Ramesseum, even managing to get into the inner rooms of the temple. The mayor of the West Bank came to assure them that all the storehouses were empty although he somehow managed to provide them with fifty-five loaves to keep them quiet for a night. The next day saw a demonstration march, including the women and children of the village, down to the temple of Sety I where the workmen believed there were more supplies to be had. The story repeated itself with increasing frequency during the next few months, with the villagers becoming more and more exasperated with the lack of action by the vizier. The impression one receives is that there was not really a lack of food at that period but simply the lack of will to ensure that the workforce were properly supplied – perhaps there was too much corruption in the bureaucracy of the time. It is even suggested by some that it was at this time that tomb robbery began in the Theban necropolis.

Trade

A large number of ostraka have survived which record the buying and selling of goods between individuals in the village. These texts are obviously of great interest to economic historians, and show that a moneyless system of trade existed in the village. If you wanted to buy something from a person you gave them other goods in exchange for it. Suppose, for example, that you were fitting out a tomb for your grandfather and wished to buy a suitable coffin for the tomb, then you might have to give in return 3 *khar* of emmer, a *keskeset*-basket, a tunic, 2 *kebes*-baskets, a mat and a *denit*-basket. The way that this exchange was calculated was that a value in *deben* (a copper weight of 0.91 kg) was established for the coffin, in this case approximately 20 *deben*.[10] Then you would give items of differing values of *deben* until you reached the agreed figure. For example the emmer was worth 6 *deben*, and the tunic 5 *deben*, and by adding items together in this way the purchaser would eventually reach a figure acceptable to the seller. Presumably either the items you gave in return for the coffin were of use to the seller or else he would use them to trade for something he required. Prices of commodities

A stall at a marketplace on the riverbank, from the tomb of Ipuy (TT217)

vary enormously and one imagines that, as today, haggling played an important role in all transactions. Also, in the case of a coffin, the amount of decoration work would cause price fluctuations: one coffin is recorded as being traded for a pig, worth only 2 or 3 *deben*. However, this may have been only one payment for a coffin which was being paid for in instalments. The most expensive coffin recorded in the documents was one worth 80 *deben* when unfinished, to which 65 *deben*'s worth of decoration was added.

Some texts speak of trade in cattle and donkeys, and it has been suggested that this indicates that the inhabitants kept such animals on land outside the village. At first sight this seems logical; however, comparison with modern-day Qurna suggests that it is perfectly possible to keep cattle and donkeys in cramped conditions within a village set on the desert. Like their modern counterparts, the inhabitants would have had to take their animals down to the cultivation to graze in the morning and bring them back in the evening. Similarly they would have had to provide them with water from the supply brought up to the village. The bones of poultry, sheep and pigs, as well as of cattle, were found in the village rubbish heaps, indicating that the villagers were regular eaters of a variety of meat, and it is likely that the animals would have been slaughtered at the village. We do know, however, that some of the workmen owned fields, and it is likely that they retained some land tenancy from the time when they, or their predecessors, first entered government employment. The variations in the numbers employed on the royal tombs, as well as the inevitable increasing size of the population, must have meant that from time to time members of the community moved out of the village, and it is likely that they would have returned to their family tenancies, although it is virtually certain that they retained their connection with the village and may have returned to it when the workforce was expanded again.

In fact, far from being totally cut off from the rest of the inhabitants of Thebes, the inhabitants of the village seem to have been regular visitors to the riverbank to buy goods there in exchange for their grain and other goods. A vivid scene from the tomb of Ipuy (TT217) depicts the area by the river, showing boats being unloaded at the riverside while women sit trading goods from the baskets in front of them. Most of their customers are carrying sacks (of grain?), while one man has a net of fish to offer. Documents show that some of the workmen owned small buildings in this area; these were apparently partly for storing goods to be traded, and it also seems that relatives of the workmen may have lived in this area; it is possible that members of the workforce who had been laid off went to trade in this area.

Religious life

To judge by the number of chapels to various deities in the village and its neighbourhood, the inhabitants of Deir el-Medina seem to have been very devout people. To the north of the village there was a small temple dedicated to Amun which had been erected in the Eighteenth Dynasty and was

Deir el-Medina, tomb of Inherkhau (TT359): damaged scene showing important kings and patrons of the necropolis: Ahmose Nefertari, Ramesses I, Nebhepetre Mentuhotep II, Amenhotep, Seqenenre

enlarged and improved by Ramesses II, and there were numerous small shrines dedicated to Amun, Ptah, Hathor, Thoth and Seshat, Khnum and Taweret, as well as several foreign deities. Particular local favourites were also revered, such as the goddess Meretseger, a cobra-goddess associated with the mountain overlooking the Valley of the Kings, and the deceased kings Tuthmose III and Ramesses II. However, from the early Eighteenth Dynasty onwards, the main focus of religious worship of the population of Deir el-Medina was the cult of Amenhotep I, particularly in the form of 'Amenhotep of the village', and his mother Ahmose-Nefertari. There does not seem to have been a temple dedicated to their worship in the village, although small shrines were set up there (p. 202), and they were depicted in the tombs.

The cult was particularly associated with the giving of oracles, which took the form of the god, Amenhotep I, responding positively or negatively to questions put to him. The mechanics of this seem to have been that the image of the god would be carried in procession by his priests, and petitioners would put questions to the god. The divine image would move to indicate 'yes' or 'no'. Since the priesthood of this cult came from the workmen themselves, it is obvious that the response would be some form of consensus between the priests who were carrying the divine image. Such processions seem to have been fairly regular events in the yearly calendar, and were usually a part of religious festivals connected with his cult. One festival involved the carrying of Amenhotep I's statue into the Valley of the Kings, and another may have been associated with the anniversary of his death.

The majority of the chapels were erected by the workmen at the northern end of the village, close to, and some of them in fact enclosed by, the later Ptolemaic temple. There was also a shrine close to some rest houses which were constructed by the workmen on the ridge between the village and the Valley of the Kings, probably dedicated to Meretseger and Ptah. In addition to these, the workmen seem to have carved a number of rock shrines on the path to the Valley of the Queens, decorated with scenes of individuals before various deities. One particularly large shrine is dedicated to Ptah and Meretseger.

The main holidays associated with the cult of Amun-Re at Karnak were celebrated within the village, as well as the festivals associated with the cult of Amenhotep I, and, not surprisingly, it seems that the Festival of the Valley (pp. 78–80) was a particular favourite of the workmen, when the great god Amun himself, together with his family, came across the river to visit the West Bank. There are a number of references to the workmen's participation in this festival, including a depiction of the arrival of the god's barque and the king officiating in the ceremonies with some senior members of the workforce present. An ostrakon records the involvement of the Scribe of the Tomb in the preparations of the Opet Festival (pp. 67–9). As well as the days of the festivals themselves which were holidays, workmen frequently appear to have taken time off brewing beer for consumption at the imminent festival. Since we know that one such festival lasted for four days, it is not hard to imagine that these events did involve the drinking of large quantities of beer, and it has been suggested that an excess of food and drink may have been a necessary part of religious festivals.

In addition to their formal religious devotion as evidenced by the large number of shrines they erected, the workmen also seem to have practised a form of ancestor cult within their own homes. Stelae showing a deceased workman, sometimes with a figure libating or censing him, were set into the walls of the second room of many of the houses. The deceased person in question seems to have been a recently dead relative of the family and this was a way of retaining a link with him after death. Similarly, small figures of the head and shoulders of a family member were set into niches of some of the houses and seem to have been the focus of an ancestor cult. Many more of these 'ancestral busts' have been found outside the houses themselves, including a very large number which were found in a series of shrines close by the workmen's rest houses on the ridge.

Disputes

Within a small enclosed community like this one, it is likely that personality conflicts were rife. In some cases this seems to be due to a person feeling he has been overlooked during promotion. One of the prime examples of this is the well-known conflict between two individuals, Amennakht and Paneb. It began when the foreman of the right 'side', Neferhotep, died without leaving behind a son to fill his office. His brother was Amennakht, who felt that he had a right by virtue of being Neferhotep's brother to be the next foreman. At this time a certain Paneb, who had until then seemingly been a mere workman, presented the vizier with a 'gift' of five slaves, whereupon the vizier immediately appointed him as the new foreman. Paneb already had a bad reputation in the village, having made death threats against many villagers, but now Amennakht, of course, had a personal grievance against him. So he prepared a list of crimes committed by Paneb and presented it to the vizier; the list included misuse of government equipment and the workmen themselves for private purposes, having affairs with the women of the village, stealing from tombs, including royal tombs, and even murder. Although some of this may be exaggeration on the part of Amennakht, there are enough other documents supporting some of the claims made against Paneb that one is forced to conclude that he probably was a bad lot. At any rate he was later replaced by a foreman called Aanakht.

This case was almost certainly out of the ordinary, and there are many examples of other disputes between individuals from the village, ranging from disputes about the settlement of property and non-payment for goods received to accusations of theft and blasphemy.

Burial places

Inhabitants were buried very close to the village, in a cemetery on the terraced hillside to the west, and workmen regularly seem to have taken time off from working on the royal tomb to work on the construction of their own tombs. The tombs they constructed for themselves were rather different from those now known as the 'Tombs of the Nobles'. They consisted of a courtyard into which was cut a burial shaft leading to the decorated burial chamber, or chambers depending on the individual's means and status. Above this at ground level there was a chapel of one or more rooms which contained a funerary stela and which was surmounted with a small pyramid made of brick and rubble and topped with a stone pyramidion. The main subterranean chamber of such a tomb usually had a vaulted roof and was very brightly decorated. We are fortunate that a number of the tombs are still in an excellent state of preservation, giving us an impression of the vivid colours employed. The decoration in the burial chambers is frequently of scenes from religious texts, scenes involving ceremonies before Amenhotep I and Ahmose-Nefertari, and depictions of the deceased's family and colleagues.

Cross-section through a workman's tomb at Deir el-Medina

Deir el-Medina, tomb of Sennedjem (TT1): deceased and wife adoring deities within a shrine

The end of an era

There seems to have been a great deal of turmoil in the Theban area at this time, even amounting to virtual civil war, and the community moved inside the walls of the nearby temple at Medinet Habu. From the end of the reign of Ramesses XI it seems that the tombs in the Valley of the Kings began to be systematically plundered, and the royal mummies moved to various locations before finally ending up in caches at Deir el-Bahari and in the tomb of Amenhotep II in the Valley of the Kings (pp. 98–100). Some confidence in the Deir el-Medina men must have returned because the scribe Butehamun and two foremen of the workmen are recorded as being involved in this important task, at the temple of Ramesses III at Medinet Habu. The house occupied by Butehamun can be seen at the rear of this temple.

Although they no longer lived in the village, former inhabitants used to return to visit family tombs and worship at the temple of Amenhotep I. The empty houses were used for storage until they decayed beyond all usefulness. What happened to the villagers after this time is not clear, as no further mention of them is made after this period. Seven centuries later Ptolemy IV built a temple dedicated to Hathor and Maat on the site of the earlier village shrines and opposite the small temple of Amun. And when Christianity reached Egypt the temple was converted into a Coptic church, and a monastery, or *deir*, was established there.

Other settlements at Thebes

Our knowledge of other settlements in the Theban area is very limited in comparison with the information from Deir el-Medina. The earliest evidence we have of habitation here is at Tarif, where remains from the early Predynastic period, the late Predynastic period and the Old Kingdom have been found.

It is clear that for most, if not all, of Egyptian dynastic history the major settlement was, as now, on the East Bank, and it is likely that it was for most of the ancient past situated around the great temple of Amun-Re at Karnak. Recent excavation work has revealed, beneath the current temple, remains of the pre-New Kingdom settlement and shown that the expansion of the temple during this period resulted in the displacement of the population from the city of the time, which was razed to the ground, to a new settlement further away from the temple. Only a few remains of the houses of the new city have been found so far, because they lie in the cultivated land, and so it is not possible to say a great deal about the layout of the city of the New Kingdom and later. However, the remains of the old city from below the temple show that it had been laid out on a grid pattern, as is familiar from other sites, and it is likely that the new settlement would have been laid out in a similar way. The Karnak complex, including as it did a number of small temples within and outside its walls, must have employed a very large number of people, both as priests and as their associated staff, and these were known to have lived in houses within the precincts. For example, a number of houses have been uncovered in the area around the sacred lake which date to the Third Intermediate Period.

With the construction of the Luxor Temple to the south during the Eighteenth Dynasty it is likely that the settlement expanded southwards. Of course, the presence of the modern town in this area again restricts the archaeological work that can be undertaken, and we know next to nothing about the town in this area. Although we cannot really do more than guess at the size of ancient Thebes, if we consider the size of the city of Akhetaten, purpose-built during the reign of Akhenaten, we can form an estimate of the possible population during the New Kingdom. It has been calculated that the population of Akhetaten was between twenty thousand and thirty thousand. It is likely that the population of Thebes would have been less than this, perhaps fifteen thousand to twenty thousand,[11] as the Akhetaten population included a large number of courtiers who would normally reside at Memphis.

Inscriptions tell us that within the walls of the temple at Karnak there was a royal palace, which was probably made of mud brick because no trace of it has yet been found. The purpose of such a palace may have been as a residence for the king when he was present within the temple. Similarly, palaces

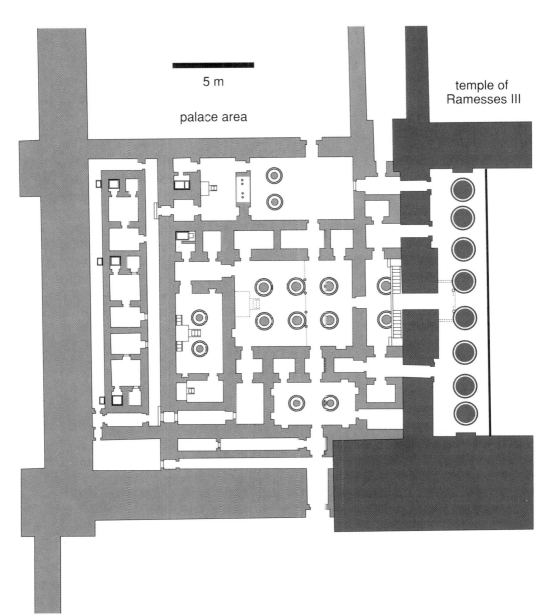

5 m

palace area

temple of
Ramesses III

Plan of the palace at Medinet Habu

have been found within the walls of all the West Bank temples from the reign of Horemheb onwards, including the Ramesseum and Medinet Habu, and they would presumably have served the same purpose there. In particular, during the Festival of the Valley, the barques of Amun, Mut and Khonsu were taken across the river to the temple of Hatshepsut at Deir el-Bahari and then on to the funerary temple of the reigning king, where they would rest overnight, and it is likely that the king would remain overnight within the temple in the palace provided for him there. It has, however, also been suggested that these palaces were designed not actually to be used but rather to provide the king with a residence in the next life.

Another important palace site lies at the southern end of the site, the area now called Malqata, to the south of Medinet Habu. This was chosen by Amenhotep III as the location for the palace and associated buildings he needed for the celebration of two of his jubilee festivals. In fact, when the time for preparing for his second jubilee came round, it was found that the first palace was not suitable and was removed, a new one being built over it. The settlement around this must have been very large, and it is not clear whether it was inhabited only briefly for the period around the jubilees or whether it was in use for an extended period. An enormous artificial lake, the remains of which are now called the Birket Habu, was constructed for the enjoyment of the royal couple.

The local inhabitants who did not live in any of these larger settlements were most likely tenant farmers, working the land which provided grain for the temples of the area, and hence for the state. Of their houses and their lifestyle we know almost nothing other than from their interactions with officialdom at the time when the temple grain was collected or from the brief glimpses we get of them as incidental components in tomb paintings or the like.

However, on the back of one of the tomb-robbery papyri (British Museum 10068) we are lucky enough to have a list of houses lying at the edge of the desert on the West Bank, apparently enumerated from north to south, starting by the temple of Sety I and continuing down to a settlement just south of Medinet Habu. The papyrus dates to year 12 of an unnamed king, who is thought to be most likely to be Ramesses XI, and it shows that there were ten houses between the Sety temple and the Ramesseum, and fourteen between there and Medinet Habu. Maiunehes, the settlement at the latter, contained 155 houses, which, it is estimated, would have accommodated a population of about a thousand people. The occupations of those listed as living at Maiunehes consisted mainly of administrators, including members of the civil service of the period, priests, craftsmen and people connected with agriculture, who comprised nearly a third of the population. The papyrus makes no mention of Deir el-Medina, and it probably also omits any dwellings nearer to the river.

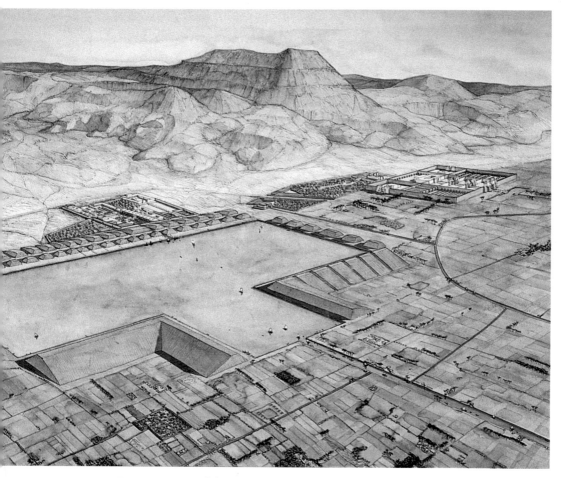

Reconstruction of the palace of Amenhotep III at Malqata

We can form an overall picture of life in the Theban area during the New Kingdom, albeit a rather sketchy one. On the East Bank there is a relatively large settlement, spreading from the area around the temples at Karnak down to the Luxor Temple, and dominated by these two complexes and the activities surrounding them, set in the surrounding farm land. The West Bank is generally much more rural in character, comprising tenant farmers working the arable land, and a number of small communities around the funerary temples at the desert edge. To the south is a larger settlement and group of administrators, whilst a bustling community resides at Deir el-Medina.

THEBES AFTER THE PHARAOHS

It is hardly possible to do justice to Thebes after 332 BC in the short space of this chapter, but it is important to make the attempt as it receives so little attention in many general publications. Egyptology has a tendency to end historical narratives with the conquest of the country by Alexander the Great in 332 BC, and this is nowhere more true than in most courses taught to students. Manetho's system of dynasties is largely to blame for this, since it also ceases at this point, and no Egyptologist has yet succeeded in escaping from his overall chronological structure. However, the material from after the Thirtieth Dynasty relating to certain aspects of the study of the culture, notably with reference to written material, then becomes so abundant that we think it is at our own peril that we ignore these later phases.

The Graeco-Roman period

A brief historical outline of this period was given at the end of Chapter 2. Although the Egyptians had been under the control of foreign powers before – the Hyksos, the Assyrians, the Persians – the periods had never been particularly long, and neither had the foreigner tried seriously to integrate its own culture into Egypt. With the break-up of the empire of Alexander the Great, Egypt was indeed independent, but none the less under the control of a non-native power. Greeks had been present in the country since at least the seventh to sixth centuries BC (for example in the colony of Naukratis in the Delta), and this meant that there was a solid base of influence on which to build. Now that Greeks were the masters, Greek governors could be put into places of influence, and it is clear that they moved more and more into positions of power; soon Greek came to rival and rapidly overtake demotic as the language of official transactions in some places. One aspect which was, however, very persistent was the use of and respect for the ancient religion and its associated architectural forms. Both the Ptolemies and Roman emperors built new temples and added to older monuments, all in styles which follow on naturally from their dynastic predecessors. Texts in these temples tend to be more informative about the rituals they represent than did earlier ones, which suggests that much of the background to the inscribing of these texts was to ensure their survival and perhaps even make them clearer to those for whom many of the old rituals were becoming difficult to comprehend.

Interior of the lid of the wooden coffin of Soter, showing a figure of the goddess Nut: the painting style is influenced by Graeco-Roman art. British Museum, EA6708

Thebes has its share of Graeco-Roman material, although most of the new temple construction was on a smaller scale than seen at major sites elsewhere, such as Dendera or Edfu. The existence of large quantities of texts, and a lesser amount of archaeological material, means that we can paint a reasonable view of life and death at this time in the 'Memnonia', as the area was most generally known.

Elite burial customs

The construction of new tombs was very rare at this time, and the addition of decoration to older ones even more so. The most elaborate burials found so far have been located in reused tombs or even houses of earlier periods, thus continuing the practices of earlier times. One intact burial of the late Ptolemaic period has been found, that of Montuzaf, found by Rhind in the late 1850s; the finds are now in Edinburgh. The precise location of this burial has never been established, but it seems to have lain somewhere at the bottom of the hill of Sheikh Abd el-Qurna, probably in the reused tomb of a New Kingdom official. Several elaborate burials were found in it, and it was a son of this man called Pamontu who probably usurped the sarcophagus of the Divine Adoratrice Ankhnesneferibre and moved it to a tomb above Deir el-Medina for his burial (see p. 137). Elite Roman burials have also been located in at least two places, one, that of the family of Pebos (c.AD 100), at Deir el-Medina, and another, of the family of Soter (first century AD) in the Nineteenth Dynasty tomb of Djehutymose (TT32).

But most of our information about burial customs in the Ptolemaic period comes from a set of textual archives which are in effect unique to Thebes.

The choachytes

These remarkable sources are known as the archives of the Theban choachytes. 'Choachyte' is a Greek term for a minor priest whose job it was to procure tombs for the dead, and then to tend their mummies, in particular to 'pour water' for them, for which service they were paid. In this sense they are the descendants of a category of priest about whom we have known since at least the Old Kingdom – the *ka* priest. They are important because a large quantity of documents in Greek or Demotic have been identified as coming from a number of Theban family archives, which contain immense amounts of information about the area. The earliest go back to the fifth century BC, while the majority date to the Ptolemaic period. The archives contain all sorts of documents: sales of houses, revenues from their work, complaints, receipts, tax payments, divisions of inheritance, legal disputes and lists are the most common. While we know about the taxes the choachytes had to pay, the texts are silent on the actual charges they made for their services.

The tombs procured by the choachytes were of two types. An area at the cultivation end of the Assasif area on the West Bank was found to be covered with small brick-built tombs of the Ptolemaic era, and there are many references in the texts to such tombs. These were among the last new tombs to be constructed at Thebes (see below for some of the Roman period). The texts also refer to rock tombs where mummies were stored, and it is clear from this that the choachytes were reusing earlier tombs as places for new burials. The best-known of these is Theban private tomb TT157, that of the high priest of Amun in the reign of Ramesses II Nebwenenef, which tomb was called 'Thunabounoun' in Greek; this is the same Nebwenenef whose small temple was mentioned on p. 91. The tomb is very large, and it is known to contain many graffiti of Ptolemaic date. Other tombs mentioned in the papyri were clearly smaller, and held bodies relating to particular families, or to groups. Such an example is 'the tomb of Herieus, the chief builder, and his brothers'; another is the tomb of the iron-workers or smiths. Lists of the mummies which were stored in these tombs are found among the archive material; often they are part of a will, and form part of a choachyte's inheritance and could be passed on from one generation to another. We assume that only the mummies which produced an income for the choachytes were recorded; presumably those for which payment had ceased were quietly buried in locations not mentioned in the documents. Robbery from tombs at this time was not unknown; a papyrus in the Louvre indicates a theft in 127/6 BC, but the items stolen were the tools which the choachytes kept there, not items belonging to the dead. The value of these tools (10 talents) was probably enough to keep a family of five for a whole year.

There is a considerable amount of archaeological evidence from tombs which supports what we read in the texts, although only in the case of the 'Thunabounoun' tomb can we equate the two sources with precision. Many tombs have been excavated which contain mummies which must be of post-dynastic date, although it is usually extremely difficult to date them more precisely as they bear no names, seem to have no burial equipment and are not placed in coffins; research into mummification is not so far advanced that a mummy can be easily dated from its method of manufacture. Our own work in tombs TT253, 254, and 294 revealed the remains of close on three hundred people, most of whom we suspect were post-dynastic in date; work in Deir el-Medina in the 1920s to 1940s revealed that this area was used as a cemetery at the Ptolemaic period as well.

The choachytes themselves probably lived mainly in Medinet Habu (Djeme in Egyptian) and also owned plots of land elsewhere on the West Bank. In 109 BC they formed a guild which they called 'the association of Amenemopet'; as they had been in existence for several centuries, we can only speculate at what threat might have compelled them to associate like this. It may be no coincidence that their records do not continue long beyond this date.

We have more specific information about a house on the East Bank which was owned by the choachytes, and which functioned as an office, and a temporary storage place for mummies on their way to burial in the west. This house seems to have stood to the south-west of the temple of Karnak, as we learn from the numerous documents which refer to it, many of which relate to lawsuits about ownership of part of it. This was part of the southern area of the city of Thebes, emphasizing the fact that the ancient town was still to the north of modern Luxor.

Roman mass burials and the settlement of Djeme

The choachyte system does not seem to have survived into the Roman period, but the presence of many mass burials clearly of that date suggests that some similar system may have existed, no record of which has survived. Large numbers of bodies of this date have been found in the Valley of the Queens and Deir el-Medina, reusing older tombs, and there are probably also examples from New Kingdom private tombs. A new cemetery of mud-brick tombs was constructed to the north of Medinet Habu in the second to third century AD, on the site of the mortuary temple of Ay and Horemheb (p. 84). This cemetery belonged to the village of Djeme, which was built in and around the enclosure wall of the Medinet Habu temples, and was still the major settlement on the West Bank, as it had been from the end of the New Kingdom.

The Ptolemaic temple of Deir el-Medina. Visible inside the enclosure are the shrines of the workmen of the New Kingdom

Medinet Habu: the walls of the settlement of Djeme

Temple construction

Ptolemaic and Roman construction at Karnak and at Medinet Habu has been mentioned earlier (pp. 65–6, 91). The primary monument of this period which can be visited today is the small temple at Deir el-Medina, dedicated, as were some of its forebears, to Hathor, and it was one of the last temples to be built inside a walled fortress-like enclosure. Ptolemies IV, VI and VIII were responsible for its construction. There was also an important Graeco-Roman cemetery at Deir el-Medina.

Two further small temples were constructed on the West Bank. Just south of Medinet Habu lies the small temple of Qasr el-Aguz, built by Ptolemy VIII for the god Thoth, and also with reference to Ptolemaic ancestors. Almost 4 km further south lies the Roman temple of Deir es-Shelwit, with decoration from the year of the four emperors (68 BC) and also from the time of Hadrian. The cult at Deir el-Bahari also seems to have been revived in Ptolemaic times; a small shrine was inserted into the middle of the remains of the Hatshepsut temple by Ptolemy VIII, and the cults there seem to have been mainly those of Imhotep (or his Greek equivalent, Asklepios) and Amenhotep son of Hapu. Both these individuals, one Memphite, one Theban, were regarded as possessing healing powers, and thus the temple became a place of pilgrimage.

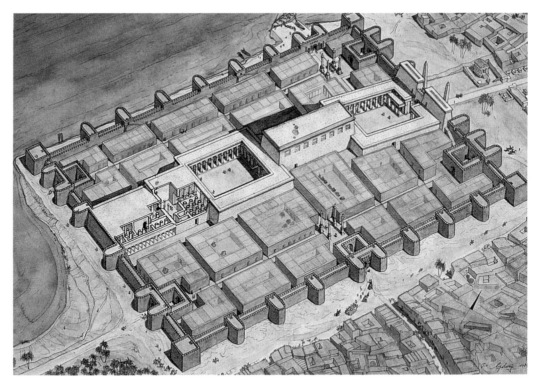

Reconstruction of the Roman camp built around the Temple of Luxor

The Roman camp at Luxor

A Roman military camp was established around the temple of Luxor very close to the beginning of the third century AD, perhaps fifty years or so after it ceased to have any remaining religious functions. The enclosure, arranged so that the temple was roughly in the centre, was built mainly of bricks, but a number of pharaonic stone blocks were incorporated into it. The entrance pylon was modified so as to serve as a gate, and images relevant to the insignia of the legion occupying it were painted in a room off the first court. From its size it seems likely that it housed about fifteen hundred men.

Tourism: Colossi of Memnon, the Osymandeion, the Valley of the Kings

We have already mentioned that the Ptolemaic sanctuary at Deir el-Bahari was a place of pilgrimage. Once Egypt became part of the classical world, word went out of the exotic things to be seen there, and it appears that there was a considerable number of visits by tourists to Thebes, particularly between the third century BC and the second century AD. Two main sights drew the eyes of the ancient tourist: the Colossi of Memnon, and the tombs in the Valley of the Kings. Visitors came from all parts of the ancient world, and from all levels of society.

They left graffiti and more official inscriptions on the Colossi, and the two statues were mentioned by a number of classical authors. Distinguished visitors were many, including the emperors Hadrian and Septimus Severus. The particular attraction of the Colossi was the fact that the northern of them was said to sing at dawn, and the myth developed around it that this statue represented Memnon (a Trojan hero, killed by Achilles in the famous war), and the sound was his call to his mother. The 'singing' apparently started after an earthquake in 27 BC; theories abound as to its source, ranging from the result of expansion of the stones at the onset of the heat of the sun through to an elaborate tourist hoax. However, the performances ceased after the statue was repaired in AD 199, in the reign of Septimus Severus.

The royal tombs were known as 'syringes'[1] to the classical travellers; approximately 2,100 graffiti in Latin and Greek, dating between 278 BC and AD 537, attest the presence of visitors in the royal tombs. They are concentrated in ten tombs, obviously those which had lain open since pharaonic times, and attest the curiosity of the age. Visitors took either of the modern routes to the valley, and often left their marks on this route. However, neither emperor who visited the Colossi seems to have gone to the valley.

Another attraction, one described in great detail by Diodorus Siculus (I, 47–50), was the large 'tomb of Osymandias', the Ramesseum. This description has been shown to be substantially accurate, and in fact sheds much light on statues and structures which are now more damaged.

The Coptic, late Roman or Byzantine period

Christianity is said to have come to Egypt very early in the new era: St Mark is traditionally credited with bringing it to Egypt, although whether he actually visited in AD 43 and 61 is questionable. It is likely that the new faith took hold among the Greek population of Alexandria before spreading to more indigenous people.

An Egyptian Orthodox Christian is referred to as a 'Copt', a corruption of an Arabic word used to refer to them. This in turn is usually derived from the Greek 'Aigyptios' (from which comes our word Egypt), thought to be based on one of the ancient names for the area of Memphis, 'Hutkaptah', 'the temple of the ka of Ptah'. The Coptic church adheres to the Monophysite doctrine, that the divine and human natures of Christ are one and the same, and has been regarded as heretical by the majority Greek Orthodox Church since the various doctrinal councils in the fourth and fifth centuries AD, culminating in the Council of Chalcedon in 451.

Egypt is the traditional home of Christian monasticism. St Anthony of Egypt (c.AD 251–356) is usually credited as the founding father of this practice, and in that period many communities sprang up, often loosely organized. Subsequent to his death in AD 321, St Pachom is particularly associated as one of the founders of the more organized type of community. But there was also persecution from the Roman emperors at various times, as under Decius and Valerian, and the most dramatic was also the last, in AD 303 during the reign of Diocletian (AD 284–305). So severe was this that the Coptic Church uses a year-dating system which counts from the accession of Diocletian. Once the Roman empire turned officially to Christianity with Constantine (AD 313), monasticism flourished; there is evidence of communities in the later reign of that emperor (c.AD 330). Many hundreds of such institutions flourished between AD 400 and 800, and we will see that Thebes was no exception. Coptic monks tended either to be in these organized monastic communities or to live as ascetic hermits, in caves or in the desert, away from most of humanity but coming into occasional contact with them. The stories of many of these monks and hermits were written down, forming the core of a collection of texts known as the 'Lives of the Desert Fathers', often called by its Latin name *Apophthegmata Patrum*.

The caves and tombs of the Theban hills presented suitable environments for those who wished not to live in a tight-knit community, and tombs all over the site, from the Valley of the Queens, through the tombs of the Nobles, to the Valley of the Kings, bear witness to the existence of anchorites from this period; a colourful Coptic sanctuary was found on the so-called Thoth Hill in the 1990s. There were also several monasteries in the Theban area, and the legacy of this can be seen in some modern place names: Arabic *deir* means monastery, and thus Deir el-Bahari means 'the northern monastery' and Deir el-Medina 'the monastery of the city'. 'Deir el-Bahari', built on top of the temple of Hatshepsut, has been examined since the late 1890s and shown to be the monastery of St Phoibammon, founded in the sixth century AD. The community which gave its name to Deir el-Medina was mainly situated in the Ptolemaic temple, while another large site on the top of the hill of Dra Abu el-Naga, known as Deir el-Bakhit, has never really been explored. A number of small communities used a group of tombs as living quarters, but many structures have suffered in the search for pharaonic remains beneath. The best excavated of all is the monastery of Epiphanius, constructed in the forecourt of Middle Kingdom tomb TT103 of Dagi and facing Deir el-Bahari, and this has revealed a wealth of information about life in Thebes in Coptic times.

Islamic Egypt

The next major change to reach Thebes, and that which was without doubt
the most momentous to affect Egypt over its long history, was the Arab conquest in AD 642. Egypt at that date owed allegiance to the Byzantine Empire
in Constantinople, but it does not appear that there was any great native
resistance to the Arabs at first. However, as time went on, the Arabs pressed
harder for the conversion of the country to Islam, and this met with various
revolts in the eighth century AD. This in turn led to a more active persecution
of Christians, which, coupled with taxation policies towards the monasteries,
must to some extent have caused the decline in a number of the communities
which is evident about that time. As more of the population converted to
Islam, the base on which the monasteries could draw for both human and
material resources continued to diminish. This decline is attested in Thebes
too, since the monastery of St Phoibammon was in the second half of the
eighth century perhaps the only active monastery in the Theban region. By
the end of that century this too had ceased to exist, and the only traces of
later activity in it are a number of visitors' graffiti which continue sporadi-
cally until the thirteenth century.

*Remains of the
monastery of
St Phoibammon on
top of the temple
of Hatshepsut at
Deir el-Bahari.
The individual beside
the tower is believed
to be Howard
Carter's brother*

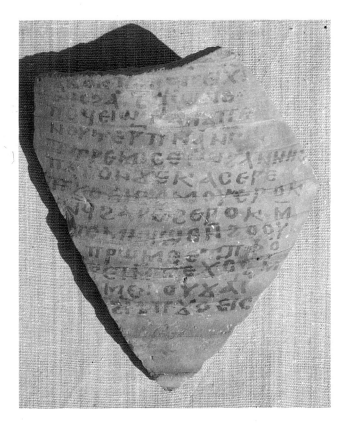

A Coptic ostrakon,
found in excavations
in the tomb of
Senneferi (TT99)

(Below)
A boat in procession
in the modern festival
of Abu el-Haggag in
Luxor

We now enter a real 'dark age' as far as events in Thebes are concerned, because medieval Egyptian history is almost entirely Cairo-centred. At some point in this obscure period an important local Muslim holy man was buried in Thebes, Abu el-Haggag. His tomb was placed in a mosque which was built over part of the First Courtyard of Luxor Temple,[2] and this mosque has great local importance, such that it has proved impossible to relocate it where it would not affect the ancient monument beneath. In fact the mosque has been surreptitiously extended at least once in the past fifty years. Each year there is a festival of the saint, which is the most important local celebration in the area, and which, with its procession of imitation boats, is surely in some faint local way a link with the Opet Festival of the New Kingdom.

The mosque of Abu el-Haggag in the First Courtyard of Luxor Temple

The occasional traveller did venture south of Cairo, such as an anonymous Italian in 1589, and two French priests who were the first to mention visits to the temples of Luxor and Karnak in 1668. As early as 1714, during a voyage by Paul Lucas, the hostility of the local population to visitors is recorded, something that would feature in most later travellers' accounts. From this point on, the history of Thebes is inextricably linked with the European search for antiquities.

The rediscovery of Thebes

We observed above that the medieval European associations with Egypt were exclusively Cairo-orientated. A particular trade between the two regions was in mummies, but not mummies for their antiquarian or even anatomical value. Ground-up mummy[3] was a prized medicine in Europe, and the major source was clearly ancient bodies from the sands of Egypt. There is no evidence, however, that this material came from Thebes.

Until this point the area of Luxor had not been equated with ancient Thebes. The man who is usually credited with making this association was Claude Sicard, a Jesuit priest who visited Upper Egypt several times between 1707 and 1721. In his letters he mentions the two great East Bank temples, and he also visited the Colossi of Memnon and the Ramesseum, as well as the Valley of the Kings. Much more is to be learned from the accounts of two travellers who visited in 1737–8, F. L. Norden and R. Pococke. Both visited some of the private tombs, and Pococke left plans of two which can still be identified. Pococke was also one of the first to describe some of the tombs in the Valley of the Kings. Both make reference to the local inhabitants, the area at this time already being known as 'Gournei' (Qurna); they gave Norden a great deal of concern, and Pococke's passage was eased only by the fact that he had a letter of introduction to the local sheikh. At this point some of the local population was living in the plain, but some might also have lived in the tombs, and it is abundantly obvious that they were aggressive and difficult to deal with. This is often put down to their nefarious practices and hard-nosed dealing in the antiquities trade, but it would appear from these early sources that it might have been deeper in their nature, possibly associated with a suspicion of all but local authority. It seems likely that the occupation of the tombs in a large way happened at around the time that Europeans were becoming interested in antiquities, so as to be nearer the sources of potential wealth. A map produced by Edward Lane in c.1826/7 marks the conventional village at the north of the site as 'ruined'.[4]

The Scottish explorer James Bruce also passed this way, and has left us a well-known, if rather over-romanticized, image of the harper in the tomb of Ramesses III in the Valley of the Kings. Bruce, who later went on to explore the source of the Blue Nile, was later known as the 'Theban liar', as a result of deep scepticism about his finds expressed by others.

The major change in the perception of Egypt by Europe came about as a result of the engineers, scientists and artists who formed part of Napoleon Bonaparte's expedition to Egypt in 1798. Public knowledge of the antiquities was first made known when the memoirs of Vivant Denon, one of the artists, were published in 1802; the publication of the great volumes of the *Description de l'Egypte* started in 1809, and between them these publications were responsible for starting the strange fascination with Egypt in the western world which is still as strong as ever today. While occasionally fanciful by today's standard of reproduction of monuments – more often than not to be attributed to the licence employed by the plate engravers back at home rather than to failings of the artists in the field – these publications were the first attempt to make scientific descriptions of monuments, and are still important today as more and more monuments are destroyed.

The interest of Europeans having been awakened, the craze for collecting antiquities began in earnest, and nowhere was a greater centre for this than Thebes. The *Description* had revealed just how many monuments there were there, and others wasted no time in starting to acquire them. And of course, the local population rapidly rose to the challenge. The main driving forces were often consular representatives of European nations, and the two most prominent were Henry Salt, the British consul, and Bernardino Drovetti, his French equivalent. Salt was responsible for obtaining the services in Egypt of Belzoni, who was to make many discoveries in Thebes and elsewhere; likewise, Drovetti had his agents, and Anglo-French political and military rivalry extended to the collection of antiquities. The memoirs of Belzoni mention frequent conflicts with Drovetti's employees in Thebes as he was trying to remove this or that antiquity, and matters even came to blows at one time near Karnak. Much has been written about Belzoni, a circus strongman who went to Egypt and was briefly an engineer there before working for Salt. Salt put together several collections, the first ones going to the British Museum, and a later one ending up in the Louvre Belzoni's first task for Salt was to bring back the large head of Ramesses II lying in the Ramesseum. In doing so he encountered much local resistance and stalling, as well as opposition from other foreigners, but the head is now in the British Museum, where it is known as the 'younger Memnon'; the body to which the head belongs has been located and studied recently by the French mission working in the Ramesseum.

Belzoni was subsequently to make many more finds, the most spectacular of which was the discovery of the tomb of Sety I in the Valley of the Kings (pp. 106–8). Various other individuals were active in Thebes collecting antiquities and acting as agents for others. Several of these are now well-known names in Egyptology circles, for example Anastasi, Athanasi and Piccinini.

Scholarly work begins and Egyptology matures

The year 1822 is the date of Champollion's decipherment of the hieroglyphic script, and it also marks the beginning of study of the monuments as opposed to the simple collection of antiquities which had gone before. Towards the end of that decade, Champollion himself went to Egypt and began copying monuments, but in the middle of the decade two even more important copying exercises had begun. Robert Hay and John Gardner Wilkinson spent much time in Thebes (as well of course as in other parts of Egypt), and they produced wonderful copies of many scenes in tombs and temples. Hay never really published his material, excellent as it was, but it is available now in the British Library, and is of the highest importance. Wilkinson published various books on Egypt, in particular his *Manners and Customs of the Ancient Egyptians* of 1837, and this drew heavily on his work in Thebes, where he had copied many of the so-called 'daily life scenes' in the private tombs; his manuscripts are now in the Bodleian Library, and contain a wealth of unpublished information. As was the custom of the time, Wilkinson built a house in Thebes, and its remains can still be seen now; the house was subsequently used by others, including Hay. James Burton was also active in Thebes at the same time, and is known for his use of the *camera lucida*.

In the 1840s an expedition was sent to Egypt by the king of Prussia, under the leadership of the first professor of Egyptology in Germany, Richard Lepsius. This marked yet another step forward in the quest for accurate recording of the monuments, and the results of Lepsius's work are one of the great outstanding academic monuments to early Egyptology. Combining the huge folio plates of his *Denkmäler* with the copious notes he made (published much later, after his death), we learn an enormous amount about Thebes; as with so many other contemporary explorers, the monuments they recorded have all too often disappeared.

The scientific history of Egyptology in Thebes can only be briefly sketched. In 1858 the Service des Antiquités was founded at the instigation of Mariette, and gradually a system of regulating the largely uncontrolled digging of monuments was put in place. Of the excavations going on at that time in Thebes, mention must be made of the work of A. H. Rhind. This Scottish lawyer travelled to Egypt in 1856–7 for health reasons, excavated in Thebes and there made a number of discoveries. The particular importance of his work was the amount of detail in which he recorded his finds, which included the intact late Ptolemaic tomb of Montuzaf (p. 200); the degree of detail far outweighed anything which had been published up to that date, and it was to be a number of years before it was to be found again.[5]

We can only really mention in passing the major milestones of archaeology in Thebes from the 1880s to 1945. Petrie did not really work very much here, but none the less undertook pioneering research on the smaller mortuary temples in 1895–6, and also began the process of scientific work at the Ramesseum. In the 1890s Edouard Naville was working for the Egypt Exploration Fund at Deir el-Bahari, and began the process of clearing and documenting the temple of Hatshepsut. The Metropolitan Museum of Art's Egyptian Expedition worked in Thebes from 1907 to 1938; it explored much of the Assasif and adjoining areas, and did some of the best recording ever done in Thebes, although most of it was not published. One branch of this expedition is particularly dear to the authors of this book, namely the graphic branch. Led by Norman de Garis Davies, it generally eschewed excavation and concentrated on the recording of the private tombs by means of line and colour facsimiles, the latter by Nina de Garis Davies, and also using the photographs of one of the best photographers ever to work in Egypt, Harry Burton. Lord Carnarvon began work in Thebes in 1908, and was soon encouraged to take on Howard Carter as his archaeologist; they made many discoveries in the tombs of the Nobles, and then moved to the Valley of the Kings, where their discovery of the tomb of Tutankhamun in 1922 is perhaps the best known archaeological find in the world.

EPILOGUE

The years following the end of the Second World War were relatively quiet in Thebes, at least in terms of archaeological work undertaken, and it was only in the 1960s that new work began again in earnest. The approach since that time has been rather different from before, and the quest for information (not objects) is now uppermost in the mind of all those who work there. Egypt has become an independent nation again, and runs its own affairs for the first time in more than two thousand years. The stress now is on co-operative working with the Supreme Council of Antiquities (SCA), as the successor to the Service des Antiquités is known.

Major campaigns of work have been undertaken by many nations, and in giving this list we hope we have omitted none: Egypt, Australia, Austria, Belgium, Canada, France, Germany, Hungary, Italy, Japan, Poland, Switzerland, UK, USA. Large programmes of work have been undertaken in all the areas of the site examined in these pages, and we have tried to incorporate the work of all these colleagues into this book.

What of the future? Pressure on a site such as Thebes is immense, but, because the site is so well known, the majority of monuments themselves are legally protected and are fortunately not directly threatened with the building, agricultural and industrial development which face so many less famous places in Egypt. However, Thebes has pressures of its own, such as tourism in normal times, and there are still outbreaks of robbery. Environmental pressures are significant: the result of the rising water table and the worldwide increases in atmospheric pollution. The greatest priority of the present is not to find new monuments but to ensure that those which are visible today are preserved for posterity. Thus visitors to Thebes are sometimes disappointed to find their favourite monument cloaked in scaffolding, but the work being done, mainly by the SCA as a result of heavy commitment by the Egyptian government, is absolutely essential for the future. Foreign missions these days are expected to include conservators and restorers among their staff wherever possible, and this is only right, so that monuments are left in a better condition than before work started on them.

We have tried to show in this book the depth and breadth of material to be found in the remains of ancient Thebes. It is now more than four thousand years since the city first came to prominence. Let us hope that we can all share in the responsibility of preserving it for at least that long again.

CHRONOLOGY

This table is based on J. von Beckerath, *Chronologie des pharaonischen Ägypten* (Mainz 1997), as simplified in R. Schulz and M. Seidl (eds), *Egypt: The World of the Pharaohs* (Cologne 1998), 528. This list concentrates on kings who are mentioned in the text of this book.

Predynastic Period

Naqada I	3700–3300
Naqada II	3300–3200
Naqada III	3200–3032

Early Dynastic Period

First to Second Dynasties	3032–2707

Old Kingdom

Third Dynasty	2707–2639
Djoser	2690–2670
Fourth Dynasty	2639–2504
Sneferu	2639–2604
Fifth Dynasty	2504–2347
Sahure	2496–2483
Niuserre	2445–2414
Djedkare	2405–2367
Unas	2367–2347
Sixth Dynasty	2347–2216
Teti	2347–2337
Pepy I	2335–2285
Merenre I	2285–2279
Pepy II	2279–2219
Seventh to Eighth Dynasties	2216–2170

First Intermediate Period

Ninth to Tenth Dynasties	2170–2020
Eleventh Dynasty	2119–1976
Mentuhotep Tepy-a	2119–?
Sehertawy Inyotef I	?–2103
Wahankh Inyotef II	2103–2054
Nakhtnebtepnefer Inyotef III	2054–2046

Middle Kingdom

Eleventh Dynasty (*continued*)	
Nebhepetre Mentuhotep II	2046–1995
Sankhkare Mentuhotep III	1995–1983
Nebtawyre Mentuhotep IV	1983–1976
Twelfth Dynasty	1976–1794/3
Amenemhat I	1976–1947
Senwosret I	1956–1911/10
Senwosret III	1872–1853/2
Amenemhat III	1853–1806/5
Amenemhat IV	1807/6–1798/7
Neferusobek	1798/7–1794/3

Second Intermediate Period

Thirteenth Dynasty	1794/3–1648
Khutawyre Wegaf	1794/3–1791/0
Neferhoteps and Sebekhoteps	
Djehuty	
Fourteenth Dynasty	?–1648
Fifteenth Dynasty	1648–1539
Apophis	1590–1549
Khamudi	1549–1539
Sixteenth Dynasty (parallel to Fifteenth Dynasty)	
Seventeenth Dynasty	1645–1550
Nubkheperre Inyotef V	
Sekhemre-Wepmaat Inyotef VI	No precise dates available
Sekhemre-Herhermaat Inyotef VII	
Sekhemre-Shedtawy Sobekemzaf II	
Senakhtenre	
Seqenenre Taa	?–1554
Kamose	1554–1550

New Kingdom

Eighteenth Dynasty	1550–1292
Ahmose	1550–1525
Amenhotep I	1525–1504
Tuthmose I	1504–1492
Tuthmose II	1492–1479
Hatshepsut	1479–1458/7
Tuthmose III	1479–1425
Amenhotep II	1428–1397
Tuthmose IV	1397–1388
Amenhotep III	1388–1351/50
Amenhotep IV/Akhenaten[1]	1351–1334
Smenkhkare	1337–1333
Tutankhamun	1333–1323

Ay	1323–1319
Horemheb	1319–1292

Nineteenth Dynasty 1292–1186/5
Ramesses I	1292–1290
Sety I	1290–1279/8
Ramesses II	1279–1213
Merenptah	1213–1203
Sety II[2]	1203–?
Amenmesse	?–1194/3
Siptah	1194/3–?
Tawosret	?–1186/5

Twentieth Dynasty 1186–1070/69
Sethnakht	1186–1183/2
Ramesses III	1183/2–1152/1
Ramesses IV	1152/1–1145/4
Ramesses V	1145/4–1142/0
Ramesses VI	1142/0–1134
Ramesses VII	1134–1126
Ramesses VIII	1126–1125
Ramesses IX	1125–1107
Ramesses X	1107–1103
Ramesses XI	1103–1070/69

Third Intermediate Period

Twenty-first Dynasty 1070/69–946/5
Nesybanebdjedu/Smendes	1070/69–1044/3
Herihor (priest king)	
Panedjem I (priest king)	1044–1026
Siamun	979/8–960/59

Twenty-second and Twenty-third Dynasty 946/5–714
Sheshonq I	946/5–925/4
Osorkon II	875–837
Harsiese (priest king)	870–850 (very approximate)
Sheshonq III	837–785
Takelot III	776–755

Twenty-fourth Dynasty 740–714

Twenty-fifth Dynasty ?–664
Kashta	?–746
Piankhy (Piye)	746–715

Late Period

Twenty-fifth Dynasty (*continued*)
Shabaka	715–700
Taharqa	690–664
Tantamani	664–?[3]

Twenty-sixth Dynasty
Psamtek I	664–610

Twenty-seventh Dynasty (Persian) 525–401

Twenty-eighth Dynasty 404/1–399

Twenty-ninth Dynasty 399–380
Hakor	393–380
Psammuthis	393–392

Thirtieth Dynasty 380–342
Nectanebo I	380–362

Second Persian period 342–332

Greek rulers 332–306
Alexander the Great	332–323
Philip Arrhidaeus	323–317
Alexander IV	317–306

Ptolemaic period 306/4–30
Ptolemy I	306/4–283/2
Ptolemy III	246–222/1
Ptolemy IV	221–204
Ptolemy V	204–180
Ptolemy VI	180–164 & 163–145
Ptolemy VII associated with Ptolemy VI in 145	
Ptolemy VIII	164 & 145–116
Ptolemy XII	80–58 & 55–51
Cleopatra VII	51–30

Roman period 30 BC–AD 330

Byzantine period 330–642

Islamic period 642–present

Divine Adoratrices in the Third Intermediate Period

Following K. A. Kitchen, *The Third Intermediate Period in Egypt*, 3rd ed. (Warminster 1995), 480.

870–840	Karomana Merytmut
c. 770	Tashakheper
754–714?	Shepenwepet I
740–700	Amenirdis I
710–650	Shepenwepet II
670–640	Amenirdis II
656–586	Nitocris
595–525	Ankhnesneferibre I

GLOSSARY

I. Shaw and P. Nicholson, *British Museum Dictionary of Ancient Egypt* (London 1995) should be referred to for more detailed information.

Akhet 'the inundation season'; see **calendar**.

ba one of a person's souls, usually shown in the form of a bird with a human head 🐦. It had its own separate existence on earth, and after death it was the *ba* that was able to travel outside the tomb and experience a form of continued existence, returning each night to be reunited with the body of its owner.

calendar the Egyptian year was divided into three seasons, *Akhet*, *Peret* and *Shomu*, having four months of thirty days each. An additional five days were added for the birthdays of Osiris, Isis, Horus, Seth and Nephthys, making a total of 365 days per year. The lack of a leap year meant that every four years the calendar slipped by about one day, so that there were regularly periods when the calendar was back to front and, for example, December occurred in *Shomu*, often translated 'summer'. Only every 1460 years did the calendar properly coincide with the seasonal year. As a result Egyptologists today tend to call the seasons by their Egyptian names rather than attempt a translation.

cartonnage a material composed of layers of linen soaked in plaster and then modelled into the required shape. It was particularly used for making mummy cases in the Third Intermediate Period.

cartouche an oval shape, representing a loop of rope (called *menesh* or *shenu*, the root meaning of which is probably 'to encircle') which enclosed two parts of the king's full names (see **royal titulary**); the name was coined by Napoleon's soldiers who likened the shape to their cartridges.

cataract an area of rapids in the course of the Nile which hinders river transport to a greater or lesser extent. The Nile has six cataracts, the first of which, at Aswan, used to act as Egypt's natural southern boundary.

demotic the form of the Egyptian language, used on documents and occasionally carved monuments, from *c.*660 BC onwards; also applied to the writing of the period which was used in place of Hieratic; from the Greek *demotikos*, 'popular'.

Ennead a grouping of nine deities. The so-called Great Ennead consisted of Atum, his children Shu and Tefnut, their children Geb and Nut, and children of the latter pair, Osiris, Isis, Seth and Nephthys.

false door a representation of a door, in carving or in paint, which acted as a doorway for the spirits of the deceased. The original simple form of a door was embellished by the Egyptians with multiple jambs, lintels and depictions.

foundation deposit a group of symbolic objects deliberately buried in association with the construction of a building or digging of a tomb, often containing model tools and samples of building materials bearing the names of the king.

Herodotos a Greek historian who included a description of his travels in Egypt, in about 450 BC, in Book II of his *Histories*.

hieratic a form of Egyptian writing, derived from hieroglyphic script, used for documents, rather than monuments, from the earliest period of Egyptian history until the development of demotic; from the Greek *hieratikos*, 'priestly'.

hieroglyphic the classic Egyptian 'picture writing' script, used on monuments throughout Egyptian history; from the Greek *hieros*, 'holy' + *glyphe*, 'carving'.

Hyksos a line of non-Egyptian rulers of Egypt forming the Fifteenth Dynasty in the Second Intermediate Period (1648–1539 BC); from Egyptian *hekau khasut*, 'rulers of foreign lands'.

ka one of an individual's souls, created at birth almost as a person's double, usually symbolized by upraised arms ⊔. During life the *ka* existed as part of its owner and received its sustenance as a part of him or her, but this ceased after death, and so food offerings were specifically made 'for the *ka* of' the deceased.

Karnak cachette a huge group of statues that had been buried, probably for reasons of security, in the courtyard in front of the Seventh Pylon at Karnak; the statues were rediscovered in 1902 and are now mostly on display in Cairo.

Manetho an Egyptian priest of the third century BC, who wrote a history of Egypt in Greek, dividing it into a series of dynasties. Although the history has not survived, it was preserved in the writings of other authors and his system of dynasties continues to form the basis of the study of ancient Egyptian history.

mastaba a square or rectangular type of free-standing tomb, made of stone or mud brick, usually with sloping sides; from the Arabic word for a low mud-brick bench, often found outside houses.

Naqada a predynastic site, 26 km north of Luxor, on the West Bank, first excavated by Petrie and used by him to date other similar sites; hence the dating terms Naqada I (also known as Amratian) and Naqada II (Gerzean). A very late phase of the latter is sometimes called Naqada III.

nome an administrative area or province. Egypt was divided into twenty-two Upper Egyptian nomes and twenty Lower Egyptian nomes. From the Greek *nomos*, 'district'.

nomarch the main administrator of a nome; from the Greek *nomos*, 'district' + *archos*, 'leader'.

opening of the mouth a ritual which brought an inanimate object (usually a mummy or a statue) to life. Spells were recited and various implements were applied to the subject to open the mouth magically (and often the eyes). Some mummies have been found with small cuts in the bandages over the mouth.

ostrakon, pl. ostraka a flake of stone, or potsherd, bearing writing or drawing (see p. 175).

Peret 'emergence of the land, "winter"'; see **calendar**.

pylon a type of gateway found in temples (see p. 45), from the Greek.

raised relief carvings on the surface of stone produced by removing the areas of background and leaving the decoration in relief. Usually very fine in quality.

red crown the crown of Lower Egypt, called *deshret*, worn singly, or in combination with the white crown as the double crown.

royal titulary The full name of an Egyptian king consisted of five parts. The oldest name was the Horus name, which identifies the king with the eldest son of Osiris. The two most prominent names in the principal periods covered by this book were written inside cartouches: the first, the *prenomen*, or throne name, was probably taken on the king's accession, and the second, the *nomen*, was that given at birth; e.g. Nebhepetre (*prenomen*) Mentuhotep (*nomen*) . The other two forms are known as the 'Golden Horus' and the 'Two Ladies' names.

***saff* tomb** a type of tomb with a pillared exterior (see pp. 146–8), possibly from an Arabic word meaning 'full of holes'.

shabti a funerary figurine which was included in burial equipment from the Middle Kingdom. At their most popular period in the late New Kingdom and Third Intermediate Period, there were typically 401 of them in a burial: one for each day of the year, and one overseer for every ten. Their main function was to undertake work in the hereafter which the deceased was called upon to do.

Shomu: 'shortage of water, "summer"'; see calendar.

stela an upright stone slab, often with a rounded top, either free-standing or carved into or painted on to rock; from the Greek *stele.*

sunk relief carvings cut into stone, so that the decoration itself is deeper than the surrounding surface. This relief is usually more visible in direct sunlight than raised relief (see above); it was cheaper than raised relief and more suited to the decoration of exposed surfaces such as the exteriors of buildings.

talatat small stone blocks, used for building during the Amarna period; see note 8 to Chapter 3 on p. 120.

uraeus the cobra image frequently found on the brow of the king, representing the protective power of the snake for the king and also the aggressive potential of the ruler. It is identified with the goddess Wadjet, the protective deity of Lower Egypt.

white crown the crown of Upper Egypt, called *hedjet,* worn singly, or in combination with the red crown as the double crown.

NOTES AND ABBREVIATIONS

Abbreviations

EEF
Egypt Exploration Fund, London, precursor to the Egypt Exploration Society, London (EES)

MMA
Metropolitan Museum of Art, New York

TT
Theban Tomb, following a numbering system devised and published in 1913

KV/VK
Valley of the Kings

QV/VQ
Valley of the Queens

1 A tour of the sites of Thebes

1 See http://www.unesco.org/whc/sites/87.htm.

2 In this book we do not deal with the cultivated and desert areas to the east of the town, as to our knowledge no exploration for ancient remains has yet been made there. This is one of the penalties of the existence of the phenomenal number of ancient remains in Thebes itself.

2 A short history of Thebes

1 Earlier Egyptological confusion as to which Mentuhotep was the first to assume royal titles, together with this problem of the names of Nebhepetre Mentuhotep, means that older books may refer to Nebhepetre as Mentuhotep I or II. We have preferred to refer to the kings of this dynasty by using two of their names to remove a possible ambiguity.

2 The official account of the expedition is translated in Lichtheim, *Ancient Egyptian Literature* I, 113–15. The other texts are available only in Breasted, *Ancient Records* I, 211–16.

3 See Lichtheim, *Ancient Egyptian Literature* I, 143; Ta-sety is the nome of Elephantine, Khen-nekhen a term for the southern nomes of Upper Egypt.

4 Translation of the whole text: Simpson, Faulkner and Wente, *The Literature of Ancient Egypt*, 77–80.

5 Kush is the general term for Upper Nubia, and at this time refers to the important culture centred at Kerma, which had control over the Nile regions at least between the second and fourth cataracts.

6 Translation of the whole text: Lichtheim, *Ancient Egyptian Literature* II, 12–14.

7 Translation of the whole text: Lichtheim, *Ancient Egyptian Literature* II, 224–30.

8 Not in any of the standard volumes of translation. See R. A. Caminos, *The Chronicle of Prince Osorkon* (Analecta Orientalia 37, 1958).

3 The temples of Karnak and Luxor

1 See p. 57; Tuthmose III may have cleared away earlier structures to make room for the buildings he wanted to construct.

2 The Open Air Museum at Karnak lies to the north of the First Courtyard. On display are many structures which were dismantled during the various phases of development of the temples and which were then used as filling within the later constructions that replaced them. The Chapel of Senwosret I, for example, was found in pieces within the Third Pylon.

3 Work on reconstructing the chapel was begun in 1997.

4 It is not clear whether there was a temple proper at Luxor at the time of Hatshepsut.

5 Such festivals, during which various rituals associated with the renewal of the king's vigour were performed, were most usually held in the thirtieth year of a king's reign.

6 Blocks bearing the name of Amenhotep III were reused during the building of the later sanctuary of this temple.

7 It should not be forgotten that the same king was solely responsible for the largest single temple in Egypt in the form of his funerary temple on the West Bank, as well as all the building works he undertook at Malqata.

8 The origin of this word is obscure. The usual explanation is that it derives from the Arabic phase for 'three hand breadths'. However another possibility is that it may be the way that the local workmen pronounced the Italian word *tagliata*, meaning 'cut stonework'.

9 High-water marks are recorded, amongst others, from the reigns of Sheshonq I, Osorkon I, Takelot I, Takelot III and Shabaka (Twenty-second to Twenty-third Dynasties).

4 The West Bank temples

1 Haring, *Divine Households*, 76.

2 Kemp, *Ancient Egypt*, 195.

3 Reconstruction by O'Connor, in Oren, *Hyksos*, 59.

4 The suggestion that the picture represents Senmut (J. Romer, *Romer's Egypt* (London 1992), 157–60) is perhaps somewhat fanciful. Interesting comments on the text are made by E. F. Wente, *JNES* 43 (1984), 47–54.

5 A reference to one of the creation myths, whereby the process began when the primeval mound rose out of the primordial sea. It may seem strange to us, but almost every Egyptian city had its own place where creation was thought to have happened; in Luxor such places were at least at Medinet Habu and on the site of the Amenemopet temple at the rear of Luxor Temple.

6 R. A. Parker, J. Leclant and J.-C. Goyon, *The Edifice of Taharqa by the Sacred Lake of Karnak* (Providence 1979), 51, 82–3.

5 Tombs of the kings

1 The tomb-robbery papyrus is translated in Peet, *The Great Tomb-robberies of the Twentieth Egyptian Dynasty*, 38. The stela is shown in Arnold, *Gräber des alten und mittleren Reiches*, Taf. 53.

2 Peet, *Great Tomb-robberies*, 38.

3 Prior to her ascending the throne as king, another burial place had been prepared for Hatshepsut in a cliff tomb which was later discovered by Howard Carter (pp. 124–5).

4 This was first thoroughly discussed by Carter and Gardiner in *JEA* 4 (1917), 130–58. Another, complete, plan was found on an ostrakon during the clearance of the tomb of Ramesses IX, and the plan on it is thought to be of that tomb.

5 The Egyptians conceived of the sun in up to seventy-five forms, but the three principal ones were as Khepri, the newborn sun, shown in the form of a scarab; Re, the mature sun; and Atum, the elderly form of the sun as it approached the end of each day.

6 Tombs of the royal family

1 Capart, Gardiner and van de Walle, *JEA* 22 (1936), 171.

2 *JEA* 4 (1917), 107.

3 This and the tomb of Hatshepsut, as well as that of the Three Princesses, are illustrated in Romer, *Valley of the Kings*, 242.

4 C. Lilyquist, 'The Tomb of Tuthmose III's Foreign Wives: A Survey of its Architectural Type, Contents and Foreign Connections', *Proceedings of the Seventh International Congress of Egyptologists* (Leuven 1998), 677–82.

5 Compare D. P. Ryan, 'Further Observations Concerning the Valley of the Kings', in Wilkinson (ed.), *Valley of the Sun Kings*, 157–63.

6 Peet, *Great Tomb-robberies*, 39.

7 Peet, *Great Tomb-robberies*, 39.

8 Many of them will be found in Kitchen, *The Third Intermediate Period in Egypt*, 40–68. There are also those for whom no burial has been found, such as the daughter of Panedjem I, Nedjemmut (Kitchen, *The Third Intermediate Period in Egypt*, 45).

7 Tombs of private persons

1 These are our estimates, based on figures from F. Kampp, *Die thebanische Nekropole*. These figures include tombs not in the normal numbering system.

2 Peet, *Great Tomb-robberies*, 39.

3 The tomb in which we have been working in the 1990s (TT99) was reused by the family of the fourth priest of Amun Wedjahor and his son Horenpe. However, the site of our work in the 1980s (TT253, 254, 294) revealed material of all periods.

4 *City of the Dead*, 31.

5 The British Museum contains a number of wonderful painted fragments from this tomb, which must have been one of the wonders of the necropolis. The original location of the chapel has never been identified with any certainty, but seems to have been somewhere in the area of Dra Abu el-Naga.

6 The papyrus is the 'Tale of the two brothers', Lichtheim, *Ancient Egyptian Literature* II, 203–4. The translator does suggest an alternative of 'loosen your braids' for 'put on your wig'.

7 Hayes, *Ostraka and Name Stones*, 21.

8 Note that this technique should not be termed 'fresco', as the paint was applied to dry plaster.

9 'Reflections on the banquet scene', in Tefnin, *La peinture égyptienne*, 29–36.

10 Assmann *et al.*, *Problems and Priorities*.

11 An example of this which comes to mind is a body wrapped only in a mat found by the Metropolitan Museum just below the tomb chapel of Senmut (TT71).

8 Living in ancient Thebes

1 This expression is often translated as 'servant in the Place of Truth'.

2 Ostrakon Berlin 12654: Černý, *A Community of Workmen*, 185.

3 Ostrakon Gardiner 221 and papyrus Turin 1923: Černý, *A Community of Workmen*, 90, 93.

4 Ostrakon Cairo 504: Černý, *A Community of Workmen*, 93.

5 Ostrakon Cairo 302: Černý, *A Community of Workmen*, 93.

6 Capart, Gardiner and van de Walle, *JEA* 22 (1936), 171.

7 Capart, Gardiner and van de Walle, *JEA* 22 (1936), 170.

8 Papyrus BM 10052: Peet, *Great Tomb-robberies*, 151.

9 1 *khar* was approximately 75 l.

10 The value of the coffin equated to 10 *khar* of emmer, or slightly less than two months' emmer ration.

11 N. Strudwick, 'The Population of Thebes in the New Kingdom: Some Preliminary Thoughts', in J. Assmann, E. Dziobek, H. Guksch and F. Kampp (eds), *Thebanische Beamtennekropolen: neue Perspektiven archäologischer Forschung* (Heidelberg 1995), 97–105.

9 Thebes after the pharaohs

1 The Greek word originally referred to a shepherd's pipe, and was elsewhere used to describe structures with corridors.

2 The tomb of his wife, originally a Christian nun, lies under the same mosque, perhaps within the remains of her church which originally lay there.

3 The word 'mummy' is probably based on an Arabic or Persian word *mumiya* meaning bitumen.

4 C. P. A. Clayton, *The Rediscovery of Ancient Egypt* (London 1982), 102–3; the village is not marked as in any particular state in the *Description de l'Egypte* twenty-five years before (11, 40).

5 *Thebes: Its Tombs and their Tenants*; assessment by Manniche, 115–16.

Chronology

1 The chronology we are adopting for this table does not recognize the possibility of a co-regency between Amenhotep III and Akhenaten. However, we feel that the case for a co-regency, perhaps as much as twelve years, is defensible.

2 The order of Sety II and Amenmesse is unclear.

3 At some point after 664 ruled in Nubia only.

FURTHER READING

Only an attempt can be made here to survey the published material relating to the subject matter of this book. The following includes both scholarly and popular publications, and thus references are given to a number of sources in languages other than English.
* marks books particularly targeted at a wider audience.

Journal abbreviations:

BIFAO:
  Bulletin de l'Institut Français d'Archéologie Orientale

JEA:
  Journal of Egyptian Archaeology, London

JARCE:
  Journal of the American Research Center in Egypt, New York

JNES:
  Journal of Near Eastern Studies

MDAIK:
  Mitteilungen des Deutschen Archäologischen Instituts Abteilung Kairo

MMJ:
  Metropolitan Museum Journal, New York

ZÄS:
  Zeitschrift für ägyptische Sprache, Leipzig

General books

*I. Shaw and P. Nicholson, *British Museum Dictionary of Ancient Egypt* (London 1995): an excellent starting place for the general reader.

W. Helck, E. Otto and W. Westendorf (eds), *Lexikon der Ägyptologie*, 7 vols (Wiesbaden 1975–88): a more wide-ranging work; although keywords are in German, articles are in English, French or German.

*J. Baines and J. Málek, *Atlas of Ancient Egypt* (Oxford 1980).

*B. J. Kemp, *Ancient Egypt: Anatomy of a Civilization* (London 1989): the best survey of the society and functioning of ancient Egypt.

*E. Strouhal, *Life in Ancient Egypt* (Cambridge 1992): a very good popular survey of society.

*R. Schultz and M. Seidl (eds), *Egypt: The World of the Pharaohs* (Cologne 1998): chapters on all aspects of Ancient Egypt and full of beautiful photographs.

*S. Aufrère, J.-Cl. Golvin and J.-C. Goyon, *Egypte restituée*, 3 vols (Paris 1994–7): presents all the major Egyptian sites in photographs and reconstruction drawings.

*W. C. Hayes, *The Scepter of Egypt*, 2 vols (New York 1953, revised 1990): an excellent survey of Egyptian material culture, based on the Metropolitan Museum's collection (much of which comes from Thebes).

*G. Robins, *Art of Ancient Egypt* (London 1997): a survey of Egyptian art.

B. Porter and R. L. B. Moss, *Topographical Bibliography of Ancient Egyptian Hieroglyphic Texts, Reliefs and Paintings*, 7 vols (Oxford 1927–) (usually abbreviated PM): the standard source for bibliography of standing monuments; the Theban volumes (I–II) are now in their second editions (1960–72).

J. Capart and M. Werbrouck, *Thebes: The Glory of a Great Past* (London 1926): long out of print

C. F. Nims, *Thebes of the Pharaohs* (London 1965): long out of print

Translations

Most volumes of translations of Egyptian texts deal with the literary texts at the expense of the monumental.

M. Lichtheim, *Ancient Egyptian Literature*, 3 vols (Berkeley and Los Angeles 1973–80): the widest-ranging selection.

R. B. Parkinson, *Voices from Ancient Egypt: An Anthology of Middle Kingdom Writings* (London 1991).

W. K. Simpson, R. O. Faulkner and E. F. Wente, *The Literature of Ancient Egypt* (New Haven 1972).

J. H. Breasted, *Ancient Records of Egypt*, 5 vols (Chicago 1906–7): still the only translations of many documentary texts.

History

General history books

*N. Grimal, *A History of Ancient Egypt* (Oxford 1992).

J. Vercoutter, *L'Egypte et la Vallée du Nil* I (Paris 1992): to the end of the Old Kingdom.

C. Vandersleyen, *L'Egypte et la Vallée du Nil* II (Paris 1995): First Intermediate Period to New Kingdom. Excellent bibliography.

D. B. Redford, *Pharaonic Annals, King-lists and Day Books* (Toronto 1987): a survey of the various king lists.

Prehistoric Egypt

M. A. Hoffman, *Egypt before the Pharaohs* (London 1991)

Old Kingdom

B. V. Bothmer, *MDAIK* 30 (1974), 165–70: Old Kingdom material from Karnak.

D. Wildung *MDAIK* 25 (1969), 212–19: ditto.

Middle Kingdom

Dorothea Arnold, *MMJ* 26 (1991), 5–48: early Middle Kingdom in Thebes.

Second Intermediate Period

D. B. O'Connor, in E. Oren, *The Hyksos: New Historical and Archaeological Perspectives* (Philadelphia 1997), 45–67: Thebes in the late Second Intermediate Period.

Reign of Amenhotep III

D. O'Connor and E. H. Cline (eds), *Amenhotep III: Perspectives on his Reign* (Ann Arbor 1998): series of important essays on many different aspects of this king and his monuments, notably in Thebes.

Amarna period

W. Raymond Johnson, *JEA* 82 (1996), 65–82: a fascinating and badly needed new approach to the period.

Reign of Ramesses II

*K. A. Kitchen, *Pharaoh Triumphant: The Life and Times of Ramesses II* (Warminster 1982): readable and informative.

End of the New Kingdom

K. Janssen-Winkeln, *ZÄS* 119 (1992), 22–37: revision of the historical sequence of the Theban rulers.

J. H. Taylor, in C. J. Eyre (ed.), *Proceedings of the Seventh International Congress of Egyptologists* (Leuven 1998), 1145–55: continuation of this revision.

Third Intermediate Period

K. A. Kitchen, *The Third Intermediate Period in Egypt*, 3rd ed. (Warminster 1995).

D. A. Aston and J. H. Taylor, in A. Leahy (ed.), *Libya and Egypt* (London 1990), 131–54: a revised view of Thebes in the later Third Intermediate Period.

Post-dynastic Egypt

*A. K. Bowman, *Egypt after the Pharaohs* (London 1986), 22–53: a succinct account of the period.

East Bank temples

General

B. E. Shafer (ed.), *Temples of Ancient Egypt* (Ithaca 1997): an excellent introduction to many aspects of Egyptian temples; Shafer's introductory chapter (pp. 1–30) includes the fundamental bibliography for the meaning and functioning of Egyptian temples.

Dieter Arnold, *Die Tempel Ägyptens* (Zürich 1992): covers all the major temples in Egypt.

Karnak

There is no single book available in English on the Karnak complex.

*J. Lauffray, *Karnak d'Egypte: domain du divin* (Paris 1979).

*C. Traunecker and J.-Cl. Golvin, *Karnak: résurrection d'un site* (Fribourg 1984).

Egypte restituée, volume II (see **General Books** above) contains a large amount of useful information.

Luxor Temple

L. Bell, in Shafer, *Temples*, 127–84: contains everything the reader needs to know, including bibliography. It also deals with the Opet Festival.

West Bank temples

General

G. Haeny, in Shafer, *Temples*, 86–126: deals with terminology and meaning of the West Bank mortuary temples.

Dieter Arnold, in Shafer, *Temples*, 31–85: covers older temples.

B. J. J. Haring, *Divine Households* (Leiden 1997): economic aspects of West Bank temples.

Beautiful Festival of the Valley

Bell, in Shafer, *Temples*, 136–7, with bibliography on p. 286 n. 38: a good summary.

J. Karkowski, *50 Years of Polish Excavations in Egypt and the Near East* (Warsaw 1992), 155–66: discussion of the Hatshepsut scenes relating to this festival.

L. Manniche, in R. Tefnin (ed.), *La peinture égyptienne ancienne: un monde de signes à préserver* (Brussels 1997), 29–36: covers the relationship between the banquet scene in the private tombs and this festival.

Nebhepetre Mentuhotep

Dieter Arnold, *Der Tempel des Königs Mentuhotep von Deir el-Bahari*, 3 vols (Mainz 1974–81).

Dieter Arnold, *The Temple of Mentuhotep at Deir el-Bahari* (New York 1979).

Sankhkare temples

Dorothea Arnold, *MMJ* 26 (1991), 5–48: so-called 'Sankhkare Temple'.

*Gyözö Vörös, *Temple on the Pyramid of Thebes* (Budapest 1998): temples on the Thoth Hill.

New Kingdom temples

G. Haeny, in Shafer, *Temples*, 86–126: provides information and bibliography about most of the individual temples.

Temple of Amenhotep III

B. Bryan, in S. Quirke, *The Temple in Ancient Egypt: New Discoveries and Recent Research* (London 1997), 57–81: about the extraordinary programme of statues in this temple.

Ramesseum

The journal *Memnonia*, published by 'l'Association pour la sauvegarde du Ramesseum', should be consulted for ongoing reports on work in the temple.

Medinet Habu

W. J. Murnane, *United with Eternity* (Cairo 1980): an excellent popular guide.

Tombs of the Kings

Old and Middle Kingdoms

Dieter Arnold, *Gräber des alten und mittleren Reiches in El-Târif* (Mainz 1976).

Vörös, *Temple on the Pyramid of Thebes* (above) mentions a possible tomb for Sankhkare Mentuhotep.

Valley of the Kings

There are numerous books on the subject, the best being:

*J. Romer, *Valley of the Kings* (London 1981).

*N. Reeves and R. H. Wilkinson, *The Complete Valley of the Kings* (London 1996): provides a copious bibliography for each tomb.

*E. Hornung, *Valley of the Kings* (New York 1990).

C. N. Reeves, *Valley of the Kings: The Decline of a Royal Necropolis* (London 1990): an important scholarly source.

There are many other scholarly publications about the Valley; examples are:

J. Romer, *MDAIK* 32 (1976), 191–206: the early tombs.

C. N. Reeves (ed.), *After Tut'ankhamun: Research and Excavation in the Royal Necropolis at Thebes* (London 1992): collection of papers.

Richard H. Wilkinson (ed.), *Valley of the Sun Kings: New Explorations in the Tombs of the Pharaohs* (Tucson 1995): collection of papers.

H. Carter and A. H. Gardiner, *JEA* 4 (1917), 130–58: publication of the plan of the tomb of Ramesses IV.

Tombs of the royal family

There is no one source book for this widely disparate topic.

Middle Kingdom

L. K. Sabbahy, *JARCE* 34 (1997), 163–6: queens of Nebhepetre Mentuhotep.

*N. Reeves, in *Minerva* 7 no. 2 (1996), 47–8: the tomb from which the diadem of Queen Mentuhotep might have come.

New Kingdom

H. Carter, *JEA* 4 (1917), 107–18: cliff tombs of the early Eighteenth Dynasty.

H. Carter, *JEA* 3 (1916), 147–54: possible burial place of Queen Ahmose-Nefertari.

J. Romer, *MDAIK* 32 (1976), 191–206: ditto.

H. E. Winlock, *The Treasure of Three Egyptian Princesses* (New York 1948): intact burials of queens of this period.

H. E. Winlock, *The Tomb of Queen Meryt-Amun at Thebes* (New York 1932): ditto.

A. Dodson and J. J. Janssen, *JEA* 75 (1989), 125–38: discussion of the cache of Tuthmoside princesses reburied in the Twenty-first Dynasty.

C. Leblanc, *Ta set neferu: une nécropole de Thèbes Ouest et son histoire* (Cairo 1989): the first volume of a series on the valley, surveying its history, by the French mission which worked in the Valley of the Queens in the 1970s and 1980s.

C. Leblanc, *BIFAO* 89 (1989), 227–47: typology and symbolism of tombs in the valley.

Divine Adoratrices

Kitchen, *Third Intermediate Period* (above), discusses the history and chronology of the Divine Adoratrices.

E. Graefe, *Untersuchungen zur Verwaltung und Geschichte der Institution der Gottesgemählin des Amun vom Beginn des Neuen Reiches bis zur Spätzeit* (Wiesbaden 1981): considers the office itself and its antecedents.

M. Gitton, *Les divines épouses de la 18e dynastie* (Paris 1984): covers similar ground.

Tombs of private persons

General

L. Manniche, *City of the Dead: Thebes in Egypt* (London 1987): the best introduction to the Tombs of the Nobles.

J. Assmann, G. Burkard and V. Davies (eds), *Problems and Priorities in Egyptian Archaeology* (London 1987): collection of papers.

J. Assmann, E. Dziobek, H. Guksch and F. Kampp (eds), *Thebanische Beamtennekropolen: neue Perspektiven archäologischer Forschung* (Heidelberg 1995): collection of papers.

*A. Mekhitarian, *Egyptian Painting* (Geneva 1954): probably the best collection of colour photographs, the majority from Theban tombs.

Symbolism

L. Manniche in Tefnin, *La peinture égyptienne*, 29-36.

N. and H. M. Strudwick, in Tefnin, *La peinture égyptienne*, 37–47.

N. Strudwick, in C. Eyre, A. Leahy and L. M. Leahy (eds), *The Unbroken Reed: Studies in the Culture and Heritage of Ancient Egypt in Honour of A. F. Shore* (London 1994): discusses the change between the Eighteenth and Nineteenth Dynasties.

Construction

W. C. Hayes, *Ostraka and Name Stones from the Tomb of Sen-mut (no. 71) at Thebes* (New York 1942): includes ostraka relating to the construction of the tomb of Senmut.

Old Kingdom

Mohammed Saleh, *Three Old-Kingdom Tombs at Thebes* (Mainz 1977): the only publication of material from the period.

Middle Kingdom

Dieter Arnold, *Das Grab des Ini-itif: die Architektur* (Mainz 1971): on the development of the *saff* tomb.

J. P. Allen, in P. D. Manuelian (ed.), *Studies in Honor of William Kelly Simpson*, 2 vols (Boston 1996) I, 1–26: reconsiders the dating of some of the owners of these tombs.

Dorothea Arnold, *MMJ* 26 (1991), 5–48: on the same subject.

H. E. Winlock, *Models of Daily Life* (Cambridge 1955): publication of the wonderful models from the tomb of Meketre

H. E. Winlock, *The Slain Soldiers of Nebhepetre Mentu-hotpe* (New York 1945): reports the discovery of the bodies near the temple of that king.

New Kingdom

F. Kampp, *Die thebanische Nekropole: zum Wandel des Grabgedankens von der XVIII. bis zur XX. Dynastie*, 2 vols (Mainz 1996): a detailed survey of all known New Kingdom tombs.

S. T. Smith, *MDAIK* 48 (1992), 193–231: survey of Eighteenth Dynasty tomb contents.

Publications of individual tombs:

The best epigraphic publications are those of Norman and Nina de Garis Davies, such as *The Tomb of Rekhmire* (New York 1943) or the five lavish volumes of the Tytus Memorial series (New York 1917–27). Excellent epigraphic and archaeological publications are produced by the German Archaeological Institute and by the Heidelberg Ramesside Tomb Project.

*Abdel Ghaffar Shedid and M. Seidl, *Das Grab des Nacht* (Mainz 1991).

*R. Gundlach et al., *Sennefer: die Grabkammer des Bürgermeisters von Theben* (Mainz 1988).

*Abdel Ghaffar Shedid, *Das Grab des Sennedjem* (Mainz 1994)

N. and H. M. Strudwick, *Tombs of Amenhotep, Khnummose and Amenmose* (Oxford 1996).

Late Period

D. Eigner, *Die monumentalen Grabbauten der Spätzeit in der thebanischen Nekropole* (Vienna 1984): the best (and only) survey of the large tombs of the Twenty-fifth to Twenty-sixth Dynasties.

D. A. Aston's publication of his dissertation on Third Intermediate Period tomb groups is in press at the time of writing.

J. H. Taylor, *Egyptian Coffins* (Aylesbury 1989): an excellent introduction to a complex subject.

M. Bietak and E. Reiser-Haslauer, *Das Grab des 'Anch-hor*, 2 vols (Vienna 1978–82).

Popular cemetery at Dra Abu el-Naga

D. Polz, in *MDAIK* 48 (1992), 109–30, *MDAIK* 49 (1993), 227–38, and *MDAIK* 51 (1995), 207–25: preliminary reports on excavations at Dra Abu el-Naga.

D. Polz, in Assmann *et al.*, *Thebanische Beamtennekropolen* (above), 25–42, on the same subject.

Living

*E. Riefstahl, *Thebes in the Time of Amunhotep III* (Norman 1964): a popular account of life in Thebes in the New Kingdom

N. Strudwick, in Assmann *et al.*, *Thebanische Beamtennekropolen* (above), 97–105: considers the possible population of Thebes.

Deir el-Medina

*M. L. Bierbrier, *The Tomb-builders of the Pharaohs* (London 1982): the best general account of Deir el-Medina.

J. Černý, *A Community of Workmen at Thebes in the Ramesside Period* (Cairo 1973): first publication by the scholar to whom we owe a great debt in understanding the site, who died before his work was fully published.

D. Valbelle, *Les ouvriers de la tombe* (Cairo 1985): uses Černý's work as a starting point.

R. J. Demarée and J. J. Janssen (eds), *Gleanings from Deir el-Medina* (Leiden 1982): collection of papers.

R. J. Demarée and A. Egberts (eds), *Village Voices* (Leiden 1992): collection of papers.

L. H. Lesko (ed.), *Pharaoh's Workers* (Ithaca 1994): collection of papers.

Papyri

T. E. Peet, *The Great Tomb-robberies of the Twentieth Egyptian Dynasty*, 2 vols (Oxford 1930): a study of many of the tomb-robbery papyri.

J. Capart, A. H. Gardiner and B. van de Walle, *JEA* 22 (1936), 168–93. Publication of the Leopold–Amherst papyrus.

W. F. Edgerton, *JNES* 10 (1951), 137–45: an interesting article on the strike texts.

Later Thebes

*A. Bowman, *Egypt after the Pharaohs* (London 1986).

N. Lewis, *Life in Egypt under Roman Rule* (Oxford 1983).

N. Lewis, *Greeks in Ptolemaic Egypt* (Oxford 1986).

R. S. Bagnall, *Egypt in Late Antiquity* (Princeton 1993).

A. Bataille, *Les Memnonia* (Cairo 1951): a fascinating pioneering account of Thebes in the classical period, which has yet to be surpassed for its broadness of scope.

S. P. Vleeming (ed.), *Hundred-gated Thebes* (Leiden 1995): collection of fascinating papers.

C. Leblanc, in *Mélanges Gamal Eddin Mokhtar*, 2 vols (Cairo 1985) II, 69–82: on the Ramesseum.

Mohammed el-Saghir *et al*, *Le camp romain de Louqsor* (Cairo 1986): on the Roman camp.

D. Monserrat and L. Meskell, *JEA* 83 (1997), 179–97: on Deir el-Medina.

J. Baillet, *Inscriptions grecques et latines de tombeaux des rois ou syringes à Thèbes* (Cairo 1920–6): on graffiti in the Valley of the Kings.

Vleeming, in *Hundred-gated Thebes* (above), 241–55: an excellent introductory study of the choachytes.

P. W. Pestman, *The Archive of the Theban Choachytes* (Leuven 1993): a detailed survey of the second and first century BC choachyte archives.

H. E. Winlock and W. E. Crum, *The Monastery of Epiphanius at Thebes* (New York 1926): contains the only real survey of Coptic activity in the area, as well as publishing the important remains of the monastery itself.

W. Godlewski, *Le monastère de St Phoibammon* (Warsaw 1986): evidence relating to the monastery at Deir el-Bahari.

The rediscovery of Egypt

Useful information on Thebes may be found in Nims, *Thebes*, Manniche, *City of the Dead* and Reeves and Wilkinson, *Complete Valley of the Kings* (above).

C. C. Gillispie and M. Dewachter (eds), *Monuments of Egypt: The Napoleonic Expedition* (Princeton 1987): an edition of part of the *Description de l'Egypte*, which describes well the Napoleonic expedition.

Belzoni's *Narrative of the Operations and Recent Discoveries within the Pyramids, Temples, Tombs, and Excavations, in Egypt and Nubia* (London, various editions): should be read by all.

S. Mayes, *The Great Belzoni* (London 1959): one of several biographies of Belzoni.

R. T. Ridley, *Napoleon's Proconsul in Egypt: The Life and Times of Bernardino Drovetti* (London n.d., possibly 1998): a biography of Belzoni's great rival.

S. Tillett, *Egypt Itself: The Career of Robert Hay, Esquire, of Linplum and Nunraw, 1799-1863* (London 1984)

J. Thompson, *Sir Gardner Wilkinson and his Circle* (Austin 1992).

Who Was Who in Egyptology, currently in its third edition by W. R. Dawson, E. P. Uphill and M. L. Bierbrier (London 1995): an indispensable resource for the history of Egyptology.

Guidebooks

There are many guidebooks for Egypt, but only two stand out as useful for the serious traveller:

W. J. Murnane, *The Penguin Guide to Ancient Egypt* (Harmondsworth 1983).

Blue Guide: Egypt (London 1983–).

Several guidebooks deal only with Thebes:

J. Kamil, *Luxor: A Guide to Ancient Thebes* (various editions).

I. Portman, *Luxor. A Guide to the Temples and Tombs of Ancient Thebes* (Cairo 1989).

Reda Ali Soliman, *The Theban Necropolis: An Esoteric Guide to the West Bank at Luxor* (Cairo 1990).

A. Siliotti, *Guide to the Valley of the Kings and to the Theban Necropolises and Temples* (Vercelli and Luxor 1996).

PICTURE ACKNOWLEDGEMENTS

Illustrations on the following pages are gratefully reproduced from the sources shown. All other illustrations are by the authors.

8–9, 66, 82–3, 86–7, 196–7, 204 from S. Aufrere, J.-Cl. Golvin and J.-C. Goyon, *Egypte restituée* (Paris 1994–7), 11, 72–3, 82–3, 158–9, 172–3

11, 53, 68, 75, 89 from or based on I. Shaw and P. Nicholson, *British Museum Dictionary of Ancient Egypt* (London 1995), pp. 287, 147, 165, 287, 242

23, 25, 49, 95, 122, 137, 155, 175, 199 courtesy of the Trustees of the British Museum, London

102, 105, 112 adapted from N. Reeves and R. H. Wilkinson, *The Complete Valley of the Kings* (London 1996), pp. 93, 99, 111, 131, 139, 147, 157, 160–1, 163, 164, 168

114, 168, 172 su concessione Ministero Beni Culturali e Ambientali – Museo Egizio, Torino – Italia

123 photo courtesy private collection

125 adapted from H. Carter, *JEA* 4 (1917), pls xx, xxi

126, 136 adapted from C. Leblanc, *BIFAO* 89 (1989), figs 3–6, 7

144, 185 photo courtesy Metropolitan Museum of Art, New York

147 (top) adapted from Dieter Arnold, *Das Grab des In-itif* (Mainz 1971), Taf. 11; Mohammed Saleh, *Three Old-Kingdom Tombs at Thebes* (Mainz 1977), pl. 2; N. de G. Davies, *The Tomb of Antefoker* (London 1920), pl. 1

149 adapted from N. de G. Davies, and A. H. Gardiner, *The Tomb of Amenemhat* (London 1915), pl. XXXIII; Epigraphic Survey, *The Tomb of Kheruef* (Chicago 1980), pl. 3

150 adapted from F. Kampp, *Die thebanischen Nekropole* (Mainz 1996), 1, 385, fig. 267; M. Bietak and E. Reiser-Haslauer, *Das Grab des Anch-hor* (Vienna 1978–82), plan 3

192 adapted from M. L. Bierbrier, *The Tomb-builders of the Pharaohs* (London 1982), p. 56

195 adapted from U. Hölscher, *The Excavation of Medinet Habu III* (Chicago 1941), fig. 29

207 photo courtesy Egypt Exploration Society, London